D1560623

STOCKTON'S GOLDEN ERA

An Illustrated History
by Alice van Ommeren

A publication of Visit Stockton and the
Greater Stockton Chamber of Commerce

HPNbooks
A division of Lammert Incorporated
San Antonio, Texas

The Port of Stockton at sunset with industrial cranes, monolithic domes and ocean vessels.

PHOTOGRAPH COURTESY OF THE PORT OF STOCKTON.

First Edition

Copyright © 2015 HPNbooks

All rights reserved. No part of this book may be reproduced in any form or by any means, electronic or mechanical, including photocopying, without permission in writing from the publisher. All inquiries should be addressed to HPNbooks, 11535 Galm Road, Suite 101, San Antonio, Texas, 78254. Phone (800) 749-9790, www.hpnbooks.com.

ISBN: 978-1-939300-88-1

Library of Congress Card Catalog Number: 2015948432

Stockton's Golden Era: An Illustrated History

author:	Alice van Ommeren
cover artist:	Vanessa Hadady
contributing writer for sharing the heritage:	Joe Goodpasture
primary photo contribution:	Bank of Stockton

HPNbooks

president:	Ron Lammert
project managers:	Daphne Fletcher, Michelle Ritter
administration:	Donna M. Mata, Melissa G. Quinn
book sales:	Dee Steidle
production:	Colin Hart, Evelyn Hart, Glenda Tarazon Krouse, Tim Lippard, Tony Quinn, Christopher D. Sturdevant

CONTENTS

Legacy Sponsors

These companies have made a major contribution to the book as part of our Legacy Program. We could not have made this book possible without their leadership and participation. These are our top contributors and we thank them for their support.

San Joaquin Delta College

www.deltacollege.edu

5151 Pacific Avenue
Stockton, California 95207
209-954-5151

www.humphreys.edu

Stockton Campus

6650 Inglewood Avenue
Stockton, California 95207
209-478-0800

Modesto Campus

3600 Sisk Road, Suite 5A
Modesto, California 95356
209-543-9411

ACKNOWLEDGEMENTS

Visit Stockton and the Greater Stockton Chamber of Commerce would like to thank the many partners, businesses, and supporters who have assisted in making *Stockton's Golden Era: An Illustrated History* a reality. This book would not have been possible without the financial support of so many proud Stockton businesses and business leaders.

We would also like to thank our author, Alice van Ommeren, whose well-known passion for Stockton history made her the obvious choice to put our great city's history into words. We would also like to thank William Maxwell, archivist at the Bank of Stockton's Historical Photograph Collection, and the Bank of Stockton for their collaboration on and support of this project and for their long-standing dedication to preserving Stockton's photographic history. Additionally we thank Ron Chapman and Bradley Steele of the Stockton Police Archives, whose photographs were a great asset to this publication. We offer sincere appreciation to all past and present historians, archivists, and librarians who have preserved Stockton's history since the beginning. Lastly we want to thank HPNbooks, and specifically Daphne Fletcher whose enthusiasm and dedication to this project was abundant.

We hope *Stockton's Golden Era: An Illustrated History* renews your pride and enthusiasm for the port city of Stockton, California, and you share that pride with your friends, family, and loved ones.

Enjoy!

Wes Rhea
CEO
Visit Stockton

Douglass W. Wilhoit
CEO
Greater Stockton Chamber of Commerce

STOCKTON'S GOLDEN ERA
6

PHOTOGRAPH COURTESY OF VISIT STOCKTON.

INTRODUCTION

Stockton's Golden Era occurred from the 1890s to the 1940s when the city was distinguished from other California cities for its strong economy and industrial innovation. Stockton reinvented itself from a supply base for gold prospectors into an agricultural transportation center. In the 1890s, its agricultural and industrial innovation combined with its riverfront location launched Stockton into its golden years as a transportation and commercial center.

This book offers residents, professionals and visitors with an overview and a glimpse of Stockton's Golden Era and an understanding of the factors that contributed to Stockton's prominence in California at the time. The chapters focus around several significant themes pertaining to Stockton's development including environmental conditions, economic forces and cultural aspects. Since this is not a comprehensive history, a selected bibliography has been included so that readers may learn more. Stockton's Golden Era was influenced by the town's beginnings, including its early settlers, the city's founder and visionary pioneers. The book reflects back on the city's early years as the structural and cultural foundation for the Golden Era.

Several institutions and individuals assisted with various aspects of the book for which the author and community is grateful. The greatest resource remains the professional and amateur historians, archivists, photographers and librarians who have documented, preserved, captured and cataloged our past so that the stories of Stockton's history can be told.

Stockton has an incredible rich history; a true source of pride.

Alice van Ommeren
June 15, 2015

CHAPTER 1

EARLY SETTLERS AND PIONEERS

NATIVE PEOPLES

❖

The dwellings that were believed to be on current Stockton land were located north of the Channel and west of Banner Island and would have consisted of clusters of huts constructed of tule mats tied to willow frames. The tule plants also provided for their diet and clothing.

PHOTOGRAPH COURTESY OF THE BANK OF STOCKTON.

The earliest people to take advantage of the rich natural resources in the area that would grow into one of the most prosperous cities in California were indigenous. The first native peoples in the Sacramento-San Joaquin Delta region were found along the San Joaquin River, which flows through the area that would become known as Stockton. This indigenous population dates back to 2500 BC and was most likely from the Hokan linguistic group, who were displaced by the Penutian language group. Of this language group, the Yokuts-speaking people were the primary tribal group that eventually occupied the area south of the Calaveras River, which is the vicinity most closely associated with Stockton. There is strong speculation and some evidence that there were at least two or three indigenous villages near the sloughs that came together at the head of the Stockton Channel.

The San Joaquin River region was the ideal location for these indigenous groups, who were primarily hunters and gatherers. They relied heavily on the waterways, including channels and sloughs, where food sources flourished. The area was abundant with wildlife including elk, deer, and antelope, which supplemented the natives' consumption of fruit, nuts, and seeds. The climate was mild and the lush vegetation provided plenty of food, as well as materials for clothing and shelter. The valley oaks that covered the landscape supplied acorns and wood, while the local rivers provided fish and waterfowl. The richness of the land certainly was an early indicator of this area's potential for success in agriculture. In the late 1700s, European explorers began exploiting and displacing the native populations, and introducing the diseases that eventually led to their disappearance.

SPANISH AND MEXICAN EXPLORERS

Spanish explorers started arriving in the region in the early 1770s. They were followed by Spanish missionaries, whose focus was converting the native population to Christianity and sending them to the various missions that were built throughout California. The missions were primarily in the coastal areas of California, but still influenced the native populations in the inland regions, including the loss of their native culture. Spanish explorer Gabriel Moraga traveled through the Central Valley in 1808, and it is speculated he named the "San Joaquin" River and Valley after "Saint Joachim", the father of the Virgin Mary. He also named the Calaveras River, which translates as "river of skulls" in Spanish. He found many skulls along this river bank of the indigenous people that had died there from famine or tribal conflict. The Spaniards explored the San Joaquin Valley and named many places, but never actually settled here. In 1822, the Mexican government became independent from Spain and it began encouraging trade in the California territory.

As Mexico acquired California, the region was occupied largely by three groups. The Spaniards were a small but powerful group made up of large landowners, mission fathers, and military officials. The Mexican settlers consisted of former soldiers and motivated colonists, who lived in the smaller towns or on the farms where they worked. In the 1820s, the native peoples of California remained the largest group, even considering how much their population had been reduced by the devastating effect of European diseases. Although the missions and rancheros had prospered, they left a deeply stratified society where most people lived an economically challenging and culturally deficient frontier life, especially in central California. The region was isolated and had been ignored by the Spanish Empire. This changed with the 1848 Treaty of Guadalupe Hidalgo, which ended the Mexican-American War, and made California officially part of the United States.

✧

The Native American contact with the new settlers and gold seekers led to a series of disruptions to the native population left in California, including violence, disease and loss of their tribes. By 1870, an estimated 30,000 native people remained in the state of California, most of them on reservations.
PHOTOGRAPH COURTESY OF THE BANK OF STOCKTON.

✧

Jedediah Strong Smith (1799-1831)—
"Old Diah," trapper and trailblazer who
charted the way for westward expansion,
camped in this vicinity along the Calaveras
River with his company of trappers on
their return from California to the Rocky
Mountains, January 3, 1826." This bronze
plaque is located on the south bank of the
Calaveras River, near the footbridge on the
University of the Pacific campus.

PHOTOGRAPH COURTESY OF RON CHAPMAN.

TRAPPERS
AND TRADERS

It was the early fur trade in California that opened up the West. In 1825, Europeans trappers were drawn to the northern and central California coast. Eventually, trappers and traders transitioned from the coastal areas to the inland regions. In 1827, Jedediah Strong Smith and his party of trappers were among the earliest Americans to travel through the Central Valley. Smith was the first white man to travel overland from the Salt Lake area into California across the Sierra Nevada and to explore westward. Smith's men found that the San Joaquin Valley, specifically the Calaveras and the Mokelumne rivers, had an abundance of wildlife for trapping beavers and elk, and even bears. The trappers brought back stories about the abundant wildlife, which enticed others to come, although most trappers never settled here.

From the 1820s to the middle of the 1840s, trappers came south from Oregon country and covered the area around the San Joaquin and Sacramento rivers with traps and transported the hides to the San Francisco Bay. The Hudson's Bay Company, a Canadian fur trading business, sent trapper Alex McLeod in 1828. He traveled to the future site of Stockton and camped near the current city hall, at the edge of what was once McLeod Lake and is now Martin Luther King Junior Plaza. This location became a popular meeting point for trappers traveling up the San Joaquin River and its various channels and sloughs. Michel LaFramboise was a French Canadian trapper who camped on the southern edge of present-day Stockton in 1832. The settlement located south of Stockton, French Camp, was named for these early pioneers. It would be another decade before a great visionary saw the potential of creating a permanent settlement that would provide the foundation for Stockton's development.

CHARLES M. WEBER

The founder of Stockton was Charles M. Weber, an immigrant born in 1814 in Steinwenden, Germany. He came to America in 1836 and arrived in California five years later with one of the first overland groups, the Bidwell-Bartleson party. He found work at Sutter's Fort, located in the future city of Sacramento, and subsequently moved to San Jose for several business opportunities. He acquired a land grant known as "El Rancho del Campo de Los Franceses" in 1845 from his business partner, William Gulnac. The 48,747-acre Mexican land grant included present-day French Camp and Stockton. It was several years later when Charles settled here, first naming the place Tuleburg. In the end, he settled on calling it Stockton, in honor of Robert F. Stockton, a military commander during the Mexican-American War. It was the first community in California to have an English name, instead of a name with Spanish or Native American origin.

❖

Left: Charles M. Weber portrait by famous photographer J. Pitcher Spooner taken on July 4, 1880. The founder of Stockton died a year later of pneumonia leaving a well planned city with generous donations of land to organizations supporting the community.

PHOTOGRAPH COURTESY OF THE BANK OF STOCKTON.

Below: Charles M. Weber's residence and garden at Weber Point taken in 1856 by photographer William Rulofson with the Otranto moored in the back. The home was built in 1851 of redwood, brick and adobe, and is one of the first permanent homes in the region. This image is one of just a few daguerreotypes left of Stockton in the 1850s.

PHOTOGRAPH COURTESY OF THE BANK OF STOCKTON.

✧

Left to right, Horace Spencer, William Dofflemyer and Raymond Hill at the dedication of Lindsay Point as a California Registered Landmark in 1969. The City of Stockton Cultural Heritage Board was created in 1966, soon after the demolition of many historic buildings during the West End Redevelopment project. The board functions to preserve historic buildings and landmark historic sites.

PHOTOGRAPH COURTESY OF THE BANK OF STOCKTON.

northeast that changed the future of the settlement forever.

The discovery of gold in Coloma in 1848 and the Stockton-area location downstream from other foothill mining locations launched the town into action as the supply center for the southern mines. Weber tried gold prospecting for a brief period but found more opportunity in supplying the miners and developing the infrastructure of a rapidly growing town. He had the land surveyed for a town by Major Richard P. Hammond in 1849. The plan included wide avenues leading to the waterfront and seventeen blocks for public lands and parks. It was his foresight and planning for a growing community that led to the town's ability to receive the invasion of boats and passengers that would arrive in the following years. Charles Weber dedicated the rest of his life, which ended on May 4, 1881, to the development of Stockton.

THE EARLIEST SETTLERS

Weber's early efforts to find settlers for the land were not always successful. The first family to settle here, near the French Camp area, was the family of David Kelsey, who had come from Oregon in 1844. The family was devastated by smallpox. Cattle ranchers John Lindsay and James Williams became the first to settle in present-day Stockton in 1844, when they established their camp at Lindsay Point, the current location of city hall. Over the next few years, Charles Weber continued to entice trappers and sailors to settle here with their families, but many felt unprotected in this undeveloped region. In 1847, Charles Weber sold all his property in San Jose and moved to settle in Stockton, along with his wife, Helen Murphy, with whom he had three children. Weber offered each settler a block of land in town and 480 acres in the country, which was an acceptable offer for many. For example, Joseph Buzell owned a block on Center Street and Weber Avenue, where he constructed the first wooden building out of logs in 1847, and also acquired a 160-acre ranch along the Calaveras River. Word of the new community began to spread slowly, but it was the discovery of gold in the foothills eighty miles to the

SOUTHERN GOLD MINES

James Marshall discovered gold at John Sutter's lumber and sawmill at the edge of the American River in Coloma, located northeast of what is now called Sacramento, on January 24, 1848. Those people already living in California were able to reach the mines before word of gold spread across the world in 1849. At first most mining was done by panning in rivers, but by 1853 mining had evolved to include extraction techniques that were more invasive to the environment, such as hydrologic mining. At the end of the Gold Rush, it was estimated that more than 300,000 people came to seek gold or associated opportunities. The Gold Rush made a substantial impact on Stockton.

By 1854, Stockton was the fourth-largest city in California, followed by San Francisco, Sacramento, and Marysville, with large numbers of sailing ships, steamboats, freight wagons, and stagecoaches arriving and departing from the waterfront. The settlement's location at the head of the Stockton Channel provided easy access to the towns connected with the southern gold mines, such as Jackson, Mokelumne, Murphys, Sonora, Groveland,

✧

The plaque located at city hall reads, "Lindsay Point—site of the first building in Stockton. In August 1844, the first settler arrived at Rancho del Campo de los Franceses. One of the company, Thomas Lindsey, built the first dwelling, a tule hut, on this site. The point was formed by the junction of McLeod's Lake and Miner's Channel."

PHOTOGRAPH COURTESY OF RON CHAPMAN.

Mariposa, and Colombia, which was known as the "Gem of the Southern Mines." The gold available in the southern mines, south of the Mokelumne River, was exhausted more rapidly than the gold in the northern mines. Many Stockton streets have names related to the Gold Rush, including Miner Avenue, and Sutter, Sonora, and Sierra Nevada streets.

*Top: This building on the corner of
Weber and Sutter streets was constructed in
1869 by John Hart and E. E. Thrift to serve
as a grocery and merchandise store. The
Hart & Thrift structure had an impressive
facade designed in the Renaissance Revival
style and accommodated two stores and
sixteen rooms. Although the building was
heavily altered over time and eventually
demolished, the facade has been
incorporated by the San Joaquin Regional
Transit District building.*

PHOTOGRAPH COURTESY OF THE BANK OF STOCKTON.

*Right: This 1850s map was produced
by the city's second surveyor, Major Richard
P. Hammond, and shows a grid system of
streets overlaying a series of channels and
sloughs, most of which were reclaimed.
The map features Banner Island and
Mormon Channel, as well as Asylum,
Miner and Fremont sloughs.*

PHOTOGRAPH COURTESY OF THE BANK OF STOCKTON.

*Opposite, top: The Yosemite Cash Store,
one of Stockton's pioneer stores, at the
intersection of Weber Avenue and San
Joaquin Street during flooding in the early
1900s. The San Joaquin County Jail and the
spires of the Central Methodist Church in
the background with the Columbia House
in the upper left, built in the 1850s with
lumber shipped around Cape Horn.*

PHOTOGRAPH COURTESY OF THE BANK OF STOCKTON.

*Opposite, bottom: A watercolor painting by
W. H. Creasey for Charles Weber provides
one of the earliest views of Stockton as the
supply base for the southern gold mines.
The view in 1849 from Weber Point shows
a tent city, a levee full of supplies and a
slough filled with ships.*

PHOTOGRAPH COURTESY OF THE BANK OF STOCKTON.

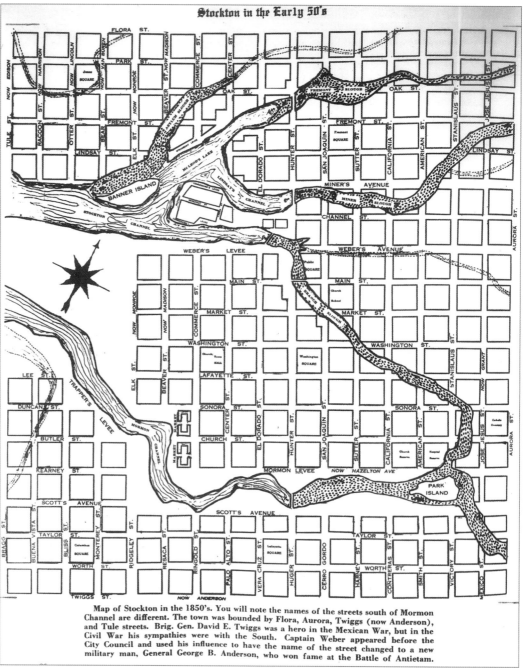

Map of Stockton in the 1850's. You will note the names of the streets south of Mormon
Channel are different. The town was bounded by Flora, Aurora, Twiggs (now Anderson),
and Tule streets. Brig. Gen. David E. Twiggs was a hero in the Mexican War, but in the
Civil War his sympathies were with the South. Captain Weber appeared before the
City Council and used his influence to have the name of the street changed to a new
military man, General George B. Anderson, who won fame at the Battle of Antietam.

SUPPLY CENTER

In 1849 sailing and steaming vessels pulled up to the waterfront to disembark thousands of gold seekers, as well as vast amounts of supplies. Boats brought many people up the waterways to participate in gold mining and returned them with their riches back to San Francisco and beyond. The settlement prospered as it became the supply center for the southern mines. The natural channel in Stockton was always considered a better resource than the river frontage for the northern mines, the settlement that would become Sacramento. In 1852, six side-wheel steamers were in regular service between Stockton and San Francisco and three of them traveled overnight. This allowed for daily mail delivery from San Francisco.

✧

Right: The mural completed in the late 1980s by Filipino artist and city muralist, Greg Custodio, on a Market Street building depicts twelve historically prominent Stocktonians. Counterclockwise from top left are Benjamin Holt, Tillie Lewis, Warren Atherton, Angelo Rollieri, Edna Gleason, Jeremiah Sanderson, Eddie Olamit, Peter Coolures, James Budd, George Shima, Charles Weber and Robert F. Stockton.

PHOTOGRAPH COURTESY OF RON CHAPMAN.

Below: James H. Budd from Stockton became the nineteenth governor of California in 1895. He was part of the first graduating class of the University of California in 1873 before starting his law practice in Stockton that included several decades of local and state political appointments. James Budd and his wife Inez lived in a beautiful Victorian on the corner of Channel and Sutter streets which was demolished in the 1950s.

PHOTOGRAPH COURTESY OF THE BANK OF STOCKTON.

Some of the earliest businesses supporting the travelers to the mines were stables and blacksmiths, but equally important were saloons, butchers, and grocery stores. In 1848, Grayson and Stephens had a general store on the Levee in one of Stockton's first wooden buildings. The area around the Levee, now referred to as Weber Avenue, and Center Street was considered the main part of town. It grew into the first commercial district bounded by Weber and El Dorado avenues, and Main and Commerce streets. Local express companies offered daily service for shipping goods to and from the communities of the southern mines and brokered gold shipments to the eastern

states. The freight wagons from Stockton were bringing the fresh food, dry goods, and mining tools to the towns located in the foothills.

OTHER PIONEERS

One of Stockton's most influential commercial pioneers was Erastus Holden. He immigrated to Stockton in 1849 and in 1853 he started the Holden Drug Store which was the first two-story brick building on the northeast corner of Main and El Dorado streets. He also served as mayor of Stockton six times and was president of the San Joaquin County Fair Board and the Copperopolis Railroad, as well as a founding member of the agricultural society. Another true commercial pioneer, L. U. Shippee, arrived in Stockton in 1856 and found his fortune as a merchant, rancher, and financier. His greatest contribution was

his involvement and foresight for the future of the community, including improving its infrastructure.

James Budd was born in 1851 and moved to Stockton in 1860. He became a lawyer in 1874 and served as the governor of California for four years starting in 1895. He successfully moved legislation through the California State Legislature to create the Bureau of Highways, an agency to build the state's roads system. The agency would later become the California Department of Transportation. He is the only governor of California from Stockton. Another pioneer and public servant was Thomas Cunningham, one of California's most famous sheriffs. He served for almost thirty years after being elected in 1871 and was associated with sending many to prison, including "Black Bart" who was a notorious stagecoach robber in California between 1875 and 1883.

✦

Above: L. U. Shippee was a leading business person and politician, as well as an innovative farmer and rancher. He served on the Stockton City Council and was the mayor in 1887. He was also the founder of the Stockton Savings and Loan Society in 1867, and later served as its president.
PHOTOGRAPH COURTESY OF THE BANK OF STOCKTON.

Left: The inside of the Holden Drug Store in the late 1800s. It was one of the earliest and longest operating businesses in Stockton, beginning in 1850. Erastus Holden went on to patent several remedies, his most popular being "Holden's Ethereal Cough Syrup."
PHOTOGRAPH COURTESY OF THE BANK OF STOCKTON.

Below: Erastus S. Holden, a popular pioneering druggist, first came to California in 1849 by way of Panama. He tried to find his fortune in the gold mines before settling in Stockton and opening the first drug store in a tent on the corner of Main and El Dorado streets in 1850.
PHOTOGRAPH COURTESY OF THE BANK OF STOCKTON.

Chapter 2

Delta Land and Agriculture

✧

A sternwheeler docked along Mormon Slough during the late 1800s when it was a navigable tributary of the San Joaquin River flowing through Stockton into the Channel. The California Paper Company is in the background, a Stockton paper mill that started in 1877.

PHOTOGRAPH COURTESY OF THE BANK OF STOCKTON.

Early explorers in the Stockton area found a region flanked by swamplands and coastal ranges on its western side and the Mother Lode and the Sierra on its eastern side. As Stockton became a settlement, it would find itself strategically located between two other future cities, Sacramento and Fresno, which developed in similar stages. The region's scenic environment was dominated by the Delta waters. Four important rivers impact Stockton—the Calaveras, the Mokelumne, the Stanislaus, and the San Joaquin. The Stockton Channel which after three miles connects to the San Joaquin River and therefore links Stockton to the San Francisco Bay and the Pacific Ocean.

More importantly, the settlement's location was at the center of one of the richest agricultural lands in the world. Stockton is surrounded by fertile land, with the Delta on its western side, providing access to many waterways. The richness of the Delta soil is attributed to it being mostly peat, which is made of decomposed vegetation. Sometimes the Delta around Stockton has been called the "Holland of America" because of the estimated eleven hundred miles of waterways and its history of land reclamation. The Delta area once encompassed much swampland, but over time, more than half of that was transformed into cultivated land.

THE RIVERS AND SLOUGHS

One of the longest rivers in California is the San Joaquin River, which winds its way west and northwest from the foothills to the Delta region, where it enters the bays of San Francisco and ends in the Pacific Ocean. During the Gold Rush, river boats coming up the San Joaquin River would turn east into the main river channel and bring supplies another two miles to the junction of various sloughs. The tides that extended upriver into town contributed to the many sloughs that lace the areas. At one point, there was an effort to name Stockton the City of Sloughs, because of the six sloughs running through the area. At the time, these natural sloughs, such as Mormon and Miner slough, were dredged into channels to better serve the riverboats. The overflowing of these rivers and sloughs, combined with the city's average elevation of just fifteen feet above sea level, caused major flooding.

Stockton's history with floods began as early as 1851, around the time of the city's founding, and includes the Great Flood of 1862 as the largest recorded flood in California history. These very early floods usually occurred because of rain in the early spring. One of Stockton's major floods occurred in 1907, when many of the levees built along the rivers broke, resulting in floodwaters as deep as four feet in many places in the city. Since there was not sufficient warning, downtown businesses did not have enough time to move their merchandise, which was often stored in basements. The catastrophic flood of 1907 led to the construction of the Diverting Canal, which leads water from the Mormon Slough to the Calaveras River north of the city. This greatly lessened the floods, although it did not prevent them entirely. In 1955, a flood on Christmas Eve covered much of the southern part of the city. This led to the building of the new Hogan Dam, which allowed for more water storage capacity, and therefore even less water flowing to the rivers and sloughs.

Above: A horse carriage at Channel Street, looking north on San Joaquin Street with the Central Methodist Church in the background. In the early part of 1907, downtown Stockton suffered from devastating floods due to an abundance of rain.

PHOTOGRAPH COURTESY OF THE BANK OF STOCKTON.

Below: The Grand Central Hotel built in 1876 on the northeast corner of Channel and California streets during the flooding in the first few months of 1907.

PHOTOGRAPH COURTESY OF THE BANK OF STOCKTON.

✧

Aerial view of the San Joaquin River as it bends through the Delta farmlands.

PHOTOGRAPH COURTESY OF THE BANK OF STOCKTON.

RICH SOIL

Stockton marks the Delta's deepest cut eastward, and sits amid farmland considered to be among the regions richest and most productive. The combination of fertile land and strategic location led to Stockton's first growth spurt and subsequent successes. Colonel Juan Jose Warner, on his visit to the valley in 1832, noted that the vast indigenous population in the area was due to the abundant supply of wild game, fresh fish, tree nuts, and plant seeds. There was little need to cultivate the soil, as so much was available by easier methods, such as hunting and gathering. The trappers who established temporary trading posts also noticed the numerous grape vines along the banks of the rivers. The Delta consists largely of fertile peat lands formed by the constant growth and decomposition of water plants. This peat produced amazingly productive farmland and, combined with irrigation, allowed for almost any fruit or vegetable to grow and flourish on the land outside of Stockton.

The acres in fruits and nuts tripled in between 1910 and 1945 and the acreage of vegetables increased seven times from 1930 to 1945, during the height of Stockton's golden years.

CLIMATE

The rich soil combined with abundant water and a mild Mediterranean climate provided the capacity to produce outstanding yields. California has a variety of climates—the weather can be windy and foggy on the coast, while it is colder and wetter in the mountains. The Central Valley, on the other hand, experiences extreme heat and a dry atmosphere during the summers. Located in the center of the state, Stockton is often spared from the extreme summer heat, as the surrounding water provides for a slightly milder climate. The winter months bring substantial rain and occasional fog to Stockton, which has a temperate climate where mild temperatures and blue skies are the most common, and perfect for abundant crop growth.

THE TREES

The area the city was founded on was once covered with forests of trees, many of them oaks. Stockton's founder, Charles Weber, made an effort to preserve some of the splendid oak forests that blanketed the area. The trees in Oak Park are typical of the forest that protected the area before it was developed.

The valley oaks, with massive trunks and limbs, are the largest North American oaks and the most characteristic native tree in the Stockton area. The abundance of trees and brush also attracted the large herds of elk and deer that roamed the area in the early 1800s. The growth of Tule along the river banks and vegetation in the plains provided the plant matter that eventually became peat soil.

✦

A Valley Oak in Oak Park on Alpine Avenue with its long and twisted outer branches coming out of large and thick limbs. Oak trees are native to California and the most common native tree in the Central Valley.

PHOTOGRAPH COURTESY OF RON CHAPMAN.

GRAIN PRODUCTION

The area's earliest and most significant industry was grain production. Grains had previously been imported from South America, but by the 1880s, the land surrounding Stockton was being cultivated with wheat, barley, and oats of higher quality than what had been imported. Wheat was the leading agricultural industry around the Stockton area from the 1870s until the 1890s, which is often referred to as Stockton's Wheat Age. Barley and oats were also grown. The area encompassing most of San Joaquin County became the largest grain-growing region in the nation, and earned the appellation of *Breadbasket to the World*. Stockton's location on the waterfront made it a hub for the grain trade, allowing for warehousing and shipping that led to profitable business opportunities for grain dealers, such as F. E. Ferrell and J. D. Peters.

MINERS TO FARMERS

After the Gold Rush, agriculture took the place of mining, with wheat and other grains becoming the most abundant crops. Many of the miners who rushed to California's foothills in the 1850s had been farmers before the Gold Rush, so when it ended, many switched back to farming as it became the focus of the economy in Stockton. Some miners also became merchants, and some

❖

Above: A crew around a grain bagging machine near the head of the Stockton Channel in the 1880s with warehouses in the background.

PHOTOGRAPH COURTESY OF THE BANK OF STOCKTON.

Below: In 1880, San Joaquin County was one of the major grain producers in the country and was supported by wholesale grain dealers such as F. E. Ferrell, located on Sutter Street near Channel Street.

PHOTOGRAPH COURTESY OF THE BANK OF STOCKTON.

decided to stay in the area for a variety of other reasons. It was during the few decades after Stockton's role as a supply center for the southern gold mines that the commerce of the city shifted from serving miners to farmers. It is during this transition that Stockton entered its Golden Era.

Stockton's Golden Era is a period in time when the city was renowned for its healthy economy and industrial innovation. The period has been defined in various ways but it approximately encompasses the 1890s to the 1940s. By the 1890s, Stockton had already transformed itself from a gateway and supply stop for miners heading to the goldfields into a center of prosperous agricultural and shipping enterprises, making it a business and commercial hub. The economic impact of farming had rippled into many industries, including manufacturing and distribution. In the early 1900s, the city even became an important destination for recreation and entertainment. The introduction of irrigation in the early 1900s allowed for the growth of specialty crops, which changed the agricultural industry significantly.

IRRIGATION AND SPECIALTY CROPS

The Swamp Land Act of 1850 was federal legislation that provided the opportunity for individuals to gain title to swampland areas from the state on the condition that the land was "reclaimed" and used for agriculture. A quarter of that available land in California was in the Delta area. The result was the creation of levees and ridges that would hold back the water to expose the land. It was Lee Allen Phillips, a lawyer and financier from Los Angeles who owned land in San Joaquin County, who was credited with the ability to reclaim the swampland surrounding Stockton on a large scale. It was between 1902 and 1907 that he moved to Stockton and organized and directed reclamation projects for farmers who were able to produce large quantities of vegetables and specialty crops. Irrigated land around Stockton increased from 18,000 acres to 245,000 acres between 1900 and 1945 and became an important factor in the city's thriving economy.

The local manufacturing of machines that dug irrigations ditches and canals saved hundreds of hours of labor. This particular machine was designed by contractor, John E. Funk, and made irrigation ditches three feet wide and four feet deep.

PHOTOGRAPH COURTESY OF THE BANK OF STOCKTON.

❖

Below: Sacks of potatoes from the George Shima ranch are being loaded on the Pioneer, *which was built in 1867 with a shallow draft to navigate the many sloughs. The Shima building at San Joaquin Delta College is named in honor of George Shima, a successful Japanese potato farmer.*

PHOTOGRAPH COURTESY OF THE BANK OF STOCKTON.

Opposite page: The Agricultural Pavilion (top) was completed in 1888 with eight pagoda towers and glass conservatories at each of the corners. A small building of watermelons (bottom) grown by the Live Oak Colony near Lodi exemplifies the types of displays for its agricultural fairs. The wooden pavilion burned to the ground on September 28, 1902.

PHOTOGRAPHS COURTESY OF THE BANK OF STOCKTON.

George Shima was a Japanese immigrant and successful potato grower who benefited from Lee Phillips's ability to purchase land, construct levees, and lease parcels. Irrigation had revolutionized farming between 1880 and 1930, turning the area's agricultural production from cereal crops to specialty crops. In the early 1900s, farmers began to plant fruit orchards and vegetable fields in addition to grains, and they shipped their produce by rail. The crops increasingly became more diversified and included beans, onions, asparagus, and celery. Around 1915, sugar beets became a successful crop as the government provided for subsidies. By 1920, farmers began to plant almond and walnut trees, as well as watermelons, tomatoes, and corn. Other fruits produced were cherries, grapes and apples. This was also a time when cattle and dairy farmers prospered.

EARLY WATER TRANSPORTATION

The rush of gold made the settlement at the head of navigation to the San Joaquin River a natural landing for the thousands of gold seekers and their abundant supplies. It also became a shipping point for other raw materials from surrounding areas, such as copper ore from Copperopolis and lumber coming from the foothills and the mountains. As early as 1849, the first steamers from San Francisco found their way to Stockton, which launched steam boating as a lucrative business. As industry shifted from gold to agriculture, river transportation adapted, and grain was hauled from the farm lands into Stockton, where riverboats and barges then transported it to other parts of the state and the country.

AGRICULTURAL PAVILION

The beginning of Stockton's Golden Era was symbolized by the building of Stockton's largest and most prominent building at the time, the Agricultural Pavilion. This architectural masterpiece occupied one square block on what later became Washington Park, and is now the cross-town freeway across from St. Mary's Church. The building was completed in 1888, was able to seat 12,000 people, and housed the county fair exhibits. Local architect Charles Beasley, who used woodwork in a variety of forms, textures, materials, and colors, designed the building in the Queen Anne Style, with eight entrance towers. Built in the shape of a Greek cross with glass conservatories in each of its four corners, it not only lit the main floor but also provided an opportunity to display the varied plant life of the county. The Pavilion was the location of many agricultural events and exhibits that celebrated the bounty of the land and the prosperity it brought to Stockton.

CHAPTER 3

WAREHOUSING AND PROCESSING

✧

A wagon train loaded with bags of wheat pulled by a steam tractor unloads in front of the Stockton Warehouse Company along the Stockton Channel in 1892.

PHOTOGRAPH COURTESY OF THE BANK OF STOCKTON.

Stockton, situated on a channel of the same name, is three miles from the San Joaquin River and seventy miles to the San Francisco Bay. In the 1850s, the population of the southern gold mines had their food, clothing, and tools shipped from San Francisco by way of Stockton. The goods were brought to the head of navigation on vessels and taken to brick warehouses, often owned by commission merchants who hired local teamsters to transport the goods to merchants in the mountain locations. The transportation hub located at the head of Stockton Channel quickly developed as the center for freight and warehouse businesses. Livery stables, shipping companies, freight companies, stage lines, and carriage makers were also established on the north and south sides of the channel terminus.

Wheat fields surrounded the city, and grain production became the main agricultural industry in the area by the late 1800s. Stockton also claimed more warehouse capacity than other California city besides San Francisco. The Farmers' Co-Operative Union owned warehouses on the south bank of the Stockton Channel, west of Monroe Street. By the 1890s, the area on the southern edge of the channel had grown to be the most industrialized part of Stockton, with large grain mills and warehouses constructed on the waterfront and lumberyards and manufacturing plants close by. The processing of agricultural materials so that they would be stored appropriately, transported conveniently, and presented appealingly became an important industry that contributed to the local economy.

THE PACKING INDUSTRY

The packing of produce became an important industry, including for packing feed and flour during the grain era, primarily in warehouses along the waterfront. Some of the mills did the packing themselves. The Sperry Flour Mill, was known for their colorful flour sacks. The growing of fruits and vegetables changed the industry. Some of the larger farmers did their own packing; others used local packing plants that also distributed the products. The California Packing Corporation was an important plant that opened on Hazelton Street in 1922. Even the production of packing materials became an industry. The National Carton Works was established in 1918 on forty acres outside of Stockton and manufactured paper packing products that were exported. Other types of packing, such as meat packing, also thrived during this era. Alpine Packing Company was founded in 1936 by butcher Josef Kaeslin from Switzerland and is still in operation.

LUMBER AND PLANING MILLS

The growth and development of the city in the early 1900s created a great demand for timber and carpenters, as well as for lumber yards and planing mills. There were several early lumber companies, including the San Joaquin Lumber Company, started in 1910 by Newton Rutherford, Charles Neumiller, and Robert Inglis. Lumber would arrive by rail and barge to a dock on the south bank of the Mormon Slough, where the Stockton yard is located to this day; it is now called Scotts Avenue. Horses and mules pulled narrow railroad carts of lumber up and down the bank and to sheds on the property. In 1933, the S. S. *Daisy Gray* became the first ocean-going ship to dock at the brand new Port of Stockton; she was loaded with 700,000 board feet of lumber for the San Joaquin Lumber Company.

Planing mills using various machines to cut and season wood from sawmills to turn it into finished lumber. One of the earliest, largest, and best equipped of these mills was

❖

In 1853, Andrew Simpson and George Gray established a lumber business on Weber and Commerce streets, which operated from that location for five decades.

PHOTOGRAPH COURTESY OF THE BANK OF STOCKTON.

Right: Established in 1891, Union Planing Mill was located at 735 S. Sutter Street.
PHOTOGRAPH COURTESY OF THE BANK OF STOCKTON.

Below: Hunter Plaza in the 1870s at the center of Stockton's early business activities.
PHOTOGRAPH COURTESY OF THE BANK OF STOCKTON.

Opposite, top: A produce market on Weber Avenue in 1905, looking east with a glimpse of the county courthouse in the middle.
PHOTOGRAPH COURTESY OF THE BANK OF STOCKTON.

Opposite, bottom: Hunter Plaza in 1876, looking northwest from the Odd Fellows building.
PHOTOGRAPH COURTESY OF THE BANK OF STOCKTON.

the P. A. Buell Planing Mill and Lumber Company, whose office was on Center and Sonora streets in the late 1800s. The mill itself covered 50,000 square feet and ten acres on the south side of Mormon Channel. The Union Planing Mill was established in 1891, originally as a windmill and water tank manufacturing and repair facility. Stockton's agricultural boom in the late 1890s led Union Planing Mill to focus on refining the building of windmills, water towers, and irrigation systems. The company began to delve into

developing more wood products during World War II, when it was asked to contribute items like military lockers and pine boxes for the war effort. After the war, the mill began specializing in residential and commercial mill work.

AGRICULTURAL MARKETS
AND FESTIVALS

The bounty from the farmland was brought into the heart of the city on a daily basis. In the early 1900s, there was a produce market

✦

In October 1909, the discovery of gold was staged at Hunter Plaza. The Rush of '49 commemorated the sixty year anniversary of the event.

PHOTOGRAPH COURTESY OF THE BANK OF STOCKTON.

at El Dorado Street and Levee, now Weber Street. Farmers would arrive each morning to set up and distribute their produce to other businesses or local households. In 1922 the city outlawed the selling of produce from trucks, which prompted the construction of the Growers Hall in 1923. Hunter Plaza was also the location of farmers' markets and other events. Charles M. Weber, envisioning a plaza in the tradition of Mexican and

Spanish towns, donated the land for Hunter Plaza to Stockton in the 1850s. The plaza was home to many important events in Stockton's history. It was the site of the 1857 California State Fair, the location of the Centennial Celebration in 1876, and the "Rush of '49," an unusual street fair that took place in 1909 and depicted a gold mining camp. In the early 1900s, Hunter Plaza hosted numerous public meetings and political rallies.

Food festivals and other celebrations of the growing season and harvest are part of many cultures, including that of the Central Valley. The Potato Day Festival was organized in 1924, after San Joaquin County set the world record for potato production, and Stockton was subsequently considered the potato center of the west. This success was largely attributed to two of the most prominent Delta potato growers, George Shima and Ching Lung. Although short-lived, the Potato Day Festival had two successful consecutive events. The festivals were celebrated at the Kroyer Motors plant on Cherokee Lane with a carnival and exhibits, as well as several ceremonies. In 1924, Friend Richardson, the Governor of California, led the parade of more than sixty floats, and the festival included special guest and renowned horticulturist, Luther Burbank. The Potato Day Festival concluded with the Potato Ball, an evening of dancing led by King Potato and Queen Delta.

✧

Luther Burbank, famous California horticulturist, is accompanied on his right by Stockton Mayor, A. C. Oullahan, in the city's Potato Day Parade of 1924.

PHOTOGRAPH COURTESY OF THE BANK OF STOCKTON.

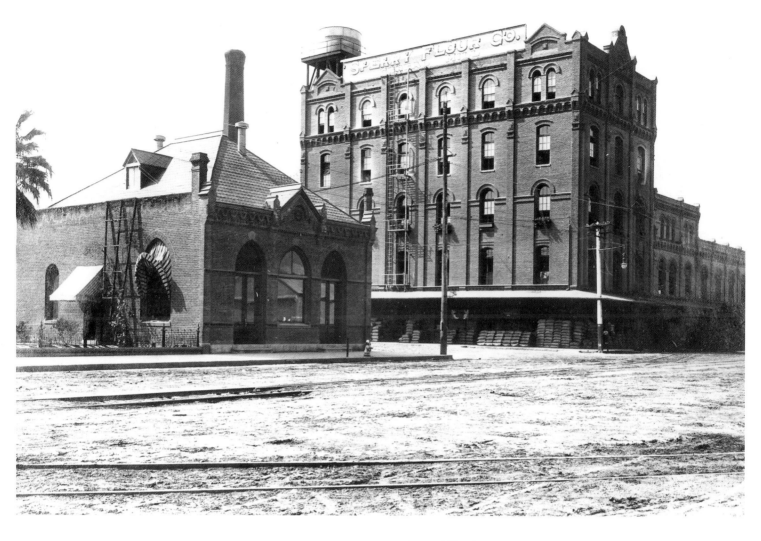

✧

Above: Sperry Flour Mill and office building facing the Stockton Channel. The company was founded in 1852 and the offices were built in 1888. It grew into a company with seventeen mills across three states and became one of the nation's most famous milling companies.

PHOTOGRAPH COURTESY OF THE BANK OF STOCKTON.

Right: The Sperry Flour Mill office building was designed by noted architect, Charles Beasley, and built in 1888 at Weber Avenue and Madison Street in the Victorian Commercial style. It is one of the oldest buildings still standing in what was the original commercial district established along the head of navigation.

PHOTOGRAPH COURTESY OF RON CHAPMAN.

FLOUR MILLS

In 1852, Stockton's first flour mill was established on the corner of Commerce and Main streets by several individuals, including Austin Sperry. In 1853 the Franklin Flour Mill was built at Monroe Street and Levee, now Weber Street, using quality machinery from England. Wheat was first imported from Napa and Martinez, but by 1856 wheat had become the San Joaquin Valley's main crop. As Stockton found itself in the center

Above: Sperry Flour Mill buildings along the Stockton Channel in 1880. The riverboat Mary Garratt, *which ran from San Francisco to Stockton, is docked on the side.*

PHOTOGRAPH COURTESY OF THE BANK OF STOCKTON.

Left: In the 1890s, Sperry Flour Company introduced a breakfast food called "Germea," a product created by extracting the germ from the California White Wheat.

PHOTOGRAPH COURTESY OF THE BANK OF STOCKTON.

✧

Above: Although the Gold Rush was over, supplying those living in the foothills with flour and grains remained important.

PHOTOGRAPH COURTESY OF THE BANK OF STOCKTON.

Opposite, top: Tillie Lewis was a businesswoman who introduced the Italian pomodoro tomato to the Stockton area and established a tomato cannery, the Flotill Cannery.

PHOTOGRAPH COURTESY OF THE BANK OF STOCKTON.

Opposite, bottom: In 1935, it took 1,500 acres of tomatoes to support the Flotill Cannery packing season. The canneries employed many Stocktonians.

PHOTOGRAPH COURTESY OF THE BANK OF STOCKTON.

of one of the largest grain-growing regions in the nation, flour mills flourished. The Stockton harbor allowed for the shipping of flour throughout the country and the world. The success of the mills was enhanced by locally manufactured harvesting equipment, most notably the "combine" that threshed, cleaned, and sacked grain. There were numerous mills, including Aurora Flour Mills and Lane's flour and feed mill. In addition, T. G. Humphreys and Perry Yaples started a barley mill in 1854 at Main and Stanislaus streets.

The Sperry Flour Mill, founded in 1852, was Stockton's first flour mill and grew into one of the nation's most famous milling companies, with seventeen mills across three states. In 1860, it became famous for its creative flour labels, such as "Drifted Snow Flour." In 1882, the mill was destroyed by fire and was replaced by the five-story Crown Mill, the largest mill of its type on the Pacific coast. Over the next few decades, Sperry acquired several other local mills, including the Golden Gate Mills, the Union Mills, and the Capital Mill, which became the largest cereal mill on the west coast. In 1920, California's wheat farmers experienced increasing competition from other states. The introduction of irrigation had already enabled farmers to shift their crops from grain to more profitable fruits and vegetables, causing a shortage of wheat crops. The Sperry Flour Mill was forced to import wheat from outside the area. In 1925 the mill moved its operations to Vallejo; it was purchased by General Mills in 1952.

CANNERIES

There were numerous canneries around Stockton by the turn of the century. The Stockton Cannery, which opened in the early 1900s, had a large workforce to can fruits and vegetables throughout the year. In following with the seasons, this cannery processed spinach, cherries, apricots, and peaches, followed by tomatoes and other vegetables. The company grew from 425 to more than 600 employees in the first few years. Stockton notoriety also increased during the Stockton cannery strike of 1937, also known as the "spinach riot." This was a conflict between the local Agricultural Workers Organization and the California Processors and Growers—between unions and growers for control over the Stockton canneries. The riots, in which both sides were armed, resulted in one death and over fifty serious injuries in front of the Stockton Foods Products plant on Waterloo Road.

One of Stockton's most industrious women was Tillie Lewis, the "Tomato Queen." She opened Stockton's Flotill Cannery on July 13, 1935, her thirty-fourth birthday. She is best known for introducing the Italian pomodoro tomato to America. In addition to tomatoes, the Flotill Cannery also canned other fruits and vegetables, baby food, and frozen juices. The company became the largest producer of C-rations for the U.S. Army during the Korean War. The plant covered over 180 acres and grew to become the fifth-largest canning business in the nation in 1951. In the same year, Tillie Lewis was named National Business Woman of the Year by the Associated Press. Tillie Lewis Foods employed more than 5,000 Stocktonians by 1974. The company was bought by the Ogden Corporation a few years before Tillie Lewis died in 1977.

WALNUT GROWERS

Walnut trees are native to California and flourished long before European or American settlers arrived. The Spanish missionaries brought nonnative species of walnut trees

✧

Most of the walnut growers were family
farmers with orchards in the Central Valley.
PHOTOGRAPH COURTESY OF THE BANK OF STOCKTON.

to California in the late 1800s that were adaptable to California's weather and soil conditions and were superior in flavor to the native species. The walnut industry had its beginnings in southern California, where ninety-five percent of the state's crop was produced in the early 1900s, which accounted for almost half of the walnuts produced in the United States at the time. In order to be treated more fairly and weather the sometimes unstable markets, growers formed the state's first grower-owned walnut cooperative in 1912, the California Walnut Growers Association. The walnut industry in San Joaquin County at the time covered only 200 acres.

In 1927 the walnut industry began to grow in the northern and central counties of the state. This was largely due to new varieties of walnuts that harvested better in those locations. The north and central counties also had inexpensive land, plenty of water, and lower taxes. The San Joaquin County Bureau was promoting the concept of growers joining a local association, as they were in other counties. In 1956, the California Walnut Growers Association, then called the Diamond Walnut Growers, chose Stockton as the best location to expand from their modest headquarters and plant in Los Angeles. They built the largest and most modern walnut facility in the world on the Santa Fe Mormon Yard, off of Charter Way by Mormon Slough in Stockton.

CHICORY AND WINE

In 1872, Charles Brandt started a chicory manufacturing business along the San Joaquin River eight miles south of Stockton, near French Camp. California Chicory Works roasted and ground chicory roots which were mixed with or substituted for coffee. In 1881, Brandt formed a partnership with his father-in-law, C. A. Bachman. The Bachman & Brandt California Chicory Factory had the finest German equipment to process chicory and used its own ship to transport the product to market. A new factory was built in 1895 and that building has been preserved; it most recently has been referred to as the River Mill. In 1892 the San Joaquin County chicory industry was considered the largest in the nation. After Bachman's death in 1903, Brandt again became plant's sole proprietor and renamed it the California Chicory Works until the business closed in 1911.

El Pinal Winery, established by George West in 1858, was the first commercial winery in the region. It was located on the east side of West Lane, which was named after George, near Alpine Road and close to the Southern Pacific railroad tracks. George West came to California in 1849, as so many others did, to discover gold. As the rush faded, he turned toward the area's rich soil and the potential for growing grapes. George became one of the most successful and famous wine growers in California. In El Pinal Winery's first decade, the grapes were mostly used for table wines; over time, the winery went on to produce more vintage products, including a port that won as a special premium wine at the California State Fair in 1867. The El Pinal Winery was forced to close in 1918 due to prohibition.

✧

Carloads of grapes being delivered to the El Pinal Winery near Alpine Road in the early 1900s.

PHOTOGRAPH COURTESY OF THE BANK OF STOCKTON.

CHAPTER 4

MANUFACTURING, COMMERCE, AND COMMUNICATION

AGRICULTURAL EQUIPMENT

As agricultural production grew in the region, the manufacturing of farm machinery and equipment quickly became Stockton's principal industry. In the late 1890s, the city distinguished itself from other California cities in the development of farm equipment by becoming the center of new inventions and revolutionizing many farm techniques. Stockton innovations included the Stockton Gang Plow and the Combined Harvester, a massive machine that cuts, threshes, and separates grain. The farm machinery that developed locally revolutionized agriculture worldwide. At the end of the nineteenth century, there were almost 300 manufacturing establishments in Stockton making manufacturing companies the city's largest employer.

✧

Matteson & Williamson was one of Stockton's first producers of farm machinery. Don Matteson pioneered the business as early as 1852 and was the first to manufacture plows, reapers and harvesters. In 1865, T. P. Williamson became a partner in the firm and the company became known for its manufacturing of harvesters, such as the "Harvest Queen," "Harvest King," and "Harvest Prince."

PHOTOGRAPH COURTESY OF THE BANK OF STOCKTON.

FARM MACHINES AND SUPPLIES

Matteson & Williamson was one of the earliest farm equipment manufacturers in Stockton. They opened in the 1850s near California and Main streets. In the 1870s, they invented the replaceable plowshare, and later received a patent for the combined harvester, or combine. The Stockton Gang Plow was developed by H. C. Shaw and improved on previous small plows by combining two or more plows on one frame and allowing for the tilling of several rows simultaneously. Harris Manufacturing and Stockton Plough and Manufacturing also built combined harvesters and other equipment for grain farming. Hickinbotham Brothers traces its origins to the Gold Rush times, when they settled in Stockton in 1852 as wagon and carriages makers. Over the decades, they transitioned from wood materials to heavy hardware. During World War II, Hickinbotham Brothers built landing barges, floating cranes, steel tugs, and supply vessels for the government.

Holt Manufacturing Company, founded as the Stockton Wheel Company in 1883 by brothers Benjamin and Charles Holt, became famous for improving and producing combined harvesters. The combined harvester was a time- and labor-saving machine that cut, threshed, cleaned, and sacked grain. By 1890, the Holt Company produced stream-driven tractors and harvesters to replace horse-drawn machines. Around 1906, Benjamin Holt invented the "caterpillar" tractor, which ran on a belt of tracks, instead of wheels. This important innovation provided better traction for heavy vehicles and led the Holt Company to switch to tank production during World War I. The Best Tractor Company took over the farm machinery market and the Holt Manufacturing

✧

Top, left: The H.C. Shaw Company dates to 1867 as one of the oldest businesses in Stockton located on El Dorado Street. Its founder, H. C. Shaw is known for his invention of the Stockton Gang Plow.
PHOTOGRAPH COURTESY OF THE BANK OF STOCKTON.

Above: Benjamin Holt (1849-1920) was the innovator of the caterpillar tractor and long term president of the Holt Manufacturing Company, a plant that covered several blocks around Aurora and Church streets. He made significant contributions to the mechanization of agriculture.
PHOTOGRAPH COURTESY OF THE BANK OF STOCKTON.

Left: Local inventions included the Stockton Gang Plow, invented in the mid-nineteenth century, allowing farmers to plow more land simultaneously with multiple plows. The efficient plows were produced locally and distributed nationally by H. C. Shaw.
PHOTOGRAPH COURTESY OF THE BANK OF STOCKTON.

❖

Above: In the 1870s, Matteson & Williamson of Stockton, improved and patented the combine harvester. The harvester was an important innovation in agricultural manufacturing as it combined the cutting and threshing of grains in a single process.

PHOTOGRAPH COURTESY OF THE BANK OF STOCKTON.

Below: John M. Kroyer was the blacksmith, bookkeeper and delivery person when he started Samson Iron Works in 1899 on the southeast corner of Washington and California streets. In the 1920s, he erected this large manufacturing plant on Aurora Street, near Jefferson Street.

PHOTOGRAPH COURTESY OF THE BANK OF STOCKTON.

Company merged with them to form the Caterpillar Tractor Company, which relocated to Illinois in 1925, leaving Stockton without a farm equipment manufacturer.

IRONWORKS AND FOUNDRIES

Ironworks and foundries in Stockton started as early as the 1850s to support the mining industry by providing materials for transportation and farm equipment. Globe Iron Works was among the early foundries in Stockton, established in 1858 at Main and Commerce streets. They had a reputation for making the finest mining cars in California, including the iron and steel Truax Automatic Dump Ore Car. Stockton Iron Works is the

city's oldest foundry, and started operating as early as 1868 under the name Farmington, Hyatt, and Company on the west side of California Street between Main Street and Miner Avenue. In the early 1900s, the foundry and machine shop moved to the north side of the Stockton Channel, where it operates today. The company was known for being the only brass foundry in the region, as well as the inventor of the clamshell dredging bucket, which was important for reclamation work in the Delta. John M. Kroyer founded Samson Iron Works around 1899 on the southeast corner of California and Washington streets. In the early 1900s, they moved to a large facility on the corner of Jefferson and Aurora streets. They became specialists in building gasoline engines, pumps, and tractors. In

Left: Globe Iron Works is one of Stockton's earliest foundries, established in 1858, at Main and Commerce streets. They began with the manufacturing of mining cars, before moving to farming equipment and eventually steam boating machinery.

PHOTOGRAPH COURTESY OF THE BANK OF STOCKTON.

1916, they changed their name to Samson Tractor Works and were purchased by General Motors the following year. Several other ironwork companies and foundries were sustained by the farm industry, including Marine Iron Works at McLeod Lake on the corner of Lindsay and Center streets and the Monarch Foundry on Oak Street.

PESTICIDE, BRICK AND POTTERY

The large farming industry in and around Stockton, as well as the city's proximity to the Delta, resulted in many pests. In the 1870s, Giovanno Milco, an immigrant from Croatia, created a pesticide called "Buhach," which is

Below: The Buhach Producing and Manufacturing Company's main office in the 1890s at Channel Street, between Center and El Dorado streets, near the waterfront. The company produced insecticide in the Merced area and distributed it from Stockton.

PHOTOGRAPH COURTESY OF THE BANK OF STOCKTON.

✧

An image from the 1890s of the National Ice Company by photographer Charles Logan. It was located on the southwest corner of Center and Taylor streets.

PHOTOGRAPH COURTESY OF THE BANK OF STOCKTON.

a powder produced from the flowers of the Pyrethrum plant. In 1873, Milco was growing the plants in Stockton and turned to successful local grain merchant, J. D. Peters, for capital to expand the business. The Buhach Producing and Manufacturing Company, whose main office was on Channel Street, acquired 300 acres near Atwater in Merced County to cultivate plants. The flowers from these plants were transported to the Stockton mill for grounding. Buhach was famous for being an environmentally safe, yet effective, insecticide. In the early 1940s, the Buhach Company went out of business when another insecticide, DDT, was developed.

As the early town suffered from many fires that burned wooden homes and structures, brick became increasingly important for construction. The first brick used in Stockton was shipped around Cape Horn from Massachusetts in 1851 for Charles Weber's chimney. Because common clays were abundant in San Joaquin County, brick was soon manufactured in Stockton. J. C. White started a brickyard in Stockton in 1851 and James Talmadge did in 1852, while Rood and Wallace ran the White House Brick Yard on Mariposa Road during those years. As

brickmaking remained an important industry during Stockton's Golden Era, small brick-yards had transitioned to large factories. In the 1920s, the San Joaquin Brick Company was making bricks from clay dredged around Robert Island. The Stockton Fire Brick Company and the Stockton Brick and Tile Company also had factories. Numerous examples of the first brick buildings built in Stockton are still standing, including Weber School and the Sperry Office.

Other types of manufacturing during the city's thriving economy included The Stockton Brick and Potter Company operating from 1891 to 1902 at Sacramento and Taylor streets. Using clay materials from nearby Tesla, they made clay sewer pipes, bricks, and pottery. They marketed their pottery as "Rekston ware", a term coined from the letters contained in Stockton Terra Cotta. In 1902 the National Ice Company at Center and Taylor announced they would be making ice and the Union Ice Company opened in 1914. A paint manufacturer built a plant on Hazelton Avenue that same year. In 1904 the Raymond Glove Factory opened on Main Street. The Western Fiber Company opened in 1905 and prepared flax for shipment to be spun into line, thread, and twine. In 1908 there was even talk of a silk mill, but it never materialized. The Stockton Box Company opened their sixty-acre plant in 1923 next to the Western Pacific railroad tracks. In the early 1900s, many of Stockton's businesses either directly or indirectly supported the agricultural industry.

BANKING

As supply center for the southern gold mines, Stockton's early banking pre-dates the city's official existence. Express companies, the predecessors of banks, offered services including large safes in which miners could deposit and transport their gold. Several express companies operated in Stockton with headquarters in San Francisco. The largest and most notorious of those first financial companies became Wells Fargo, whose office was on Center Street between Main Street and Weber Avenue.

Stockton's first actual bank was a canvas structure on Center Street, erected in 1849 by the T. Robinson Bours and Company. A fire burned the tent, so the bank built one of Stockton's first downtown brick structures in 1853. The bank reorganized as the San Joaquin Valley Bank and eventually became part of the Bank of Italy, now the Bank of America. The Commercial and Savings Bank, another early bank that merged with the Bank of Italy, built a ten-story Renaissance-style structure in 1915 that now serves as Cort Towers.

✧

The Masonic Temple on El Dorado between Bridge Place and Channel streets was completed in 1884 and demolished in 1933. The three story brick building and the barge unloading bricks exemplifies Stockton as a brick city during the late 1890s.

PHOTOGRAPH COURTESY OF THE BANK OF STOCKTON.

Right: In 1907, the San Joaquin Valley Bank opened this building on the west side of Hunter Square. The Bank of Italy bought the San Joaquin Valley Bank in 1917.

PHOTOGRAPH COURTESY OF THE BANK OF STOCKTON.

Below: The interior of the Union Safe Deposit in 1898, located at 30 N. San Joaquin Street with its money vault, teller cages and adding machines.

PHOTOGRAPH COURTESY OF THE BANK OF STOCKTON.

After the gold rush, the riches of the surrounding farmland brought tremendous economic opportunities to Stockton. The agricultural commerce and industrial development that followed created a need for security and safety in financing and banking. Some banks failed and many merged. Buildings from several of the early banks are still on Main Street, including the Union Safe Deposit Bank and the Farmers and Merchants Bank. The Bank of Stockton, originally called the Stockton Savings and Loan Society, was the first savings bank in Stockton and is now the oldest banking institution in California still operating under its original charter.

PHOTOGRAPHERS AND NEWSPAPERS

Stockton has historically been known for its good newspapers and newspapers often indicate a city's success. Stockton's first weekly newspaper was the *Stockton Times*, which was first issued in 1850 and was soon followed by several competitors, including the *Stockton Journal*, the *San Joaquin Republican*, and the *Evening Post*. There was a series of other papers published in Stockton over various periods. In the 1880s, the *Evening Herald* and the *Evening Mail* were

popular because of their emphasis on political headlines. In 1888, Irving Martin and William Denig started the *Commercial Record* in a basement on Parker's Alley near Hunter Street; it would later become the *Stockton Evening Record*. In 1895, Irving Martin bought out his partner and changed the paper's name to the *Stockton Record*.

Several important pioneer photographers recorded the early settlement and subsequent growth of Stockton from a supply center to an industrial city. The earliest photographers included Benjamin Batchelder, Isaac Locke, William Stuart, and J. Pitcher Spooner. By the 1860s, they had their own studios or galleries and created many of the portraits of early Stocktonians. The civic and commercial development that took place during

✧

Above: Stockton Savings and Loan Society building was completed in 1908 at San Joaquin and Main streets. This eight-story classical revival style building became known as the first skyscraper in Stockton. The bank was chartered in 1867 and became the Bank of Stockton in 1958.
PHOTOGRAPH COURTESY OF THE BANK OF STOCKTON.

Left: John Pitcher Spooner came from an apprenticeship in San Francisco and opened his own studio at 171 Main Street in 1870 which he operated until 1900. Here he is with his portrait camera in 1892.
PHOTOGRAPH COURTESY OF THE BANK OF STOCKTON.

✧

Below: The Stockton Daily Evening Mail building on Sutter Street between Market and Main streets. The first paper of the Evening Mail was issued in 1880, it quickly became a leading newspaper.

PHOTOGRAPH COURTESY OF THE BANK OF STOCKTON.

Opposite, top: Stockton Record started in 1895 and was the only newspaper in town by 1939. The Record moved to its current Market Street location in 1910.

PHOTOGRAPH COURTESY OF THE BANK OF STOCKTON.

Opposite, bottom: Local operators of the Pacific Telephone and Telegraph Company in the 1920s at its location on the corner of San Joaquin and Channel streets.

PHOTOGRAPH COURTESY OF THE BANK OF STOCKTON.

Stockton's Golden Era supported their practice as photographers. They also captured some of the cultural aspects of the beginning of Stockton's golden years. J. Pitcher Spooner can take most of the credit for doing so, as he documented many of Stockton's cultural institutions. V. Covert Martin, under the apprenticeship of Charles Logan and J. Pitcher Spooner, was both a commercial photographer and newspaper photographer. He captured much of the later part of Stockton's Golden Era, from 1920 to 1945.

Commercial artists also made valuable contributions to capturing Stockton's golden years. Ralph Yardley, Stockton's most famous illustrator, was born in 1878 and moved to San Francisco for art school and a career as an artist for the *San Francisco Examiner*, among other newspapers. In 1921, he returned to his hometown and began a long career as an illustrator at the *Stockton Record*. He was best known for his daily editorial cartoons, but his most popular contribution was the "Do You Remember?"

series that delved into the city's past through detailed drawings. Yardley would often work from old photographs to provide highly detailed glimpses of the city's bygone days. This weekly series was very popular and ran for two years beginning in 1924. Today, these drawings are a valuable visual history of Stockton.

TELEPHONE AND RADIO

As early as 1852, telegraph lines were installed between Stockton and San Francisco. In 1881 telephone service was established in San Joaquin County and the Stockton Telephone Company became the tenth telephone office in the state. This was only five years after Alexander Graham Bell invented the telephone. The Sunset Telephone and Telegraph Company took over in 1884 and moved to its own building on the corner of San Joaquin and Channel streets in 1892. They developed the first long-distance phone line from San Francisco to Stockton, before extending to other northern California cities. In 1907, the Pacific Telephone and Telegraph Company took over the exchange. From 1890 to 1930, the approximate span of Stockton's Golden Era, the company grew from 351 to 16,000 subscribers.

The first commercially licensed radio station in Stockton, and one of the first in the nation, was KWG, which launched in November of 1921. KJQ was licensed in December of that same year but was deleted in 1925. KWG remained on the air until 1999 when it was sold. Many other commercial radio stations started during and after Stockton's Golden Era, including KJOY in 1946 and KSTN in 1949. The KGDM station started

in 1926 at the Peffer Music Store on Channel Street. This popular radio station operated under those call letters until 1957, when it changed to KRAK. The radio had an important impact on the city's culture, as a new form of entertainment with influences of consumerism and travel. By 1930, more than half of American families had radios.

CHAPTER 5

DISTRIBUTION AND TRANSPORTATION

HORSES AND CARRIAGES

✧

Livery stables were some of the first
commercial enterprises, Wolf's Livery &
Feed on Sutter Street around 1890.
PHOTOGRAPH COURTESY OF THE BANK OF STOCKTON.

Stockton has been a distribution and transportation center since the Gold Rush days. In 1948, the traffic along the river in Stockton increased dramatically where eager gold seekers shored their boats and headed for the mines. Stage coaches, pack animals and horses bore the burden of the increasing demand to transport passengers and freight to the mines. The establishment of livery stables, such as the Avenue Stable on Weber Avenue, was one of the first business developments in Stockton. Andrew Wolf and A. J. Colburn operated stables on Main Street. In 1856, there were four stables operating within three blocks. In order to support the stables, saddle and harness shops flourished, as did black smiths. The need for transporting passengers and freight also led to an important carriage- and wagon-building industry in Stockton.

By the late 1800s, there were at least ten wagon and carriage plants in Stockton. John Fairbanks made the first wagon in Stockton in 1851 and William P. Miller built the first freight wagon in 1852. Miller had his carriage plant at the southwest corner of Channel and California streets. It was rumored he salvaged the wood and the metal from the many abandoned ships in the channel and sloughs to build his carriages. He became famous for manufacturing "The Stockton," one of the biggest freight wagons built in the West. Milton P. Henderson, eventually known as a hardware dealer, established himself in 1869 and became famous for supplying the wagons that pulled the borax out of the Death Valley mines, as well as for selling wagon replacement parts. Many of these Stockton carriage plants made wagons and shipped them by steamers throughout California and the West.

EARLY WATER TRANSPORTATION

Stockton owes much of its prosperity to its location at the head of the channel that bears its name. As the world rushed to the gold mines in 1849, many came to Stockton by water and abandoned their boats as they headed for the mines on land. The first boats to enter Stockton were whale boats powered by sails, they took as many as three days to make the journey from San Francisco. One of the first vessels on the San Joaquin River was the sailing sloop, *Maria*. It was loaded with thirteen tons of supplies in San Francisco in 1848 before traveling to the head of the Stockton Channel. As industry shifted from supply center for the gold mines to agricultural distribution center, so did river transportation.

Agricultural products that were grown, processed and stored in Stockton were exported from the wharves of the Stockton Channel. Schooners were vessels with flat bottoms that would carry huge loads on their decks.

Sturdy vessels with flat bottoms had the ability to navigate shallow waters, including Stockton's sloughs. There were five sloughs that came together at the head of the Stockton Channel. In the 1870s, Stockton developed a public transportation system when it exchanged passengers between steamships with riverboat companies on the west side of the Stockton Channel and freight on a rail of a railroad company on the east side of the Channel.

✦

Above: William P. Miller Carriage Manufacturing located on the corner of Channel and California streets, 1890.
PHOTOGRAPH COURTESY OF THE BANK OF STOCKTON.

Below: Schooner loaded with bark from the oak forests of the northwest to be used for the tanning process at the Pacific Tannery, 1890.
PHOTOGRAPH COURTESY OF THE BANK OF STOCKTON.

STEAMBOATS AND RIVERBOAT COMPANIES

✧

Above: The Mary Garratt, *built for the California Steam Navigation Company in 1878, loaded with bags of grains at the Stockton Channel.*

PHOTOGRAPH COURTESY OF THE BANK OF STOCKTON.

Right: The J. D. Peters, *a famous riverboat built in 1889, at the end of the Stockton Channel at the California Navigation Company docks.*

PHOTOGRAPH COURTESY OF THE BANK OF STOCKTON.

Opposite, top: The Head of Navigation in the 1890s with schooners and steamships to carry freight and passengers, Sperry Flour Mills in the background.

PHOTOGRAPH COURTESY OF THE BANK OF STOCKTON.

Opposite, bottom: The Stockton Channel from the El Dorado Street bridge during the delivery of mail and transportation of workers in 1923.

PHOTOGRAPH COURTESY OF THE BANK OF STOCKTON.

There was such a demand for passage and freight to the gold mines during the Gold Rush that the river transportation industry flourished. In 1848, the first steam powered ships reached the head of the channel in Stockton. Many of the early steamboats were side-wheelers, since they could navigate the river more successfully. The California Steam Navigation Company, later the Navigation and Improvement Company, was organized in 1854. The company purchased all the river steamers at the time and monopolized river transportation in Stockton. They were headquartered across the channel at Weber Avenue and Commerce Street. The Union Transportation Company was founded in 1892. At the turn of the century during the height of the golden years, these two major Stockton steamboat lines eventually merged to become the California Transportation Company.

✧

Above: The steamers, Captain Weber *and* J. D. Peters, *at the head of the Stockton Channel in 1912, buildings from left to right the Masonic Hall, the Hotel Stockton and the San Joaquin County Courthouse.*

PHOTOGRAPH COURTESY OF THE BANK OF STOCKTON.

Right: In 1927, the Delta Queen *and* Delta King *were the largest steamships built in Stockton before the completion of the Deep Water Channel.*

PHOTOGRAPH COURTESY OF THE BANK OF STOCKTON.

The *T. C. Walker*, a riverboat that accommodated 226 passengers, was built in 1885 and ran between Stockton and San Francisco until the 1930s. The boat was named after an influential riverboat captain and president of the California Steam Navigation Company, who navigated the San Joaquin River. The *J. D. Peters* was an 880-ton sternwheeler built in 1889 at the Jarvis Shipyard in Stockton and named after a prominent local grain merchant. For almost fifty years, this steamer traveled between Stockton and San Francisco carrying freight and passengers, before retiring and being used for small excursion trips.

The steamboat was destroyed in a grass fire in 1965. The *T. C. Walker* and the *J. D. Peters* have both been preserved on the big screen when used in the filming of *Steamboat 'Round the Bend*, which was released in 1935 and starred Will Rogers.

DELTA QUEEN AND DELTA KING

The largest and most luxurious stern-wheelers ever built, the *Delta Queen* and *Delta King*, were constructed by the California Transportation Company along the Stockton Channel. In 1924 the hulls, decks and steam engines were prefabricated in Scotland and brought to Stockton for assembly. The two steamers were dedicated on May 20, 1927, and providing luxurious passenger service from Sacramento and San Francisco. The building of highways resulted in increased train, auto, and truck transportation forcing these distinguished riverboats out of service around 1940. These two sternwheelers were the last river steamers built in California and the last passenger-carrying sternwheelers built in the United States. These identical twins have been restored and preserved,

the *Delta Queen* currently in Chattanooga Tennessee and the *Delta King* in Sacramento. They are on the National Register of Historic Places and the *Delta Queen* is also a National Historic Landmark. They serve as symbols of commercial and industrial development during Stockton's Golden Era.

STEAMBOAT RACES

Although riverboat races were common, a Golden Empire Centennial celebration in Stockton in 1938 led the mayor of Sacramento, Tom B. Monk, to challenge the Ralph W. Fay who was the mayor of Stockton to a steamboat race. The race pitted the *Delta Queen* owned by Sacramento, against the steamboat named *Port of Stockton*. The mayors were the captains of the sixteen-mile highly publicized steamboat race, which Stockton won. Sacramento claimed unfair advantages by Stockton related to shipping weight, which led to another race on April 22, 1939. The *Delta King* was Stockton's entry this time against Sacramento's *Delta Queen*, and Stockton won again. Thereafter, river transportation declined as road and rail transportation became more popular for transporting freight and passengers.

✧

Local steamers on the Delta used for the filming of the Steamboat Round the Bend *starring Will Rogers, released in 1935.*
PHOTOGRAPH COURTESY OF THE BANK OF STOCKTON.

RAIL TRANSPORTATION

✧

Above: The Southern Pacific Railroad Station at Sacramento Street, between Main Street and Weber Avenue, 1909.

PHOTOGRAPH COURTESY OF THE BANK OF STOCKTON.

Below: The Santa Fe Depot around 1900, built in California's unique Mission Revival Style and similar to other train depots along its route.

PHOTOGRAPH COURTESY OF THE BANK OF STOCKTON.

Opposite, top: Southern Pacific Railroad passenger service on Weber Avenue, between Hunter and San Joaquin streets, 1890s.

PHOTOGRAPH COURTESY OF THE BANK OF STOCKTON

Opposite, bottom: Streetcar of the Stockton Electric Railroad Company, founded in 1891, at the end of California Street at Alpine Street and Oak Park.

PHOTOGRAPH COURTESY OF THE BANK OF STOCKTON.

Stockton was the center of freight and passenger rail transportation in the San Joaquin Valley and had three transcontinental railroads and numerous small railroad lines, which were instrumental in Stockton's development from pioneer town to industrial city. The railroad became the chief mode of exporting crops since refrigerated cars were able to hold produce. The depots were the city's portals to the world as people, information, and products flowed through railroad stations. The city's first passenger depot, a wood-frame building, was completed in 1869 by the Western Pacific Railroad, the railroad that later became the Central Pacific Railroad and then the Southern Pacific Railroad. In 1869

the rail connected Sacramento to San Francisco via Stockton. This was a significant link for the city, because several months earlier Sacramento had become the western end of the first transcontinental railroad, the Central Pacific Railroad.

In 1898, the Santa Fe Railroad came to Stockton and built a depot at San Joaquin and Taylor streets, which is now the oldest railroad station in the city. It served as the northern terminal of the San Francisco and San Joaquin Valley Railroad, or the "Valley Road." The railroad tracks passed through Fresno on their way to the end of the San Joaquin Valley, near Bakersfield. In 1900 the Santa Fe operated three trains a day between Stockton and San Francisco. Oak Park in Stockton became a popular resort area for San Franciscans and, in 1904, the Santa Fe offered Sunday excursions from San Francisco. In 1909 the Western Pacific became the third transcontinental railway line to reach Stockton, running from Oakland to Salt Lake City. During Stockton's Golden Era, Stockton was the only city in California to have three transcontinental railroad connections.

Some of the smaller local railroads and shorter lines included the Stockton and Copperopolis Railroad, which traveled into the foothills of the Sierra Nevada. It provided transportation for the copper brought back to Stockton for distribution. The railroad started on the Weber Avenue tracks to the waterfront in 1870, and reached the town of Milton, a few miles from Copperopolis. There were numerous other railroad lines, such as the Stockton and Visalia Railroad, which reached Stanislaus County in 1872. The Stockton Terminal and Eastern Railroad began going to Linden in 1910 and the Tidewater Southern Railway went to Modesto in 1912. The railroad lowered the cost of transportation and provided easier access to some of the more remote areas that had materials and products to distribute.

STREETCARS AND TROLLEYS

Streetcars are as much of Stockton's history as riverboats and railroads. At the height of Stockton's streetcar era in the 1920s, there were twenty-eight miles of track crisscrossing downtown with as many as forty streetcars in operation. Streetcar service began in Stockton in 1874 with horse and mule drawn cars. A typical car was drawn by a mule and could accommodate many passengers. The first lines of the Stockton Street Railway Company ran along Main and California

✧

Miner Avenue became a popular location for auto dealerships beginning in the 1920s. The Renney Motors here in 1953 on the corner of Miner Avenue and Sutter Street.

PHOTOGRAPH COURTESY OF THE BANK OF STOCKTON.

streets. Streetcars were a convenient mode of transportation for travelers arriving by riverboat or railroad, because they provided access to popular recreational destinations. The California Street line extended from downtown to Oak Park, which was then known as Goodwater Grove. Another line traveled south on San Joaquin Street to the Mineral Baths, now McKinley Park. In 1892, electric streetcars, often referred to as trolleys, replaced the horse-drawn streetcars.

By 1906, two such streetcar companies served the city, the Stockton Electric Railroad Company and the Central California Traction Company. Tracks were converted, cars were modified and lines were extended. Trolleys enabled Stocktonians to visit the thriving downtown business district, which was filled with fashionable stores and famous theatres. The last track was built in 1924 by extending the Tuxedo Line from Oxford Circle along Kensington Avenue, to the College of the Pacific, as it was called at the time. As competition from automobiles and buses increased during the 1930s, ridership of the trolleys began to decline. After more than sixty-five years of service in Stockton, streetcars made their last run on September 28, 1941. The original rails and cars have disappeared but vestiges and fond memories remain. The brick car barn for the California line can be seen on California Street, just south of Alpine Avenue.

AUTOMOBILES AND ROADS

As it did in most other California cities, the automobile revolution had a considerable impact on Stockton beginning in the 1910s. In the 1920s, there were over fifty auto service stations, more than forty garages and twenty-seven auto dealers in the Stockton area. In the early 1900s, the Stockton Automobile Company became one of the first auto companies and Pacific Garage became one of the first garages. The first auto wash opened in 1920 on Market Street. Increasing competition among companies and dealers led to numerous show rooms and repair shops being built along El Dorado Street and Miner Avenue. The automobile fueled many other businesses such as auto camps, auto rentals, tire shops, auto repair shops and auto painter shops during Stockton's Golden Era.

The increase of traffic also led to changes in the streets and roads, which had been gravel and dirt but became streets, oiled and asphalted lanes. The county and city roads later linked to highways and turnpikes. The road improvements also led to adaptation, such as the underground diversion of Miner Avenue where it crosses a railroad track. In 1912, an automobile ride from Stockton to Sacramento took approximately four hours. Howell Taxi was the first taxi stand in Stockton and was established in 1908 in front of the Commercial Hotel on Main Street. Commercial buses also gained popularity in the 1920s, and the California Transit Company located on El Dorado Street provided Stockton's first such services.

STOCKTON FIELD AND THE AIRPORT

One of the earliest pilots to land a plane in Stockton was Lincoln Beachy whose biplane landed on the San Joaquin County Fairgrounds race track in 1914. It was thereafter that biplanes began to be used for crop dusting and contributed to the development of air freight, which was used for transporting agricultural products across the country. World War II brought an increased demand for industrial production, military training and supplies and three military installations were built near the city. Stockton Field was an Army Air Force transport base and training facility from 1940 to 1945 located on the site of the current Stockton Metropolitan Airport. The Stockton Field trained about 200 pilots every two months. In 1944 the facility was consolidated and purchased by the United States Army and used as a logistical aviation hub due to its proximity to other facilities.

In December 1946, under a joint license, the City of Stockton and San Joaquin County

resumed operating the Stockton Field as the Stockton Municipal Airport. The airport comprises about 1,000 acres of land, and a small portion of those acres was annexed by the Army as a depot for maintenance, storage and shipping. On July 8, 1957, the City of Stockton had transferred its interest in the Stockton Municipal Airport to San Joaquin County. Sharpe Army Depot Field Annex was vacated in 1973, ending the Army's presence on the field. This led all of the land and buildings to revert to San Joaquin County, and to the subsequent full conversion to a civilian airport.

✧

Above: In the 1970s, the Stockton Metropolitan Airport's administrative offices, restaurants, lounge and a banquet rooms served three airlines.
PHOTOGRAPH COURTESY OF THE BANK OF STOCKTON.

Below: Metropolitan Room Restaurant and Flight Deck Bar at the Stockton Metropolitan Airport, 1960s.
PHOTOGRAPH COURTESY OF THE BANK OF STOCKTON.

Home of Moses Rodgers, a former slave from Missouri, on San Joaquin Street. The historic landmark was built in 1898 and illustrates Moses' success during the Gold Rush as a pioneer in mining engineering.
PHOTOGRAPH COURTESY OF THE BANK OF STOCKTON.

CHAPTER 6

IMMIGRATION AND LABOR

AFRICAN AMERICAN PIONEERS

African Americans contributed to the development of Stockton from the very beginning. In 1849 the Gold Rush drew many African Americans from across the country that were free, or seeking to buy their freedom working the mines. After the rush a number of them settled in Stockton, specifically west of Center Street, between Mormon Channel and Weber Avenue. Stockton's founder, Charles Weber, donated property to various groups to build their religious institutions or places of worship. African Americans used the land from Weber to build the African Baptist Church, also known as the Second Baptist Church, and the African Methodist Episcopal Church, which were two of the first African American churches in Stockton. African American children were not allowed to attend public schools, so they organized their own school in 1860. The school was incorporated in the Stockton school district in 1863, although remained a segregated facility until full integration in 1879.

The Gold Rush brought a diverse population of people to Stockton from a variety of ethnic and cultural backgrounds. Those groups that stayed and settled each carved out a particular function in the community with many of them well established by the time Stockton entered its most industrious era in the 1890s. Members of the African American community established small businesses in the service industry, such as barbershops and wagon services. Many also found opportunities in the farming industry. There were also a few large employers that hired African American workers at the beginning of this era, including Wells Fargo, the Sperry Flour Mill, and the El Dorado Brewing Company. African Americans were the only non-white people who could purchase land, so investing in property was common. African Americans bought property throughout the city, much of it was concentrated in the city's commercial center.

HISPANIC SETTLERS AND WORKERS

In the early 1850s, Hispanics represented an important part of Stockton's population. Many were born in Mexico, but natives of Spain and Central and South American countries also came to Stockton. During the first few years of the city's history, there were several Hispanic-owned businesses in Stockton. The most notable was Manuel Ainsa's general merchandise store, which in 1850 was located on Main Street between El Dorado and Center streets. Ainsa owned additional land parcels downtown and was an important business resource for Hispanic pioneers in Stockton. As industry shifted to agriculture after the Gold Rush, many Hispanics worked as farm laborers, while some continued pursuing business opportunities. Theodore Cruz, a Mexican immigrant, operated an eatery called the Mexican Restaurant at the northwest corner of Hunter and Market streets in 1878. Marcelo Negrete came to Stockton from Mexico in 1895 to become an acclaimed harness maker.

Severe inflation in Mexico that doubled the cost of living, combined with the Mexican Revolution, forced many Mexicans to immigrate to America looking for work during the first few decades of the twentieth century. Most Mexican immigrants found work in agriculture, but many also worked on the construction of railroads. America's involvement in World War I created a farm labor shortage, which led to a large number of contract workers arriving from Mexico. Industry had used Mexican contract workers before, but not on a large scale. They provided low-cost labor and were able to return easily to their native and nearby country after the war. They endured social discrimination and economic abuse but many stayed after the war to take advantage of the continuous labor opportunities. In 1942 another severe shortage of laborers led the United States to contract again with Mexico for labor under the Braceros Program. On September 29, 1942, the first braceros arrived to work in the fields of Stockton.

CHINESE IMMIGRANTS

Thousands of Chinese from the Kwangtung province came to Stockton during the 1850s, due to a combination of political and economic unrest in China and the discovery of gold in California. After the Gold Rush, many found opportunities in railroad and reclamation projects and settled in Stockton. By 1880, the city was home to the third-largest Chinese community in California. The earliest Chinese community in Stockton was located on Channel Street between Hunter and El Dorado streets. Fire destroyed much

✧

Above: California pioneer and civil rights worker William Robison (1821-1899) was born a slave in Virginia and made Stockton his home after finding success with hauling freight for express companies, including Wells Fargo.

PHOTOGRAPH COURTESY OF THE HAGGIN MUSEUM.

Below: Northern edge of Stockton's Chinatown, looking west on Market Street in the 1940s.

PHOTOGRAPH COURTESY OF THE BANK OF STOCKTON.

✧

Right: The original On Lock Sam Restaurant was started on E. Washington Street between Hunter and El Dorado streets in 1898.

PHOTOGRAPH COURTESY OF THE BANK OF STOCKTON.

Below: Quan Yaks Chinese and Japanese Bazaar in the early 1890s, first located on Hunter Street and later on Main Street.

PHOTOGRAPH COURTESY OF THE BANK OF STOCKTON.

of this original settlement and the community moved to the south bank of Mormon Slough. Later, the center of commerce and social activity for the Chinese community moved to East Washington Street between Center and Hunter streets. The area was well known for its residences, restaurants, stores, and gambling houses.

The Chinese were culturally different from other immigration groups at the time and faced discrimination at various levels, including through ordinances and laws. The discriminatory laws, including the Chinese Exclusion Act of 1882, restricted immigration and prevented the Chinese from buying property. After the turn of the century, American-born Chinese were allowed to purchase land and own buildings. The Lincoln Hotel, built in 1920 by the Wong brothers on El Dorado Street, was considered one of Stockton's finest hotels of the time. During the 1960s, redevelopment and construction of the Crosstown Freeway destroyed most of the original Chinatown, but there are some reminders of its illustrious past. The promenade on Chung Wah Lane was built on the site of the original Chinatown and Chinese family associations are still located in the area, a reminder of their resilience and perseverance.

ITALIAN ENTREPRENEURS

Italians were among the first Europeans to navigate and explore the California coast in the 1830s, mainly as fisherman and not necessarily as settlers. In 1849 the discovery of gold brought its share of Italians to the gold mines, including to the southern mines. After the Gold Rush, Italians were able to transition more easily to the agricultural opportunities because of the similar environment and climate as in their native land. The "Italian Gardens" created in San Joaquin County allowed them to grow fruits and vegetables which were sold in downtown Stockton and its surrounding towns. The creation of Italian Gardeners Society in 1902, initially established as a mutual aid society, is an example of their collaboration and support to their own community.

The Unification of the Italian States in 1861 was followed by political, social and economic unrest in Italy leading many to immigrate to America. In 1869, the largest number of Italian immigrants in the United States, mostly from northern Italy, lived in California. A second wave of immigration occurred the 1880s, at the beginning of Stockton's Golden Era. Italians faced minimal discrimination, compared to other immigrant groups, and combined with their existing farming skills and business expertise allowed for relatively easy integration into society. Italian immigrants and pioneers made a huge impact to the culture, agriculture and business in Stockton.

JAPANESE FARMERS

The unstable price of rice, shrinking food supply, and the raiding of farms had taken a toll on Japanese peasants during the later years of the Tokugawa Shogunate regime. The end of the regime in 1867 lifted many of Japan's restrictions, including opportunities for travel outside the country. The continuing plight of the farmers and the lure of opportunities in California led many Japanese to immigrate to Stockton in the late 1800s. In California, the Chinese Exclusion Act of 1882 also impacted the existing labor supply, providing an even greater need for the Japanese settlers. Many Japanese immigrants worked hard and efficiently as farm laborers. Their skill at farming and the opportunity to save money allowed many to have their own farms over time. Japanese farmers prospered, largely because of their ability to diversify from the existing crops and traditional harvesting techniques.

Although the 1912 Alien Land and Naturalization Act prevented Japanese people from owning land, they prospered by leasing much of the fertile land surrounding Stockton. Japanese settlers in Stockton formed a strong and independent community by establishing their own newspaper, forming community associations, and establishing a Buddhist

The Nippon Hospital on Commerce Street was built in 1919 by the local Japanese community after the influenza outbreak.
PHOTOGRAPH COURTESY OF RON CHAPMAN.

✧

Above: Filipinos migrated to Stockton because of the farm opportunities in the Delta region, 1920s.

PHOTOGRAPH COURTESY OF THE BANK OF STOCKTON.

Below: The Daguhoy Lodge of the Legionarios del Trabajo purchased this building on Hazelton Avenue in 1937 to be used for a Filipino meeting hall, it is a Stockton historic landmark today.

PHOTOGRAPH COURTESY OF THE BANK OF STOCKTON.

FILIPINO COMMUNITY

In 1898, America colonized the Philippines, which drove immigration from the Philippines to Hawaii and other American states that had thriving agricultural industries. In the 1920s, many Filipinos working in Hawaii's sugar plantations began to immigrate to Stockton and the Delta region for better wages and more year-round work opportunities. The 1924 Immigration Act excluded Japanese and Chinese laborers from working, which put Filipino nationals in high demand for agricultural work. By the late 1920s, Filipinos had become the largest ethnic group engaged in the county's farm labor force. Several Filipino labor leaders, including Larry Itliong, played important roles in organizing Filipino farm workers to unionize and strike to improve agricultural working conditions during the 1930s.

Stockton Filipinos were discouraged to reside or travel north of Main Street, so they built their own community south of Main Street. The six-block area centered on LaFayette and El Dorado streets included

church and school. By the 1920s, Stockton had one of the largest Japanese communities in the United States. Japanese culture and food permeated Stockton during the city's Golden Era. The attack on Pearl Harbor in 1941 and the subsequent placement of Japanese Americans in relocation and internment camps had a significant and lasting impact on the Japanese American community. The Japanese were released from these camps after the war, and were able to become American citizens in 1952, for some after three generations of being in America.

restaurants, stores, shops, dancing halls, and social clubs. By 1946, Stockton's Little Manila was the largest community of Filipinos outside of the Philippines and an important social and business destination for those who lived and worked in the San Joaquin Delta area. In the late 1950s, the city initiated the West End Redevelopment as an effort to revitalize the downtown area and demolished many buildings located in Little Manila. The physical destruction and the displacement of the Filipino community had a devastating impact on Stockton Filipinos.

OTHER MIGRANT AND IMMIGRANTS

The migration from across the country and the immigration from outside the country have been an integral part of Stockton's successes and its rich cultural diversity today. It was the Chinese, Japanese, Filipino and Mexican immigrants who assembled the railroad track, built the levee systems and harvested the crops. The African Americans and the Italians have been in Stockton since the Gold Rush and went on to establish businesses in the service and farming industry to support the city during its thriving economy of the early 1900s. Another group whose contribution has been important is the Sikhs from East India who came here in the early 1900s and began farming outside of Stockton. In 1912, they established the first Sikh Temple in the United States on Grant Street in Stockton. Another group, although not ethically or racially diverse, are the displaced farmers from the Midwest during the Dust Bowl of 1934 who found work in the Stockton area, or started their own businesses.

✧

In 1912, the first Sikh Temple in the United States was established on this Grant Street lot. This brick Sikh Temple building was constructed in 1929.
PHOTOGRAPH COURTESY OF THE BANK OF STOCKTON.

CHAPTER 7

INDUSTRIES
AND DEVELOPMENT

TANNERIES

✧

A 1890s view of the Pacific Tannery, a
major industry in Stockton located at
El Dorado and Oak streets.

PHOTOGRAPH COURTESY OF THE BANK OF STOCKTON.

The abundance of cattle in the area surrounding Stockton, combined with the demand for leather goods from miners and stables, spurred the opening of several tanneries in Stockton by 1856. These early leather-making businesses included the Pioneer Tannery near the State Hospital grounds, the tanneries of Graham & Stewart on the north side of the main Stockton Channel, and H. R. Porter along Mormon Slough. The tanneries used the bark from local black oak trees to create tannic acid, which in combination with the gelatin from the hides produces leather. The Stockton Tannery on Scott's Avenue between Hunter and El Dorado streets and the Pacific Tannery at El Dorado and Oak streets grew into one of the largest tanneries on the West Coast.

The Pacific Tannery, which was located along where Martin Luther King Plaza is now, was once McLeod Lake. This one-block site provided the tannery with direct access to the Stockton Channel. German immigrants Charles and Jacob Wagner, who had come here during the Gold Rush, established the Pacific Tannery in 1856. Stockton founder Charles Weber sold the land for the tannery to the Wagner family. The leather processed by the company eventually was shipped all over the world. In the 1920s, overseas market competition for the tanning industry forced the closure of the Pacific Tannery, which was at that time was referred to as the Wagner Leather Company. The facility transformed into Pacific Storage in 1932. Today, the engine and pump room of the tannery built in 1876 still stands on Oak Street.

BREWERIES

Brewing was one of Stockton's earliest industries. In the early 1850s, Philip Niestrath ran the City Brewery and David Mickie operated a small brewery on Weber Avenue. There were others, such as the San Joaquin Brewery and the Humboldt Brewery, but most of them were short-lived. The most successful brewery was the El Dorado Brewing Company, founded by the Rothenbush family in 1853. It grew into a large production facility on the block between American, Stanislaus, Park, and Oak streets. They produced the award-winning "Valley Brew," which was delivered to many local restaurants and saloons in the Central Valley. They remained in business during the Prohibition Era by manufacturing ice, sodas,

✧

The El Dorado Brewing Company was founded by the Rothenbush family in 1853. The brewery received early recognition for producing "steam beer" which was marketed under "El Dorado Beer." The brewery grew into a large production facility, located on the block between American and Stanislaus, and Park and Oak streets.

PHOTOGRAPH COURTESY OF THE BANK OF STOCKTON.

and a "near beer" called Special Valley. The California State Fair in 1953 recognized the El Dorado Brewing Company for making a single product for more than a century at the same location by the same family.

GLASS AND WOOL

In 1902, the Pacific Window Glass Company became the first glass factory built west of the Mississippi. The sand used to make the glass was three-quarters quartz and one-quarter clay, and was mined in Tesla, a town near Livermore. The sand was transported by railroad to the factory, located on South Hunter Street, now McKinley Park, to be transformed into window panes. The business became extremely important when the 1906 San Francisco earthquake created a great demand for glass. In 1907 the company employed about 200 skilled workers. A temporary office on Post Street in

San Francisco allowed for expedited orders of what was considered the highest-quality glass on the West Coast.

Another Stockton industry that prospered during Stockton's Golden Era was the production of woolen blankets and cloths. Stockton Woolen Mills was located just south of the Mormon Channel, at Lincoln Street. A sheep owner and two others who had experience in the manufacturing of textiles started the mill. Wool production encouraged some of the early Basque migration from the Basque Country, which is partially in the north of Spain and the south of France. The capacity of the plant doubled in the 1890s as much of its focus went toward blanket manufacturing. The factory was taken over by E. H. Tyron, a wool dealer out of San Francisco, and renamed Tyron Wool Scouring Plant. The business closed in 1933 during the Great Depression.

❖

Below: The Pacific Window Glass Company was built south of what is now McKinley Park in 1902.

PHOTOGRAPH COURTESY OF THE BANK OF STOCKTON.

Opposite, top: Stockton Woolen Mills as viewed from the Mormon Channel near Lincoln Street in the 1890s.

PHOTOGRAPH COURTESY OF THE BANK OF STOCKTON.

Opposite, bottom: In 1891, the Stockton Woolen Mills manufactured blankets and flannels, with two carding machines, nine looms and hundreds of spindles.

PHOTOGRAPH COURTESY OF THE BANK OF STOCKTON.

Above: Officer Benjamin Cassidy directing traffic in 1926 on Main Street at California Street.

PHOTOGRAPH COURTESY OF THE BANK OF STOCKTON.

Right: The Medico-Dental building was constructed in 1927 and the twelve-story structure was devoted exclusively for medical and dental offices.

PHOTOGRAPH COURTESY OF THE BANK OF STOCKTON.

The city's earliest businesses were clustered around the waterfront, a convenient location for trade and transport to the gold mines. By 1851, the area had been devastated by a series of floods and fires and businesses had started migrating towards Hunter Square and Main Street. The period during which the bulk of construction occurred in this new downtown ranged from the 1880s to the late 1930s. The devastating floods of 1907 were followed by a burst of commercial construction downtown, with five high-rise buildings built between 1910 and 1917, including the Medico-Dental Building, the California Building, and the Bank of Stockton. At the same time, an intense period of hotel and apartment construction took place, which led to the construction of various two- to four-story commercial structures, many along Main Street.

MAIN STREET

The earliest buildings on Main Street were wood-framed grocery and provision stores, saddle and harness shops, and hardware and machinery merchants. Horse-drawn carts and buggies traveled the unpaved road while pedestrians used the wooden sidewalks. As Stockton grew into an industrial city by the late 1800s, streetcars were running down Main Street and the presence of banks, hotels, and theaters attracted a steady flow of visitors. Main Street boasted several skyscrapers by the 1930s and it became the center of Stockton's leading shops and prominent businesses. The pioneer stores were replaced by larger retail stores, including the Owl Drug Company, J. C. Penney, and Woolworth. Nevertheless, many specialty shops and small businesses remained. Construction downtown declined significantly by the 1940s as the city grew outside of its center and the economy slowed.

STOCKTON STREETS

Stockton founder Charles Weber donated the streets and public squares to the city on August 28, 1851, almost a year after the city's incorporation. Weber named most of the streets and the parks based on names from the second city survey by Major Richard P. Hammond. Many of the public parks have patriotic significance, such as Independence, Fremont, and Washington parks. In the northern part of the city, a series of streets were named after common plants, such as Flora, Poplar and Magnolia streets. In the west, the streets were called after animals from the region, including Beaver, Elk, and Otter streets. Weber named the Mormon Channel after prominent Mormon and California settler Sam Brannan, whose party transported goods up the channel. To the south of Mormon Channel, the streets were named after Civil War generals and battles, such as Scott, Taylor, Butler, Twiggs, and Lee streets.

As early as 1850, attempts were made to pave the adobe streets of Stockton because they were dusty in the summers and muddy in the winters. By 1860, Main Street and

Hunter Square were graded and graveled. At that same time, the French Camp Turnpike or the "Old French Camp Toll Road" was developed, improving road transportation from the region south of Stockton into the city. Although the downtown streets were graveled by 1900, wagons were still sprinkling water during the summer to settle the dust. By that time, street names were being changed to presidents, such as Madison, Harrison, and Lincoln. Charles Weber even requested to have Jose Jesus Street, named by him in honor of his Native American friend, changed to Grant Street. In 1925, North Street became Harding Way, East Street was renamed Wilson Way, South Street became Charter Way, and West Street turned into Pershing Avenue.

✤

Top: The Hotel Clark was located on the southeast corner of Market and Sutter streets, adjacent to it was a "pee wee" eighteen hole miniature golf course which was a popular pastime during the Depression.

PHOTOGRAPH COURTESY OF THE BANK OF STOCKTON.

Above: The lobby of the Hotel Clark which was considered one of the top three hotels in Stockton during the 1920s.

PHOTOGRAPH COURTESY OF THE BANK OF STOCKTON.

✧

Right: The Newell Home on San Joaquin Street in the Magnolia District, built in 1888 and a fine example of the Queen Anne style architecture.

PHOTOGRAPH COURTESY OF THE BANK OF STOCKTON.

Below: The entrance gates to Tuxedo Park, a development completed by 1919 along Pacific Avenue, west of the Miracle Mile.

PHOTOGRAPH COURTESY OF THE BANK OF STOCKTON.

RESIDENTIAL DEVELOPMENT

In 1850, Stockton was one square block bounded by Flora, Aurora, Edison, and Anderson streets. In the early 1870s, the city limits were extended to a four-square-mile block bordered by what are now Harding Way, Wilson Way, Charter Way, and Pershing Avenue. At that same time, the Magnolia District just north of the downtown business district became one of the first residential developments. Prior to that time, most families lived outside the city on farms and ranches but there was an increasing societal shift during the early 1870s to move closer to churches, school, and social activities. The large homes in the Magnolia District had impressive living spaces that included attics, basements, and porches. The residences, many of which are still there, represented the prevailing architectural styles of the time. They were often adorned with ornate woodwork, brick chimneys, and stained glass over their main entrances.

The growth and development of residential areas north of the city's epicenter continued from the late 1800s to the 1920s, during Stockton's Golden Era. These more affluent developments included Victory Park, Tuxedo Park, and Bours Park. The Bours Park area was developed in 1912 to become an exclusive community in a six-block area with elaborate entrance gates. Its twenty acres of land were once owned by investor and capitalist Benjamin W. Bours, and they served as his homestead in 1860. This upscale neighborhood symbolizes Stockton's wealth during the prosperous economy of the early 1900s. The automobile revolution led to more road and further residential development around the city. In 1909, the Morada subdivision was built in the northeast part of the city. Many subdivisions bordered the city and most were gradually annexed into the municipality over the decades.

✧

Bours Park at the corner of San Joaquin and Hunter streets, an architectural treasure trove of residential homes.

PHOTOGRAPH COURTESY OF THE BANK OF STOCKTON.

DOWNTOWN HOTELS

The Imperial Hotel was designed by local architect Charles Beasley and completed in 1898 for the Rothenbush family, owners of the El Dorado Brewing Company.

PHOTOGRAPH COURTESY OF THE BANK OF STOCKTON.

Stockton's hotel history dates back to the town's very beginnings. The St. Charles Hotel, first called the Stockton House, was built in 1849 on the north shore between Center and El Dorado streets and considered one of the finest earlier hotels. The three-story building that accommodated as many seventy people burned to the ground in 1871. The many travelers coming to Stockton by water or rail before the 1900s required numerous accommodations. The Yosemite House and the Imperial Hotel were some of the other leaders in providing lodging before the turn of the century. The Imperial Hotel, designed in the lavish Victorian Eclectic style, was constructed in 1898 at Aurora and Main streets. It was the first hotel to have hot and cold water in each of the guest rooms and was considered the city's finest hotel until the Hotel Stockton was constructed.

Although residential development grew outward, it also continued downtown, especially for the working class. In the early 1900s, living in downtown Stockton far outweighed the cost and effort required to reside outside of town. Downtown meant easy access to work, transportation, shopping, banking, and entertainment. The Commercial and the La Verta hotels were built in the 1870s on Main Street. These and many other residential hotels provided essential housing to newcomers and laborers in Stockton's prosperous agricultural industry. The Commercial Hotel, although now heavily altered, was one of Stockton's finest hotels in the late 1800s. The hotels served a transient population of skilled laborers, as well as white- and blue-collar workers. The Main and the Terry hotels reflect the city's commercial activity after the 1907 floods.

Above: The Hotel Terry in 1956 with the Katten-Marengo department store on the ground floor. The hotel was built in 1912 and designed by architect Glenn Allen in the Commercial style with Classical details such as color tile work and leaf cresting.
PHOTOGRAPH COURTESY OF THE BANK OF STOCKTON.

Below: The Commercial Hotel built in 1874 in the Classical Revival style. It was one of the earliest first-class hotels in the late 1800s and included a dining room for eighty people. The facade has been significantly modified.
PHOTOGRAPH COURTESY OF THE BANK OF STOCKTON.

HOTEL STOCKTON

✦

Right: Aerial view from the top of the courthouse of the Hotel Stockton located on the corner of El Dorado Street and Weber Avenue at the head of the Stockton Channel, where the Weber Baths were at one time.

PHOTOGRAPH COURTESY OF THE BANK OF STOCKTON.

Below: The Roof Garden was a distinctive feature of the Hotel Stockton. This garden pavillion was located on the west side and included a fountain and pergolas in each corner, guests could watch the sunset over the Stockton Channel with Mount Diablo in the background.

PHOTOGRAPH COURTESY OF THE BANK OF STOCKTON.

Stockton experienced tremendous commercial growth in the early 1900s, which included the construction of many more hotels. The Hotel Stockton, built in 1910, was near some of California's greatest theaters and was close to downtown retailers and the business district. This first-class hotel with 252 rooms provided fine dining and rooftop dancing, as well as convenient lodging for travelers to the Sierra Nevada and the Mother Lode. The Hotel Stockton is rich with architectural innovation; it is California's first example of commercial mission revival style. The five-story hotel was also the first steel-reinforced concrete construction in the Central Valley. The hotel's most distinctive interior feature is its lobby, which includes what was one of the largest public fireplaces in California when it was built. The Hotel Stockton symbolizes the city's prominence in California and also represents a masterpiece of historical hotel architecture.

✧

Below: The Hotel Stockton, not long after its completion in 1910. The city landmark is considered one of California's most outstanding example of Mission Revival architecture.

PHOTOGRAPH COURTESY OF RON CHAPMAN

CHAPTER 8

ENTERTAINMENT AND RECREATION

THEATERS

✧

Above: The Avon Theatre building, located on the southeast corner of Main and California streets, opened in 1882 with the play Hazel Kirke.

PHOTOGRAPH COURTESY OF THE BANK OF STOCKTON.

Opposite, top: The Fox Theatre opened in 1930 at 242 E. Main Street and became a popular venue for movie and stage productions.

PHOTOGRAPH COURTESY OF THE BANK OF STOCKTON.

Opposite, bottom: The interior of the Fox Theatre is adorned with tall columns, beautiful chandeliers and elaborate ornamentation and seats more than 2,000 people.

PHOTOGRAPH COURTESY OF THE BANK OF STOCKTON.

Stockton was one of the greatest theater cities in California, with a reputation for providing world-class entertainment. The city's strategic location between San Francisco and the southern gold mines attracted numerous touring theatrical groups. Stockton's theatrical history began in 1850 in a renovated room of the Stockton House, the city's first hotel, which was located on El Dorado and Channel streets. By 1851, Stockton's waterfront was surrounded by the Corinthian Theatre, located in the Corinthian Building, and the magnificent El Placer Theatre, situated over the El Dorado Saloon. The famous Stockton Theatre opened in 1853 and operated for thirty-seven years on the southeast corner of Main and El Dorado streets until it burned down in 1890. Theaters contributed to the social and cultural development of the city, especially during the subsequent golden years.

The Avon Theatre was completed in August of 1882 and occupied two floors of the building on the corner of Main and California streets. The Avon, which was also used for boxing events, was forced to close in 1892 because it was unable to compete with the elegance of the Yosemite Theatre. Erected in 1892, the Yosemite Theatre on San Joaquin Street between Weber and Main streets was Stockton's most extravagantly decorated theater. The first theater with electrical lights, it hosted dramatic plays, musical productions, band concerts, and political events. These grand theaters, such as the Yosemite and the Stockton theatres, hosted many famous entertainers. The city continued to produce many more theaters, particularly during the golden era of motion pictures, beginning in the 1920s.

Right: The Yosemite Theatre Building on San Joaquin Street viewed from the top of the courthouse around 1905. In the 1920s, it was converted into the State Theater.
PHOTOGRAPH COURTESY OF THE BANK OF STOCKTON.

Below: In 1952, people lined up for almost a block at the Esquire Theatre at Main and American streets to see Francis Goes to West Point *starring Francis the Talking Mule.*
PHOTOGRAPH COURTESY OF THE BANK OF STOCKTON.

STOCKTON'S GOLDEN ERA

MOTION PICTURES

Motion pictures in Stockton were introduced in the 1920s. In the first few years, the number of movie theatres grew to twenty, as well as several vaudeville houses. Ones of the most popular and beautiful theater buildings of that time period was the Fox Theatre, originally occupied by the T & D Theatre, which was built in 1917. The T & D Theatre was renamed California Theatre in 1923, and was closed and demolished in 1929. The Fox California Theatre, now called the Bob Hope Theatre, was built in 1930 by the Fox West Coast Theatre circuit. Another popular venue was the Esquire Theatre, which opened in 1946 and was operated by Blumenfeld Theatres before closing in 1954.

Stockton once served as a popular location for shooting movies, starting with the filming of *Steamboat Round the Bend* in 1935. Although it was not until the late 1940s, after the second World War, that it attracted its share of the movie business. Movie producers and directors traveled to Stockton to take advantage of its great location with easy rail and

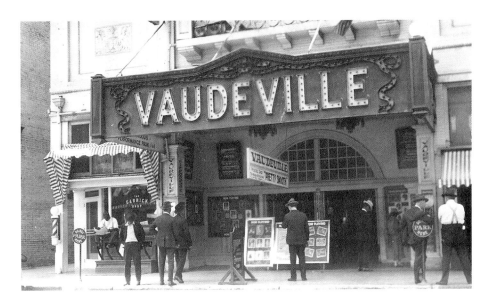

freeway access, and low production costs. One of the most famous movies filmed in Stockton was *All the King's Men* starring Broderick Crawford and John Ireland. The film received three Academy Awards in 1950, including Best Picture and forever preserved Stockton's landscape of the 1940s on the big screen. By the late 1950s and 1960s major movies were being filmed here, including *Cool Hand Luke* and *The Big Country*.

Above: Many early theaters played vaudeville, showed musicals and moving pictures, including the Hippodrome Theatre located at 21 N. Sutter Street. The theater was demolished in 1922.

PHOTOGRAPH COURTESY OF THE BANK OF STOCKTON.

Below: All the King's Men was filmed in Stockton in 1948 using local residents as extras, something fairly unknown for Hollywood at the time. This is a scene towards the end of the movie showing actor John Ireland at the steps of Stockton's City Hall.

PHOTOGRAPH COURTESY OF THE BANK OF STOCKTON.

THE STOCKTON SYMPHONY

Manlio Silva created the Stockton Symphony Orchestra in 1926, during a time when Stockton was notorious for its band concerts, nightclubs, and vaudeville shows. It hosted its first concert with twenty local musicians for the Stockton Musical Club, an organization that planned a series of concerts during the year. Five months later, the Stockton Symphony Orchestra opened their first season at the California Theatre on Main Street. Over the years, they also performed many concerts at the Stockton High School Auditorium on San Joaquin Street, which was able to seat 2,400 people. Today, the Stockton Symphony is the third oldest continuously performing orchestra in California, exceeded only by the San Francisco Symphony and the Los Angeles Philharmonic in longevity.

The Symphony's founder had dreamed of leading his own orchestra while growing up on the Italian Riviera. After graduating from the Conservatory of Chiavari near Genoa, Manlio Silva immigrated to the United States in 1909. Manlio Silva was a pharmacist by trade and with his brother, Tullio Silva, ran the Genova Pharmacy originally located on Center Street. By 1924 he was gathering area musicians to play in the orchestra, including Tullio, who was a fine musician himself. Manlio was passionate about the orchestra and is credited with much of its existence and success, because he assumed much of its financial burden during slow times. Manlio was the Symphony's first music director, conductor, and manager, and he held those roles until his retirement in 1957. The Symphony was later led by Korean maestro Kyung-Soo Won for several decades.

CIRCUSES, PARADES AND FAIRS

Entertainment was an important component of Stockton when it served as a supply center. From the very beginning, circuses and circus parades were an important part of the community's entertainment. W. H. Foley's

ring of finely trained horses performed in front of the Stockton House on June 24, 1850. Henry C. Lee's South American Circus gave its first Stockton performance in 1853 and used the location as its winter headquarters because of the relatively warm climate. The Sells Brothers Circus, a popular circus show company, settled on the San Joaquin County fairgrounds as its winter training base for several years in the early 1900s. Many of the larger circus shows, such as Ringling Brothers and Barnum & Bailey, performed in Stockton annually between 1900 and 1925.

Stockton was a patriotic city during its Golden Era and never missed an opportunity to have a grand parade on Main Street, including on California Admission Day, Independence Day, and Veterans Day. The parades continued until the late 1940s, when interest in them began to decline in favor for new and different ways of celebrating. Banking and retail buildings as well as farmers' markets, street fairs, concerts, and carnivals historically surrounded Hunter Plaza, located in the shadow of the courthouse. Hunter Plaza was home to many important events in Stockton's history, including the California State Fair in 1857. On July 4, 1876, the Plaza was the location of the Centennial Celebration.

PUBLIC PARKS

In 1851, Charles Weber deeded all the surveyed streets and channels, as well as the public square sites, to the city. As the founder of Stockton, Weber dedicated ten parks called Weber Squares. These original parks, or village squares, in Stockton are a little more than two acres each and were selected for preserving open land within the growing town. Thereafter, four additional parks were designated as such by the city. Independence Square, located at Market and Aurora streets, was a baseball field and circus ground in the early 1900s. Weber personally named each of the town squares something with patriotic significance, such as Fremont Square, Columbus Square, and Constitution Square. Today, these parks still provide the city with beautiful trees and open spaces.

✧

Above: Manlio Silva was the founder of the Stockton Symphony Orchestra in 1926, and became its passionate leader for the next three decades.

PHOTOGRAPH COURTESY OF THE BANK OF STOCKTON.

Below: A parade of elephants on Weber Avenue in the early 1900s. These parades were a way of celebrating and promoting the circus in town.

PHOTOGRAPH COURTESY OF THE BANK OF STOCKTON.

After the turn of the century, the city acquired some of the larger parks from companies that were developing the areas for housing, including Victory Park in 1914 and American Legion Park in 1912. The city purchased Oak Park, formerly Goodwater Grove, from the Southern Pacific Company in 1918. The thirty-acre park filled with valley oak trees was popular and drew visitors from across the state. Goodwater Grove got its name because of the abundance of water that was able to be drawn from its well. The Southern Pacific Company made it famous as a picnic ground, running excursions on Sundays from San Francisco to Stockton. Amenities in the park included a bowling alley, a dance pavilion, a clubhouse, and a playground. The city added a swimming pool in 1925 and a baseball field in 1927. The baseball field was renamed Billy Hebert Field in 1953, after the first professional baseball player killed in action during World War II. Hebert had played in various baseball leagues in the Stockton area.

RECREATIONAL AREAS

American Legion Park, which is often called Yosemite Park today, is the land area surrounding Yosemite Lake. Yosemite Lake was created in 1912 because of the need for dirt to be used as infill in Yosemite Terrace, a subdivision west of Yosemite Street. The water flowing from Smith Canal caused a waterhole to develop, which eventually turned into Yosemite Lake. Smith Canal was built around 1890 to connect the North Street Canal with the San Joaquin River and prevent flooding. Yosemite Lake was privately owned but the public swam and boated there, with lifeguard service provided by the city. The popular Yosemite Boat House resided on the south bank until 1919, when it was moved to the north shore. Housing developed around the lake and the surrounding private land. Yosemite Lake, now owned by the city, was closed to public use in 1946 due to unsanitary and dangerous conditions, but American Legion Park remains open.

The Stockton Municipal Camp at Silver Lake is about a hundred miles east of the city in Amador County, on the historic Carson Pass Highway. The lake is at about 7,287 feet in elevation and sits at the base of Thunder Mountain, surrounded by large granite and beautiful peaks. The municipal family camp

✧

Above: The Haggin Museum was built in 1931 by the San Joaquin Pioneer and Historical Society with support from the McKee family. The beautiful brick building with Corinthian pillars is located in Victory Park and houses a fine art and local history collection. The museum is named after Louis Terah Haggin, an attorney who donated his art collection to the museum.
PHOTOGRAPH COURTESY OF THE BANK OF STOCKTON.

Below: The north bank of Yosemite Lake in American Legion Park in 1932, a popular venue for swimming and boating.
PHOTOGRAPH COURTESY OF THE BANK OF STOCKTON.

❖

The Stockton Mineral Baths, built in 1893, were formerly known as the Jackson Natural Gas Well Baths. These popular baths were located at the south end of San Joaquin Street, where McKinley Park is today.

PHOTOGRAPH COURTESY OF THE BANK OF STOCKTON.

concept originated in Los Angeles in 1915, when the city built three municipal camps in the mountains. The idea spread among large and prominent cities, including Stockton. Stockton's Silver Lake Municipal Camp was created in 1921 to provide families with affordable cabin vacations and planned camp activities, as well as outdoor recreational activities such as hiking, swimming, and fishing. The camp features a lodge and rustic wood cabins with baths. The camp has also been used as a youth camp since the 1940s.

STOCKTON MINERAL BATHS

Stockton was once the site of several renowned mineral baths. The current site of the Hotel Stockton was formerly occupied by the Weber Baths, which were the first mineral baths in Stockton. Built in 1883, the Weber Baths boasted a substantial swimming tank and more than forty dressing rooms. Stockton's abundance of natural gas wells allowed for a steady and continuous flow of warm water into the baths. The gas actually pushed up therapeutic mineral water

containing iron, sulfur, magnesium, soda, and salt. Stockton's most famous mineral baths were the Jackson Baths, built in 1893 at the present location of McKinley Park. Three wells supplied water to one large pool and several smaller pools, which were surrounded by swings, a trapeze, slides, springboards, and 150 dressing rooms.

The Jackson Baths included twelve bath houses for private parties, a clubhouse for entertaining, and a grand stand for musical concerts. The 13-acre resort destination also featured lawn areas with picnic tables and barbecue pits, and even had a small zoo and a scenic railway. After substantial renovations in 1920, the resort was renamed the Stockton Mineral Baths, and the expanded pool became the largest swimming tank in the world. Architect Glenn Allen designed the four-story lighthouse tower with a statuary and fountain at its base, two Venetian bridges at either side of the circular pool, and several slides and waterfalls. Private pavilions, wading pools, and sandy beaches made this Stockton's most popular attraction of the time. These wells dissipated by the 1940s and the Stockton Mineral Baths closed thereafter.

LOUIS PARK AND PIXIE WOODS

Louis Park is situated on the San Joaquin River where Smith Canal comes in toward Yosemite Lake, in the heart of Stockton. Its location is also known as Dad's Point, a piece of land named after fisherman squatter Dad Kreiger. The 14-acre property was bought and donated to the city to be used as a park and playground by the Louis family, in memory of their son Charles H. Louis. The Louis family has strong links to the early history of Stockton. With its shade trees and wide open spaces, the park is ideal for family outings and large group picnics. During Stockton's Golden Era, one could see the steamers and the ocean vessels go by on their daily trips to San Francisco.

Additional acres were added over the decades, and Louis Park now contains 37 acres, some of which remain undeveloped. The developed area contains facilities, playgrounds, and a large number of picnic tables and benches. Pixie Woods, a children's amusement park, was added to the park in 1955. Although it is owned by the City of Stockton, the park was created with and has been sustained by fundraising and donations. Pixie Woods is on a 3.5-acre site within Louis Park and has many attractions, including three amusement rides. This area has been developed from an often-flooded terrain covered with native willows into an important riverside park with unlimited possibilities for marine recreation. Louis Park is one of Stockton's most popular park areas.

✧

An aerial view of Pixie Woods, built in 1955 and located in Louis Park along the San Joaquin River and Smith Canal.
PHOTOGRAPH COURTESY OF THE BANK OF STOCKTON.

CHAPTER 9

PUBLIC AND COMMUNITY INSTITUTIONS

CITY OF STOCKTON

❖

Top: The Stockton Memorial Civic Auditorium completed in 1925 and dedicated to Stockton soldiers killed in World War I.

PHOTOGRAPH COURTESY OF THE BANK OF STOCKTON.

Above: In 1851, city council approved the city seal as designed by Stockton's first mayor, Samuel Purdy.

PHOTOGRAPH COURTESY OF THE CITY OF STOCKTON.

Commodore Robert F. Stockton met Charles Weber in southern California when he was released after being a prisoner of the Mexican forces. Commodore Stockton oversaw the military operations associated with the conquest of California during the Mexican War. After hearing about Captain Weber's plans to settle on the waterfront property, the naval officer promised to advocate for him and provide assistance. Although Weber first called his settlement Tuleburg, because of the numerous tules growing along the riverbanks, he eventually changed its name to Stockton because he was impressed by the commander's generosity. The commander's promises never materialized, however. Stockton officially became a city on July 23, 1850, and was the first American-named city in California since most other place names were of Native American or Spanish origin.

The city of Stockton grew as it entered the twentieth century, leading to many community and civic improvements. The second courthouse stands out as an exemplary and stately government building, as does the civic center. The design of Stockton's civic center was drawn from the "City Beautiful" movement. The civic auditorium and city hall, both completed by 1926, are the most significant buildings of one of the finest civic centers in northern California. These two structures, with their massive columns, decorated friezes, and cornices, are designed in grand classical style and both face a public plaza. Prior to the plaza's construction in 1947, the site had a lake fronting both buildings. The public library's architecture is more modern, because plans to construct it did not develop until 1964, when the "City Beautiful" movement had ended. The prominence of the civic center demonstrates the importance of Stockton during its Golden Era.

✧

Above: Aerial view of McLeod Lake at Stockton's civic center, before being filled in the 1940s, with the Memorial Civic Auditorium on the left and city hall on the right.

PHOTOGRAPH COURTESY OF THE BANK OF STOCKTON.

Left: City hall was built in the Renaissance Revival style, a rectangular building with symmetrical facades and classical Ionic order columns.

PHOTOGRAPH COURTESY OF THE BANK OF STOCKTON.

Stockton Police Department in the 1915 Main Street parade.
John L. Briscoe, third department officer to die in the line of
duty two years later, is in the second row, second from the right.

PHOTOGRAPH COURTESY OF THE STOCKTON POLICE DEPARTMENT.

STOCKTON
POLICE DEPARTMENT

The Stockton Police Department was established in August of 1850 which immediately led to the appointment of William H. Willoughby as the city marshal, Stockton's first law enforcement officer. In 1861, the city council reorganized the police department and eliminated the city marshal position. The department was now headed by a chief of police, and George E. Taber was the first to hold office. In 1890, the fourteen police officers began wearing regulation uniforms and badges. In 1894, the Stockton Police Department moved to the first floor of the county's newly built and magnificent courthouse. Local law enforcement certainly was influenced by Stockton's Golden Era, as the Stockton Police Department reached several milestones. In 1912 the department

purchased its first motorized vehicles and with new motorcycles established one of the first dedicated traffic sections in California. The agency moved to the first floor of the Masonic Temple in 1915 and to the basement of city hall in 1924, where it remained for almost five decades.

STOCKTON FIRE
DEPARTMENT

Fires were a serious threat during Stockton's earliest settlement days, as structures were primarily made of cloth and wood. The Weber Bucket Brigade was the first organized group of firefighting volunteers. In 1849, Stockton's first significant fire swept through the business district along the waterfront. Because of the devastation caused by this blaze, fire protection became an essential component of city planning. The result was

✧

The fire on June 24, 1914, destroyed the Taylor Milling Company, a five-story mill building, and several waterfront warehouses. It was one of Stockton's largest and most famous fires during the golden years.

PHOTOGRAPH COURTESY OF THE STOCKTON FIRE DEPARTMENT.

the establishment of the Weber Engine Company in 1850, which was soon followed by others, including the Eureka Engine Company and the San Joaquin Company. This early competition made the Stockton Fire Department one of the most progressive. In 1862 it was the first inland city in California to purchase a steam engine and it was among the first fire departments in the United States to master the chemical fire engine in the 1870s. Professional firefighters had replaced the volunteers by 1888 and the department became fully mechanized in 1924 when its last horses were retired.

POSTAL SERVICES

The Stockton Post Office was established in 1849 to deliver mail to mining camps. Homes and business did not have mail delivery until the 1890s. The first government-owned post office in Stockton was built in 1902 at Market and California streets as a two-story sandstone building and was the city's main post office for more than thirty years. After the post office relocated, the building was used as the city's Hall of Records before being demolished in 1965. Since 1933 the post office and

federal offices have occupied the building at San Joaquin and Lindsay streets with a two-story block structure built in the Classic architectural style typical of federal buildings in the 1920s. Architectural characteristics of the "Federal Building" include the raised foundation, stonewalls, colonnades, and the stepped railing cap. The post office building was built by the Works Progress Administration (WPA), which employed out-of-work laborers during the Depression.

✧

Above: Stockton's most significant fire in the downtown commercial district occurred on July 29, 1923. The fire spread and substantially damaged the Commercial and Savings Bank building.
PHOTOGRAPH COURTESY OF THE STOCKTON FIRE DEPARTMENT.

Below: Stockton's first post office building was built in 1902 at Market and California streets.
PHOTOGRAPH COURTESY OF THE BANK OF STOCKTON.

COUNTY COURTHOUSES
AND CITY LIBRARIES

From the time it was founded, Stockton has procured services from San Joaquin County, including the use of its courthouses. The first courthouse, built in 1853 on land donated by city founder Charles M. Weber, included a prominent dome containing a bell and clock. It served the city and county until 1887. The second courthouse, completed in 1890, was an architectural masterpiece designed by Elijah E. Myers, a noted architect of several state capitols. The dome of the three-story courthouse with the Statue of Justice perched on top dominated the Stockton skyline for over seventy years and afforded panoramic views for visitors. Because the building had deteriorated, the controversial decision was made in 1961 to demolish and replace this second courthouse that today is still considered Stockton's grandest and noblest building. It was a measure of the wealth, pride, and aspiration of one of California's most important cities at that time.

Opposite, top: The first courthouse, designed in the Roman Doric style, was dedicated in 1854 built on land donated by Charles Weber.

PHOTOGRAPH COURTESY OF THE BANK OF STOCKTON.

Opposite, bottom: The second San Joaquin County Courthouse was completed in 1890, built with local bricks and faced with high quality granite from Placer County.

PHOTOGRAPH COURTESY OF THE BANK OF STOCKTON.

Left: The courthouse was designed with four entrances and the interior included two wide stairways that extended to the third floor. The building had spacious hallways with tall columns and high ceilings with flooring made of tiles imported from Belgium.

PHOTOGRAPH COURTESY OF THE BANK OF STOCKTON.

Below: A panoramic view of Hunter Plaza looking east down Hunter Street. The dome of the courthouse dominated the Stockton skyline for over seventy years

PHOTOGRAPH COURTESY OF THE BANK OF STOCKTON.

Another important public institution, the library system, was developing around the time that the first courthouse was built. In 1854, the Stockton Library Association became the first of many local library associations. In 1878 the Rogers Act authorized cities to collect taxes to establish free public libraries. A decade later, the Stewart Memorial Library was constructed at Hunter and Market streets on land donated by Charles Weber. The library was endowed by businessman Frank Stewart and designed by famous architect Charles Beasley. This library with Greek-style architecture was the third-largest

library in the state and was considered truly magnificent. As the city rapidly grew in the 1890s, the need for a larger building was evident. After only three years, the Stewart Memorial Library was replaced by the Hazelton Library. It was not until 1965 that the Hazelton Library was torn down. The columns were saved and moved to the front of library at the University of the Pacific.

PRIMARY AND SECONDARY EDUCATION

In 1852, two years after Stockton's incorporation, a city ordinance initiated the formation of the public school system that included the appointment of a city superintendent and a board of education of schools. The first free public school in Stockton opened on March 1, 1853, with the then-common segregation of boys and girls. Franklin School, the first school building, was constructed by the Stockton School District in

1859. At the end of that year, there were 200 students attending four public schools, two grammar, and two primary schools in the area. In 1870 high school classes were being taught for the first time, but in elementary school buildings. The only surviving school building from the first few decades of Stockton's existence is Weber School on Flora Street and it was erected in 1873.

In 1904 shortage of classroom space led to the construction of Stockton High School at California and Vine streets. The Anglo Classic-style building was designed by local architect George Rushforth and held twenty-four classrooms. The grounds included expanses of lawn and flowerbeds, as well as a greenhouse and a botanical garden. The growing student population forced continuous expansions on the ten-acre Stockton High School campus. A science building, gymnasium, and swimming pool were built behind the main building in 1914, and a 2,400-seat auditorium was completed in 1928. The last of the buildings constructed on this campus and still standing today, was referred to as the Language Arts Building and had a cafeteria in its basement. Stockton High School's main building was condemned in 1966 and demolished in 1967.

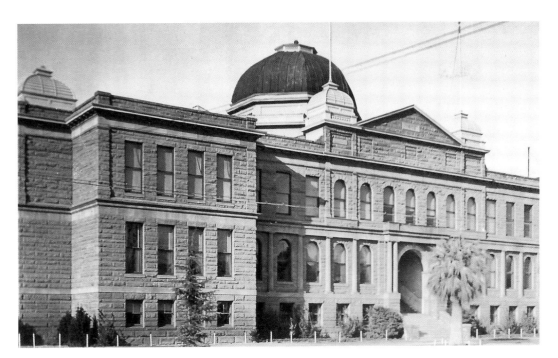

Opposite, clockwise starting from the top:

The Hazelton Library was built in 1895 on the northeast corner of Market and Hunter streets. Covered in white marble, this building housed the library for almost seventy years.
PHOTOGRAPH COURTESY OF THE BANK OF STOCKTON.

The reception desk of the Hazelton Library, built of marble with a large gallery behind it. The gallery had bronze railings and oak stairs with reading rooms on each side.
PHOTOGRAPH COURTESY OF THE BANK OF STOCKTON.

The San Joaquin County Jail was completed in 1893 to hold seventy-five prisoners and was referred to as "Cunningham's Castle" after Sheriff Thomas Cunningham and due its' fortress-like architecture and design.
PHOTOGRAPH COURTESY OF THE BANK OF STOCKTON.

The Stewart Memorial Library on Hunter Street, between Main and Market streets opened in 1889. The architectural style is a combination of medieval and classic Greek, with granite pillars, marble caps and large "bulls-eye" windows.
PHOTOGRAPH COURTESY OF THE BANK OF STOCKTON.

Above: The first El Dorado School was built in 1898 at the corner of El Dorado and Vine streets. The three-story wooden building had eight classrooms, a full basement and an assembly hall.
PHOTOGRAPH COURTESY OF THE BANK OF STOCKTON.

Left: The domed main building was the first structure of the Stockton High School campus built in 1904 at the corner of California and Vine streets.
PHOTOGRAPH COURTESY OF ALICE VAN OMMEREN.

HIGHER EDUCATION IN STOCKTON

In 1851, the University of the Pacific, California's first chartered institution of higher learning, was established in Santa Clara. The private college, founded by the Methodist Church and initially named California Wesleyan College then College of the Pacific and eventually University of the Pacific, moved to San Jose in 1871 and merged with Napa College in 1896. In 1920, President Tully C. Knoles recommended that the college move to Stockton based on the increasing competition for students in that area with other schools, such as Santa Clara University, Berkeley, and Stanford. In 1924 the college moved to its current location in Stockton along the Calaveras River and became the first private university in the Central Valley. An innovator and leader in higher education, the University of the Pacific has made significant contributions to Stockton's community.

Opposite, top: The Conservatory of Music building on the University campus opened in 1927 and was the first accredited professional school of music in the western United States, later renamed for Faye Spanos.

PHOTOGRAPH COURTESY OF THE BANK OF STOCKTON.

Opposite, bottom: Smith Memorial Gate was named for Harriet M. Smith, the mother of J. C. Smith who donated the original forty acres of the college.

PHOTOGRAPH COURTESY OF THE BANK OF STOCKTON.

Above: In 1949, San Joaquin Delta College relocated from its location on the College of the Pacific campus to this forty-three acre site on Pacific Avenue.

PHOTOGRAPH COURTESY OF ALICE VAN OMMEREN.

Left: The San Joaquin Delta College sign and logo at the front entrance of the college on Pacific Avenue.

PHOTOGRAPH COURTESY OF ALICE VAN OMMEREN.

Stockton was famous for its private schools early in its history. The Stockton Business College and Normal Institute was established in 1875 on the corner of California and Channel streets and was considered quite prestigious on the West Coast. John R. Humphreys, Sr., took over the college and reestablished and renamed it Humphreys College. The Western School of Commerce, located at San Joaquin and Channel streets, taught shorthand and other business skills.

It began operating in 1901, when it took over from another school called the Gas City Business College. In 1920 the Western School of Commerce merged with Heald Business College. San Joaquin Delta College had its beginnings in 1935 on the campus of the College of the Pacific, now called the University of the Pacific. San Joaquin Delta College moved to its current location in 1949, and as a community college grew to become the largest educational institution in Stockton.

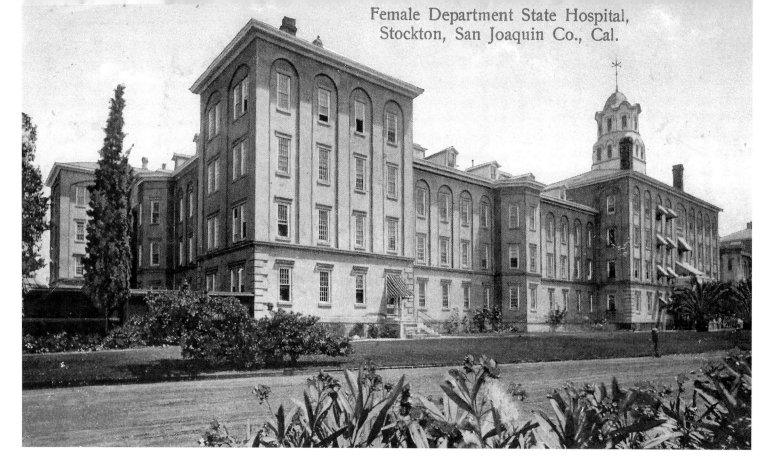

Female Department State Hospital,
Stockton, San Joaquin Co., Cal.

✦

Above: The Insane Asylum of California was built on California Street in 1852. This 1909 postcard shows the Female Department used to house female patients.

Below: The Male Department was built in 1875 and partially destroyed by fire in 1938 before being replaced in 1949. The Insane Asylum was eventually renamed the Stockton State Hospital.

PHOTOGRAPHS COURTESY OF ALICE VAN OMMEREN.

Male Department,
State Hospital San Joaquin Co.,
Stockton, Cal.

HOSPITALS

Although the hardships of life in the mines created a need for medical services, hospitals were not established until state and local government were formalized. In 1851, the Legislature passed an act to create three general hospitals, to be located in Sacramento, San Francisco, and Stockton, to care for the physically and mentally ill. Charles Weber donated one hundred acres along California Street for the Stockton State Hospital. In 1853 the Stockton hospital was ordered by the California Legislature to only treat mentally ill patients. It was renamed the Insane Asylum of the State of California and became the first publicly supported psychiatric institution in the West. Many buildings and facilities were constructed on the grounds, but overcrowding remained an issue at the end of the century. The state hospital continued to expand through Stockton's Golden Era and by 1953, it was serving about 4,600 patients.

The first county hospital was erected in 1879 at Wilson Way and Hazelton Avenue. The two-story main building and other hospital buildings on the thirty-six acre site burned in a fire on June 3, 1892. This led to the completion of the French Camp facility in 1895, where the county hospital resides today. Although there are many private hospitals in Stockton, St. Joseph's Hospital is the oldest in continuous operation. It was established by Father William B. Connor, first as a rest home for elderly men, in 1898. The original two-story brick building was expanded and a main hospital wing was added in 1918. A third floor was built ten years later. The additions and renovations continued over the decades. Another private hospital, Dameron, was founded by Dr. John Dameron in 1912 and is still in operation today on Lincoln and Magnolia streets.

✧

Above: The southern-style "Magnolia Mansion" was built in 1900 on the State Hospital Grounds at California and Acacia streets, serving as the superintendent's residence until 1975.

PHOTOGRAPH COURTESY OF RON CHAPMAN.

Below: The original thirty-five-bed facility of Dameron Hospital, founded in 1912, at Lincoln and Magnolia streets.

PHOTOGRAPH COURTESY OF ALICE VAN OMMEREN.

Right: The Central Methodist Church was built in 1891 at Miner Avenue and San Joaquin Street. In 1958, the building was sold, and eventually demolished, as a new church was completed at Pacific Avenue and Fulton Street.

PHOTOGRAPH COURTESY OF THE BANK OF STOCKTON.

Below: This is the original, although heavily remodeled, Temple Israel on Madison Street. The building was constructed in 1855 near Miner Avenue and El Dorado Street and moved to this location in 1905.

PHOTOGRAPH COURTESY OF THE BANK OF STOCKTON.

Opposite: St. Mary's Catholic Church on Washington Street is one of the oldest churches in Central California. It was built in sections with the nave and square bell tower built in 1861 and the Gothic spire, facade and stained glass windows added in 1893.

PHOTOGRAPH COURTESY OF THE BANK OF STOCKTON.

Christian leaders and ministers began holding religious services in Stockton as early as the Gold Rush period. The first church service in Stockton likely took place on July 12, 1849, on a ship docked along the levee. Methodists, Presbyterians, Baptists, and Episcopalians were among the first religious groups to organize church communities and construct buildings in Stockton, which happened as early as 1850. St. Mary's Catholic Church on Washington Street was built in 1861 on land bestowed by Charles Weber; it is the oldest non-residential building in Stockton today. Several other places of worship in town are more than a hundred years old, including Trinity Lutheran Church, First Congregational Church, and Temple Israel. In 1912, immigrants from Punjab, India, established the first Sikh temple or Gurdwara in the United States in Stockton.

In 1895, at the beginning of Stockton's Golden Era, the city had about twenty religious organizations and many of them were housed in important and magnificent structures. These included one of the finest brick structures ever built in Stockton, the Central Methodist Church, which was once located at Miner Avenue and San Joaquin Street. One of the churches is St. John's Episcopal Church which was built during Stockton's golden years and today still stands on the corner of El Dorado Street and Miner Avenue. The building dates back to 1892 and was designed by a San Francisco architect in the style of an old English cathedral with a cruciform shape. Built in 1923, toward the later part of the city's thriving economy, the First Presbyterian Church on Vine Street is one of the most beautiful Gothic Revival structures in the region.

✧

The Earle *(635) and the* Thompson *(627)*
at the Naval Supply Annex located at
Rough and Ready Island.

PHOTOGRAPH COURTESY OF THE BANK OF STOCKTON.

CHAPTER 10

BEYOND THE GOLDEN ERA

END OF THE GOLDEN ERA

A writer for the *Overland Monthly*, an influential California magazine of culture and literature, in 1895 said, "Stockton is destined to become the Chicago of the West and the commercial center of the interior." It was the beginning of Stockton's Golden Era, a period when the city was renowned for its healthy economy and industrial innovation because it was surrounded by an agricultural revolution. A series of factors slowed Stockton's industrious growth during the 1930s, and by 1940, Stockton's golden years had come to an end. The Stock Market Crash of 1929 was significant to Stockton and the rest of the country, because it initiated the decade-long Great Depression. The cities most impacted by the economic downturn were those supported by the manufacturing industry. The Depression also slowed construction, and farming communities saw a large drop in crop prices. Stockton's economy retained some stability during the Depression, mostly due to the continued deepening of the Stockton Channel, which created maritime opportunities.

The automobile revolution and its influence on the commercial transportation industry also affected Stockton's economy. The changes in wheeled transportation that took place during the Depression included the manufacturing of buses and trucks and the construction of roads and highways. Vehicular transportation grew faster and less expensive for transporting certain goods, which created competition with the water and rail transportation industry, an important part of the Stockton economy. Shipbuilders in Stockton had prospered through World War II, but production declined after the war ended in 1945. Military businesses shifted back to manufacturing farm machinery, and shipbuilders attempted to transition to building boats and barges. The Depression brought an increase in the number of migrants looking for now-sparse labor opportunities in a once-prosperous area. The economy's impact on the city's poor also drove the need for lower-cost housing, making the downtown area vulnerable to urban blight, and creating a visual reminder of less prosperous years.

IMPACT OF WAR
ON LOCAL INDUSTRY

Because of its significant contributions during World War I, most notably from the war tanks built by Stockton's Holt Manufacturing Company during that time, Stockton became a strong contender for becoming the West Coast supply center for World War II. In addition, the dredging of the Stockton Channel and its physical connection to a railroad made the city attractive to the 1940s wartime industry. The established manufacturing sector in Stockton went into wartime production, most significantly in the shipyards. Stockton companies received government contracts because of their inland location, which was outside of naval shooting range. In turn, these shipyards contracted with local business for supplies and other services. During the war years, civilian goods production and local military installations fueled the local economy.

During World War II and under the U.S. Army jurisdiction, the Port of Stockton established the Stockton Ordnance Depot and the Naval Supply Annex. The Stockton Ordnance Depot was a military installation that provided vehicle repair services and supplied machinery parts until 1956. The Naval Supply Annex on the Port's Rough and Ready Island was the first Navy depot built to accommodate cargo on pallets. The Marginal Wharf provided access to three major modes of cargo transportation: water, rail, and truck service. The Port was the location of the world's largest continuous concrete wharf, which was able to berth thirteen ships at one time. Because of its value as a supply center, Stockton was considered to be one of the top military targets in California. After the war, many civilians were hired at Sharpe's Army Depot outside Stockton, an installation that shifted from storing supplies to repairing supplies as they returned from the seas. The Navy Supply Annex built on Rough and Ready Island was eventually phased out in 1995 and transferred its production to the Port of Stockton.

The Pearl Harbor attack by the Japanese in 1941 shook the nation for many reasons, including its occurrence on American soil. Japanese Americans were now seen as threats, even if they had been in America for generations. In 1942 wartime orders from President Roosevelt led to the relocation of Japanese Americans to internment camps. The San Joaquin County Fairgrounds was designated as one of the fifteen temporary detention centers in the country. The Stockton Assembly Center, built with 125 barracks, held the large Japanese population from Stockton and the surrounding area. After more than five months, many of the 4,000 inmates held in Stockton were transferred to the Rohwer Relocation Center, a permanent center in Arkansas that closed after the war ended in 1945. During World War II, the Army base at the Port of Stockton also functioned as a prisoner of war (POW) camp, which mostly held Germans. The camp closed in 1946 after having housed thousands of prisoners.

✧

Top, left: Two Navy battleships at the Naval Supply Annex in Stockton.
PHOTOGRAPH COURTESY OF THE BANK OF STOCKTON.

Top, right: Navy vessels lined up at the wharves of the Naval Supply Annex located on Rough and Ready Island at the Port of Stockton.
PHOTOGRAPH COURTESY OF THE BANK OF STOCKTON.

Below: The ability of the port to accommodate large ocean-going ships led to the development of additional wharves and warehouses in the 1930s to process the sacked cargo.
PHOTOGRAPH COURTESY OF THE BANK OF STOCKTON.

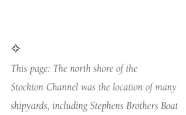

This page: The north shore of the Stockton Channel was the location of many shipyards, including Stephens Brothers Boat Builders which began operating in 1902.

PHOTOGRAPHS COURTESY OF THE BANK OF STOCKTON.

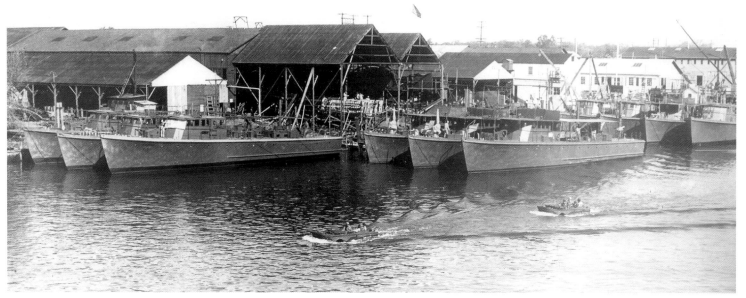

SHIPBUILDING

In the early 1940s, nine Stockton ship-yards build docks, ships, and boats to support the World War II effort. At the height of the war, the shipyards employed about 10,000 people with Pollock-Stockton Building Company as the largest shipyard employing almost half of them. George Pollock was a construction engineer who built Shasta Dam north of Redding, and Tower Bridge in Sacramento. His strong relationships with those government agencies led him to go into shipbuilding. The Pollock company converted a field along the Stockton Channel into two deep basins, allowing for the construction of sectional dry docks in its shipyard. Dry docks were a valuable innovation in World War II, as they were movable and could be used to repair ships at sea. Hickinbotham Brothers was one of several other shipyard companies that built water vessels, including tugboats, for the military during World War II.

One of the other shipyards supported by the war effort was Colberg Boat Works. In 1896, William Colberg started a fleet of boats that carried passengers and light freight to serve isolated farms on the islands in the Delta. They also delivered the mail for free until they got a government contract in 1928 to be paid to do it. Besides building boats for the war, Colberg also built many of the sightseeing, cruise boats and ferries for the San Francisco Bay. Stephens

✧

Above and below: Colberg Boat Works, which was started in the late 1890s, was located just east of Stephens Brothers Boat Works, at 848 W. Fremont Street. The company operated for almost a century producing pleasure boats and military craft.

PHOTOGRAPH COURTESY OF THE BANK OF STOCKTON.

*Right: The Stockton Deep Water Channel
was officially opened on February 3, 1933,
when the first deepwater ship, the
S. S. Daisy Gray, arrived.*

PHOTOGRAPH COURTESY OF THE BANK OF STOCKTON.

*Below: Aerial view of the Port of Stockton
in 1975 looking east with ocean vessels
along its docks, as well as a glimpse of the
Interstate 5 bridge over the Stockton
Channel in the upper left corner.*

PHOTOGRAPH COURTESY OF THE BANK OF STOCKTON.

STOCKTON'S GOLDEN ERA

Brothers Boat Builders was in business from 1902 to 1987 and built some of the finest wooden cruiser boats ever assembled. For the Korean War in 1954, they prepared the minesweepers for delivery. Although Pollock's shipyard only existed during the war years, Colberg and Stephens' yards persisted. Colberg Boat Works and Stephens Brothers are the only two physically remaining shipbuilding yards in Stockton.

PORT OF STOCKTON

In 1871 an attempt was made to construct a deeper water channel from Stockton to the Pacific Ocean, to accommodate larger boats. The lack of government funding and the beginning of World War I delayed construction until 1927. As funding was reinstated, the digging of the canal from the previous depth of 15 feet to a new depth of 26 feet began. In 1933 the Port of Stockton officially opened as California's first inland sea port with the arrival of the S. S. *Daisy Gray*. In 1932 the city approved establishment of a port district with its own authority and elected the first five members of the board of port commissioners. In 1935, an application was approved to increase the depth of the channel to 35 feet.

Because it took more than five decades to accomplish, the creation of the Port of Stockton was the city's greatest development in the 1930s. The port included three wharves, constructed with transit sheds, three brick warehouses, and its first grain terminal. By 1938, four more wharves and transit sheds had been added, with nine additional brick warehouses and an expanded grain terminal. Thousands of ships from all over the world had already been at the Stockton seaport, which was at the center of agricultural and industrial trade. The Port of Stockton became one of the first harbors on the West Coast to handle bulk materials when its bulk terminal was constructed in 1952. The port has remained successful over the decades.

✧

Aerial view of the Port of Stockton and the massive grain elevators loading a large ship. The grain elevators and storage silos were built in 1955 and have become an icon of the port.

PHOTOGRAPH COURTESY OF THE BANK OF STOCKTON.

DEPARTMENT STORES

As a supply center, Stockton has a long history in the retail and merchandising business. The Hale's Dry Goods Store, located on the corner of Main and San Joaquin streets between 1883 and 1915, sold dry goods and clothing, among other things. The Yosemite Cash Store and Holden Drug Store were Stockton's earliest clothing and apparel stores. The Sterling was a popular clothing store located at the southwest corner of Hunter and Main streets. The store opened in 1905 and remained in business until the

Right: The J. C. Penney department store began operating in the 1920s on Sutter Street but by the 1930s it had moved to this popular location on Main and California streets until its relocation to the Weberstown Mall in the 1960s.

PHOTOGRAPH COURTESY OF THE BANK OF STOCKTON.

Below: The F. W. Woolworth store opened the first Stockton franchise at 422 E. Main Street. Lerner Shops, a chain of stores selling business clothing for women, was located at the corner of Main and Sutter streets.

PHOTOGRAPH COURTESY OF THE BANK OF STOCKTON.

◆

Left: The Katten-Marengo department store at Main and California streets in the 1960s. The three story building was once the Avon Theatre, built in 1882. At one time it was converted to J. C. Penney, then later a Mode O'Day before becoming the Katten-Marengo store.

PHOTOGRAPH COURTESY OF THE BANK OF STOCKTON.

Below: The S. H. Kress building on Sutter Street is a four-story building completed in 1930 and designed by architect John G. Fleming. The S. H. Kress building was decorated with terra cotta elements and provides for one of Stockton's finest Art Deco facades.

PHOTOGRAPH COURTESY OF THE BANK OF STOCKTON

early 1960s. In 1914, the F. W. Woolworth Company opened their first franchise in Stockton. The store immediately experienced competition from new franchise stores, such as the Owl Drug Company and J. C. Penney. Independent clothing stores, including the Wonder, Mode O'Day, Katten-Marengo, and Bravo McKeegan, continued to thrive until the 1960s.

The S. H. Kress store in Stockton was completed in 1930, during the Depression, as part of an American chain of five-and-dime retailers developed by Samuel Henry Kress. The Kress franchise was known for its quality and affordable house-hold merchandise, but also for its enticing store environment. Samuel Kress was an art collector and emphasized constructing buildings with fine architecture. Late 1800s Kress buildings were distinguished by light bricks and terra cotta fronts. The later stores, such as Stockton's, were redesigned in the modern art deco style. The Kress logo was distinct and always prominently displayed on the building. The interior store design included popular soda fountains, but also provided a relaxed atmosphere while displaying large amounts of merchandise. Today, the Kress building on Sutter Street is a reminder of a once-thriving downtown commercial center.

THE MIRACLE MILE

✦

Above: The entrance from Pacific Avenue into the residential community of Tuxedo Park in 1934. The subsequent phase became the development of the Miracle Mile shopping area, resulting in a unique neighborhood blending residential with commercial.

PHOTOGRAPH COURTESY OF THE BANK OF STOCKTON.

Opposite page: The stretch from Castle Street and Harding Way was called the Miracle Mile in the late 1930s boasting grocery stores, restaurants, paint stores, hardware stores, clothing stores and even gas stations.

PHOTOGRAPH COURTESY OF THE BANK OF STOCKTON.

The automobile led to increasing residential and business development outside of downtown. Until the early 1900s, the area that is now known as the Miracle Mile was at the southernmost end of Lower Sacramento Road, surrounded by fields and orchards. One of the first residential expansions along this road, a neighborhood of sixteen homes referred to as Tuxedo Park, was built in 1914. As serviceman returned home after World War I, the demand for housing increased and the number of residences in Tuxedo Park doubled. In the early 1920s, developer Joseph Plecarpo successfully lobbied votes to annex a section of the main road of this growing residential area for shopping and named it the Miracle Mile. In 1924 the University of the Pacific

was built and Lower Sacramento Road was renamed Pacific Avenue. The commercial growth complemented the residential and university development in the area

Joe Plecarpo decided to specifically name the one-mile stretch from the University to Harding Way the Miracle Mile. He likely got the idea from a similar stretch known as the Miracle Mile on Los Angeles's palm-lined Wilshire Boulevard, and this is the reason that some palm trees were planted in the area. The shopping area itself stretched from Castle Street to Harding Way and boasted grocery stores, restaurants, hardware stores, clothing stores, and even gas stations. It was the first shopping area of its type as the city grew north. Over the decades, the Miracle Mile saw many changes as businesses came and went, but its most prosperous time was the 1950s.

✧

Opposite: The "L" at Lincoln Center lights
up at night and has been a landmark on
Pacific Avenue since the 1950s to one of the
areas most popular shopping centers.
PHOTOGRAPH COURTESY OF RON CHAPMAN.

LINCOLN CENTER

Lincoln Center is one of the area's unique shopping centers; it was built in 1951, at the beginning of the golden age of American shopping centers. The postwar decade brought suburbanization, largely due to the popularity of the automobile. Developers felt less restricted by the need to accommodate public transportation and began taking advantage of the increased mobility that individuals enjoyed. The combination of increased consumer buying power and federal tax advantages that favored investment in commercial buildings spurred shopping center development. Lincoln Center began as a premier shopping and dining experience featuring independent family-owned shops and thrived for many decades. Following the opening of Lincoln Center, Lincoln Properties built more than 700 homes nearby, which they called Lincoln Village.

Lincoln Village was inspired by Greenlaw Grupe, Roy Sims, and four others who envisioned a community with homes, schools, recreation areas, and commercial areas. The Grupe family had its beginnings in the Gold Rush of 1849, providing freight transport from Stockton to the Mother Lode. The group of developers bought a 1,800-acre parcel from the estate of pioneer Benjamin Holt, and named the street next to its location along Pacific Avenue after the pioneer. Lincoln Center was created before the city developed around it, which is one of the reasons that the shopping center today does not belong to Stockton, but exists only as an unincorporated area of San Joaquin County. The Center started with sixteen stores and had four grocery stores in its history, including Black's Market, followed by Gaines Market, Don Quick's, and now Podesto's. Lincoln Center is now located on both sides of Benjamin Holt Drive and covers more than thirty-five acres.

SELECTED BIBLIOGRAPHY

Baltich, Frances. *Search for Safety: The Founding of Stockton's Black Community.* Stockton: Artprint Press, 1982.

Boda, Joyce. *Pioneer Leather Tanners: A History of the Wagner Family.* Stockton: Eureka Printing Company, 1997.

Boda, Joyce. *Our Fair 1860-2000: An Illustrated History of the San Joaquin County Fair.* Stockton: Eureka Printing Company, 2000.

Bonta, Robert & Spencer, Horace. *Stockton's Historic Public Schools.* Stockton: Stockton Unified School District, 1981.

Cort, Dan. *Downtown Turnaround: Lessons for a New Urban Landscape.* Pacific Grove: Park Place Publications, 2010.

Crow, Leslie. *High and Dry: A History of the Calaveras River and its Hydrology.* Stockton: Stockton East Water District and Lodi Printing Company, 2006.

Davis, Olive. *Stockton: Sunrise Port on the San Joaquin.* Woodland Hills: Windsor Publications, 1984.

Gohlke, Mary Jo. *Remarkable Women of Stockton.* Charleston, South Carolina: The History Press, 2014.

Haggin Museum. *Ralph O. Yardley: Stockton's Inkwell Artist Extraordinaire.* Stockton: San Joaquin Pioneer and Historical Society, 1987.

Hardeman, Nicolas P. *Harbor of the Heartlands: A History of the Inland Seaport of Stockton from the Gold Rush to 1985.* Stockton, Holt-Atherton Center for Western Studies, University of the Pacific, 1986.

Kasser, Daniel. *Downtown Stockton.* Charleston, South Carolina: Arcadia Publishing, 2005.

Kennedy, Glenn A. *It Happened in Stockton 1900-1925, Volume I-III.* Stockton: Private Printing, 1967

Mabalon, Dawn B. *Little Manila is in the Heart: The Making of the Filipina/o American Community in Stockton, California.* Durham, North Carolina: Duke University Press, 2013.

Martin, Covert V. *Stockton Album Through the Years.* Stockton: College of the Pacific and Stockton College, 1959.

Minnick, Sylvia Sun. *Samfow: The San Joaquin Chinese Legacy.* Fresno: Panorama West, 1988.

Payne, Walter A. (ed). *Benjamin Holt: The Story of the Caterpillar Tractor.* Stockton: The Holt-Atherton Pacific Center for Western Studies, University of the Pacific, 1982.

Shebl, James. *This Great Work: The 85 Year History of St. Joseph's Hospital.* Stockton: St. Joseph's Hospital of Stockton, 1984.

Spencer, Horace A. *The Railroads of San Joaquin County: An Elementary School Source Book.* Stockton: San Joaquin County Superintendent of Schools, 1976.

Struhsaker, Virginia L. *Stockton's Black Pioneers.* Stockton: Pacific Center for Western Studies, University of the Pacific, 1975.

Swenson, Bert E. *A History of the Stockton Recreation Department, 1910-1947 (Master's Thesis).* Stockton: Department of Education, College of the Pacific, 1950.

San Joaquin County Historical Society and Museum. *The San Joaquin Historians.* Lodi: San Joaquin County Historical Society and Museum, 1963-2014.

Tinkham, George. *A History of Stockton.* San Francisco: W.I. Hinton & Company, 1880.

Thompson, John & Dutra, Edward A. *The Tule Breakers: The Story of the California Dredge.* Stockton, California: University of the Pacific and Stockton Corral of Westerners International, 1983.

Van Ommeren, Alice. *Stockton in Vintage Postcards.* Charleston, South Carolina: Arcadia Publishing, 2004.

Ward, Barry J. *Stephens Bros: Boat Builders and Designers.* Stockton: Haggin Museum, 2002.

Wik, Reynold M. *Benjamin Holt and Caterpillar: Tracks and Combines.* St. Joseph, Michigan: American Society of Agricultural Engineers, 1984.

Wood, Coke R. & Covello, Leonard. *Stockton Memories: A Pictorial History of Stockton, California.* Fresno: Valley Publishers, 1977.

INDEX

✧ PHOTOGRAPH COURTESY OF VISIT STOCKTON.

PHOTOGRAPH COURTESY OF VISIT STOCKTON.

STOCKTON'S GOLDEN ERA

SHARING THE HERITAGE

Historic profiles of businesses, organizations, and families that have contributed to the development and economic base of Stockton

PHOTOGRAPH COURTESY OF VISIT STOCKTON.

STOCKTON'S GOLDEN ERA

QUALITY OF LIFE

Healthcare providers, foundations,

universities, and other institutions that

contribute to the quality of life in Stockton

CALIFORNIA STATE UNIVERSITY

STANISLAUS STOCKTON CENTER

California State University Stanislaus serves a diverse student body of more than 9,000 at two locations in the Central Valley— a beautiful 228 acre campus in Turlock and the Stockton Center, located in the city's historic Magnolia District. The CSU Stanislaus Stockton Center represents San Joaquin County's only public higher education institution above the community college level.

Widely recognized for its dedicated faculty and high-quality academic programs, the University offers more than 100 majors, minors and areas of concentration, along with twenty-four master's degree programs and a doctorate in educational leadership.

CSU Stanislaus opened as Stanislaus State College in 1960, with a faculty of fifteen and fewer than 800 students at the Stanislaus County Fairgrounds in Turlock. The institution moved to its current location in 1965, gained university status and its present name in 1986, and opened its Stockton Center in 1998.

The University's presence in Stockton began in 1974 with an educational center in the State of California Building downtown. Nineteen classes were offered during the first year of instruction. In 1981 the University relocated to the Locke Center at San Joaquin Delta College and, in 1991, expanded to portable classrooms on the Delta campus.

In 1996 the University collaborated with other interested parties to establish the Stockton Center on the grounds of the former State Hospital site. In 2000 the Stockton Center Site Authority, a joint powers authority between the CSU and the city of Stockton, was established to oversee development of the Center.

The Stockton Center occupies two buildings on the 102 acre site known as University Park. Academic programs and services are located in Acacia Court. This building houses the Stockton Office of Enrollment Services, faculty and staff offices, an array of student services, classrooms, computer labs and teaching labs, distance-learning classrooms, student lounge, study areas, and a library access center. The second building is Stockton's historic Magnolia Mansion, located across the street from Acacia Court.

The faculty, staff, administrators and students of CSU Stanislaus are committed to creating a learning environment that encourages all members of the campus community to expand their intellectual, creative and social horizons. As stated in the school's mission statement, "We challenge one another to realize our potential, to appreciate and contribute to the enrichment of our diverse community, and to develop a passion for lifelong learning."

To facilitate this mission, CSU Stanislaus promotes academic excellence in the teaching and scholarly activities of its faculty, encourages personalized student learning, fosters interactions and partnerships with surrounding communities, and provides opportunities for the intellectual, cultural and artistic enrichment of the region.

The current dean of the Stockton Center is Ashour Badal. Other deans, directors and provosts who have helped shape the University or the Stockton Center over the years include Kenneth Shrable, Douglas Taylor, George A. Condon, Richard Alter, Rodolfo Arevalo, Jessie Garza-Roderik, Diana Demetrulias, Cynthia Morgan, and Dave Hamlett.

The average Stockton Center student is a thirty-two year old adult, employed full-time, who is returning to college to complete an undergraduate degree or pursue a graduate degree, certificate or credential. Many students have completed their lower-division coursework at a community college and have transferred to the Stockton Center to complete their degrees. Stockton Center students report that they choose the center for its programs, location and affordability.

The Stockton Center offers upper-division courses that earn students full academic credit and lead to selected baccalaureate and master's degrees and credentials. Currently, courses are offered in psychology, sociology, business, public administration and teacher education. The Stockton Center also offers criminal justice and social science degree programs through University Extended Education. Many students attending classes in Stockton can complete their degrees without the need to commute to the main campus in Turlock. Most classes are offered in the late afternoon and evening, making it convenient for working adults.

The University is divided into four colleges:

- The College of Business Administration consists of three departments: Accounting and Finance; Computer Information Systems; and Management, Operations and Marketing. One undergraduate degree program is offered, with several concentration options and three graduate degree programs.

- The College of the Arts, Humanities and Social Sciences believes university education in the twenty-first century must be responsive to the complexities and challenges of a constantly changing world. Central to the college's mission is fostering an appreciation and understanding of the value of lifelong intellectual pursuit.

- The College of Education, Kinesiology and Social Work is dedicated to preparing professionals who are life-long learners, equipped with the skills, knowledge and abilities needed to address the challenges facing schools, social service agencies and communities.

- The departments in the College of Science form a scientific community dedicated to providing students the intellectual and technological capacity to contribute to and succeed in their academic and scientific pursuits.

The Princeton Review consistently ranks CSU Stanislaus among the Best Colleges in the Nation, and Time Magazine recently ranked the University twenty-eighth in the nation for access, affordability and graduation rate. Unlike larger, impersonal campuses, CSU Stanislaus feels friendly and welcoming. Although enrollment has grown to more than 9,000, most classes have fewer than twenty-one students, providing more opportunities for one-on-one relationships between students and professors.

CSU Stanislaus is a member of the NCAA Division II and fields fourteen men's and women's athletic teams in the California Collegiate Athletic Association. The University's teams consistently compete for conference and national championships while maintaining high academic standards for its student-athletes.

Meeting planners and corporate trainers find the academic atmosphere of the Stockton Center campus to be conducive to interaction and learning. Rooms are available seven days a week, during both daytime and evening hours. Rates are affordable, and an expert staff is available to assist in planning your next meeting.

As it faces the future, the faculty, staff and students at the CSU Stanislaus Stockton Center remain deeply committed to achieving the school's mission and vision through this pledge:

"We inspire all members of the campus community to demand more of self than we do of others to attain new knowledge and challenge assumptions.

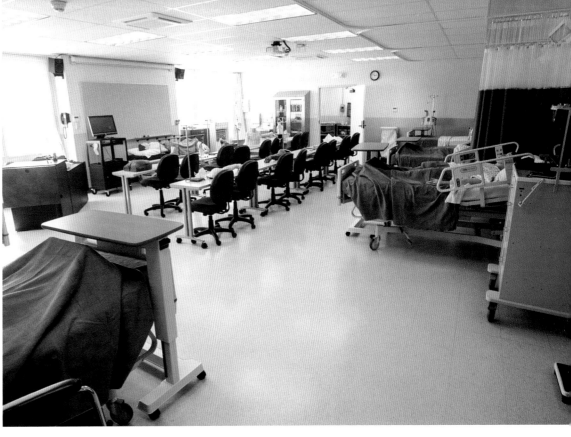

"We challenge one another to be fully engaged, responsible citizens with the ethics, knowledge, skills and desire to improve self and community.

"We value learning that encompasses lifelong exploration and discovery through intellectual integrity, personal responsibility, global self-awareness, grounded in individual student-faculty interactions.

"We are a student-centered community committed to a diverse, caring, learning-focused environment that fosters collegial, reflective and open exchange of ideas.

"We, as students create the collegiate experience through initiative, participation, motivation, and continual growth to meet the demands of self and others.

"We, as faculty, elicit, nurture and enhance the different voices of ourselves, students and communities through deliberate engagement, continual discovery and ongoing transformation.

"We, as staff and administrators, contribute to the learning environment by demonstrating the knowledge, skills and values that serve and support the University's mission." For additional information about the CSU Stanislaus Stockton Center, please visit www.csustan.edu/stockton-center.

SAN JOAQUIN DELTA COMMUNITY COLLEGE DISTRICT

✧

Above: Pacific Avenue entrance.

Below: Central Campus Koi pond.

Bottom: Lawrence and Alma DeRicco Student Services Building.

The Board, administration, faculty, and staff of San Joaquin Delta Community College District are steadfast in their dedication to help the diverse student population of the District to reach their education and career goals. Delta's commitment to serving students includes programs and courses in Career and Technical Education (CTE) and job training; retraining for new careers; preparation for Associate in Arts (AA) and Associate in Science (AS) degrees and transfer to four-year colleges or universities; and opportunities for personal enrichment. The College provides a wide array of opportunities for students to gain leadership and work experience through academic, student support, and student activities programs. The College offers over 100 certificate and degree programs and provides day, evening, and online classes. Delta's highly qualified and dedicated faculty and staff have two primary goals: Student Success and Student Equity!

The College of the Pacific, a private Methodist-funded school located in Stockton, known today as University of the Pacific, provided the impetus that led eventually to the establishment of San Joaquin Delta College.

The roots of Delta College can be traced back to September 1935 and the formation of Stockton Junior College in union with the College of the Pacific (COP). In an unprecedented arrangement, junior college students had their freshman and sophomore years' tuition paid through the Stockton Unified School District. Because COP was a private college, special legislation was required from the state legislature to permit the transfer of public funds to pay tuition.

The economic difficulties faced by both the public school district and COP during the Great Depression sparked the need for the successful arrangement. The program provided education that would otherwise be difficult or unattainable, and it helped Pacific weather the economic hard times.

Major changes began to occur in 1939 as the nation neared World War II. Federally-funded courses provided technical programs such as radio technology, pilot training, and reserve officer training to improve national defense. Following December 7, 1941, both Stockton Junior College and College of the Pacific mobilized to confer early degrees and

expand into defense work. In addition, the college contracted with the Navy to offer a V-12 Collegiate Training Program and the Army Signal Corps to expand its radio program.

In 1944 the Stockton Unified School District purchased forty-three acres of land with plans to develop a "Stockton College" campus. While the arrangement with Pacific was to continue, it was clear that the rapid growth of enrollment would require more traditional classroom space and to house an ambitious trade and industry program in cooperation with major local manufacturers.

A sophisticated instructional program was designed around work furnished by the manufacturing firms in model shop environments. Students were required to take both core academic classes and trade-related academic classes. Stockton College was regarded as the junior college with the most comprehensive technical and vocational curricula in the western United States and became the model followed by other colleges west of the Mississippi and throughout California.

In 1951, Pacific and Stockton Unified separated and Pacific resumed its freshman and sophomore classes on a private-pay basis with classes separated from junior college students. Meanwhile, Stockton College held separate classes either in classrooms rented from Pacific or on its own newly-constructed campus.

As the years passed, talk of forming a separate junior college district with its own governing board became more frequent. As part of the unified school district, Stockton College was essentially a small part of a much larger entity. Faced with expanding enrollment and a limited revenue base due to the low property valuations in Stockton, its governing board was hard-pressed to satisfy all of the needs of the district. The decision to transition "Stockton College" into an area-wide college with an expanded tax and enrollment base became a reality when voters approved that change in 1963. Thus was born "San Joaquin Delta Community College," which serves San Joaquin County and portions of four surrounding counties.

San Joaquin Delta College now rented the old "Stockton College" campus from the Stockton Unified School District, but immediately began planning to relocate on its own permanent campus and to raise the necessary funds for its construction. The land for the new campus, once the old State Hospital Farm site, was acquired in 1968; a vigorous bond campaign that financed part of the construction followed. The first building was ready for classes in 1973.

The campus was completed in 1975. It was designed around five centers with independent student services, libraries, snack bars and lounges, and a center administration. Students in various disciplines were to attend major classes at a specific center. Center activities were designed to give each of the complexes a unique character. The hope was that students would identify with core faculty, counselors and support staff in order to provide a more personal college experience. All of these facilities are built around a center courtyard area that contains the main library, student union, large lecture-hall forums, art gallery and administrative center. Over time, the center concept was abandoned in order to be more cost-efficient with centralized services and greater flexibility in housing programs.

The performing arts are housed in three theaters: Atherton Auditorium, which serves as,

✧

Above: Science and Mathematics Building.

Below: Delta College veteran graduates at the Stockton Arena.

the home of the Stockton Symphony Orchestra; Tillie Lewis Theatre; and the Alfred H. Muller Studio Theater. The Center for Microscopy and Allied Sciences building is dedicated exclusively to electron microscopy laboratories and classrooms, one of only two such community college programs in the nation.

With the passage of 2004's $250 million Measure L Bond, the College took a giant step into the future with campus renovations, new buildings, and a new campus at Mountain House near Tracy.

The Measure L-funded South Campus at Mountain House opened its doors in 2009. Mountain House features over 30,000 square feet of modular classroom and lab environments. The campus offers a full range of general education classes and opportunities to pursue AA/AS degrees with "jobs of the future" as its focus. Plans are now in the works for construction of another educational center in the northern part of San Joaquin County.

Among the first Measure L projects completed were the renovated athletic fields for baseball, football and new venues for soccer,

softball and track throwing events. Delta College indeed has some of the finest athletic venues in the community college system.

The Lawrence and Alma DeRicco Student Services Center was opened in 2009. The center serves as Delta's "one stop shop" for student services. Busy students appreciate the convenience of having Admissions and Records, Financial Aid and Counseling Services (among others) in one location. Measure L also provided for the renovation of the Goleman Library, featuring a striking new exterior design, classrooms and modern library technologies that create a student-friendly hub for learning. Always looking to the future, a new Data Center was completed in 2011 to meet the district's advanced technology needs for years to come. The college also built new shop facilities for its diesel/heavy equipment and automotive programs, which include the Caterpillar "Think Big" apprenticeship program.

Opened in 2014 is the new state-of-the-art Science and Mathematics Building, which replaced the outdated Cunningham Building. The striking three-story center features a 70,000 square foot laboratory core, with 20,000 square feet of classrooms on each floor. To augment academics, the building includes high-tech Smart Room lecture halls, computer labs and a Resource Center for studying and tutoring. The Science and Mathematics Building will remain an example of Delta College's commitment to educate students for careers in Science, Technology, Engineering and Math "STEM" programs for years to come.

The campus is also home to a Child Development Center, which provides opportunities for students seeking certification in early childhood education. The center also provides childcare for children of students enrolled at Delta College.

With agriculture education an important component of the valley's economy, Delta College leads the way with a 160 acre farm laboratory in Manteca.

San Joaquin Delta College, accredited by the Western Association of Schools and Colleges-Accreditation Commission of Community and Junior Colleges, provides excellent postsecondary undergraduate studies for nearly 20,000 students. The school provides Associate

✧

Above: Diesel Technology.

Below: Delta College Electron Microscopy.

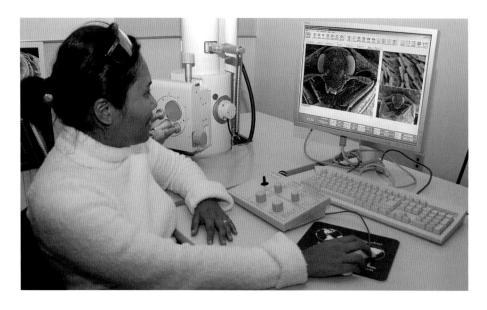

degrees and career technical education certificates through six divisions: Agriculture, Science and Mathematics; Applied Science, Business and Technology; Arts and Communication; Health Sciences; Humanities, Social Science, Education, Kinesiology and Athletics; and Languages, Library, and Learning Resources.

The College has a full program of academic and student support services such as tutoring centers, computer laboratories, L. H. Horton Art Gallery, a full-service library, enrollment services, veterans services, financial aid and scholarships, a CalWORKs program, a career and transfer center, Disability Support Programs and Services (DSPS), Extended Opportunity Programs and Services (EOPS), a variety of programs for underserved populations (AFFIRM, CARE, Puente, HSI STEM, Mini-Corps, MESA, and YESS), learning disability services, and general counseling services.

The campus features a full-service and online bookstore, food services, police services, work experience services, and a Workforce Investment Board funded WorkNet Center, which provides an array of employment services.

In partnership with the Lodi Unified School District, Delta College houses the high achieving Middle College High School and partners with Stockton Unified in the Stockton Early College Academy. Currently, the college is also working with Manteca Unified and Calaveras Unified School Districts to offer classes in those regions.

Delta College supports an extensive athletic program that includes football, men's and women's basketball, baseball, softball, men's and women's golf, men's and women's soccer, men's and women's swimming and diving, men's and women's track and field, women's volleyball, men's and women's water polo, and wrestling. Delta College teams are always among the best in the California Community College Athletic Association. It is not unusual for Delta's teams to compete for CCCAA championships year in and year out!

Delta College's other services include Community Education, which offers classes, workshops and programs for adults, with opportunities for personal growth, professional development, cultural enrichment, and recreational enjoyment. Programs for adults

include the Stockton Institute for Continued Learning (SICL), a learning-in-retirement program for older adults, and Kids College, which serves students from age two to seventeen. Kids College workshops are designed to teach new and meaningful skills, as well as excite students about learning and creativity.

Delta College's Small Business Development Center (SBDC) is at the forefront in assisting local entrepreneurs grow their businesses. Through free and affordable training, consulting, and a wide range of programs, the SBDC is available to help district residents launch or expand their businesses.

The faculty, staff, and students of San Joaquin Delta College envision a community of lifelong learners, passionately pursuing and achieving ever-higher educational goals, and fully appreciating the diverse and dynamic world around them.

For more information about San Joaquin Delta College, visit www.deltacollege.edu.

Charles Bloch, Delta College historian and retired Delta College faculty member, wrote the historical contribution for this article.

✧

Above: Irving Goleman Library.

Below: The Lady Mustangs play in the Bucky Layland Softball Complex.

HUMPHREYS
COLLEGE

For more than a century, Humphreys College has been dedicated to providing effective instruction and related learning experiences for its students. The prestigious independent college, with campuses in Stockton and Modesto, offers certificate, associate, bachelor, master and juris doctor degrees in five broad academic areas: law, business, education, human services and liberal arts. The college views itself primarily as a teaching institution.

Although there is evidence that a predecessor school existed as far back as 1875, the college dates its founding from the fall of 1896 when John R. Humphreys, Sr., took over academic administration of the Stockton Business College, Normal School and Telegraphic Institute.

Humphreys College was the first institution of higher education in the San Joaquin Valley and has been in continuous service to the region for 118 years. Until 1924 the college was the only institution of higher learning in the area.

"The philosophy and objectives of its founder have remained with the college," explains Dr. Robert Humphreys, grandson of the founder, and president since 1980. "We are a small, independent college dedicated to post-secondary education and to serving the educational needs of our students and community.

"The founder believed that any sound program must first be concerned with meeting the educational needs of the individual student and, second, with ensuring the program contains elements of general and career or professional education. The college has maintained this simple philosophy throughout its long service to the community," Humphrey adds.

The founder of the college died in 1937 and his son, John R. Humphreys, Jr., who had served as academic administrator, became the second president.

The school's name changed several times over the years. It was known as Gas City Business College before it was acquired by the Western School of Commerce in 1901. A few years later it was named Stockton College of Commerce and then became Humphreys College in July 1947 when it was reorganized and incorporated as a nonprofit educational corporation under the California Education Code.

In 1950, school trustees established a non-accredited, four-year night law school.

✧

Above: Founder John R. Humphreys Sr., 1868-1937.

Right: Humphreys class, c. 1908.

Below: The original location in 1896. Corner of California and Channel Streets in Stockton.

The school took the first steps toward accreditation of the law school in 1973 and accreditation was granted in 1983. Today, the school's Laurence Drivon School of Law offers a professional program of education leading to the Juris Doctor degree, preparing students for the California State Bar examination and the practice of law. The school has deliberately kept tuition affordable, providing an extraordinary value for an excellent legal education. The School of Law attracts recent college graduates as well as those returning to college after several years. Many of these students hold full-time jobs while pursuing their studies.

In 1966, Humphreys College moved from downtown Stockton to an eight acre campus about five miles north of downtown. The campus is one block east of Pacific Avenue, one of Stockton's major thoroughfares.

The main academic building houses several classrooms, computer labs, bookstore and administrative offices. The west campus is composed of four buildings, which house the Academy of Business, Law and Education, a charter high school operated as a subsidiary nonprofit corporation. Both the main and west campuses have outdoor courtyard areas with ample space for students to study, eat lunch, or gather with friends. Recently, the physical plant was expanded by approximately 24,000 square feet consisting of two new buildings constructed on vacant campus land. The library building houses the law and undergraduate libraries as well as the administrative offices of Humphreys College Laurence Drivon School of Law. The classroom building includes eight classrooms, as

well as eighteen faculty offices, administrative offices and a student lounge. A central courtyard provides an attractive place for students to gather and socialize outside and is served by a wireless Internet network. Another 15,000 square feet facility was added in 2010 to provide ten additional classrooms.

The college's two libraries are major learning centers, not only for students and faculty, but also for alumni and the community. Extended hours of operation provide a convenient and easily accessible community resource. A branch of the Stockton Public Library is located directly across the street from the college with a large general collection which is available to all students. Because of the proximity to the public library, the college does not attempt to duplicate its general holdings, but rather is able to focus its own collection to support the college's curricula in liberal arts, accounting, business, early childhood education and the legal disciplines: court reporting, paralegal studies, criminal justice and law.

The college libraries open stacks and reading area provides easy access to reference and circulating collections. Periodicals, DVDs and videos are available on request in the circulation area. Requests for interlibrary loan of monographs and periodicals, state, federal and international government publications may be made at the reference desk. The library also provides students access to several online databases, with access to numerous peer-reviewed journals, magazines and newspaper articles.

The law library collection, available on open stacks and online, exceeds the minimum set by the Committee of Bar Examiners. It provides primary source material as well as

✧
Left: The current campus as it appeared when built in 1966.

Right: Dedication of new campus in 1967.

secondary resources and more than twenty major law periodicals. An in-depth collection of tax services is available for students and practitioners of accounting and law.

In 1972, Humphreys College was accredited by the Western Association of Schools and Colleges (WASC), accrediting commission for community and junior colleges. In 1992 the college was accredited by the Accrediting Commission for Senior Colleges and Universities of WASC, making all certificates and degrees granted by the college (including the law school) accredited.

John R. Humphreys, Jr., retired as president in 1980 and Robert G. Humphreys became the school's third President. Thus, three generations of Humphreys have maintained the leadership of the college since its founding.

In 1987, Humphreys College began offering courses through Modesto Junior College, eventually establishing a campus in Modesto. The branch campus is located in north Modesto in Stanislaus County. Facilities include classrooms, computer laboratory, faculty offices, bookstore, student lounge and reference library. Rooms and apartments for students are available within walking distance of the campus.

The school has enjoyed significant growth since 2007 with total enrollment at one time exceeding 1,200. Most of Humphreys' students are from San Joaquin and the seven neighboring counties, although some are from outside the valley and several foreign countries.

Realizing that a 'one-size-fits-all' approach to learning does not meet the needs of all students, the professors at Humphreys take the time to understand how students learn best. These approaches may include team projects, individual presentations, hands-on practice or online learning. Simply put, Humphreys is a college where learning works the way the student needs it to.

The college prepares students for careers and professions through a high-quality educational experience directed to the specific and changing needs of students from diverse ethnic, cultural, economic and educational backgrounds, using current technology and

methods. Programs include career-oriented education strongly informed by the liberal arts, with a growing international and global perspective, and focused toward enhancing students' life skills.

Whatever the student's goal, Humphreys has a program that will prepare them to go farther faster. The school's interdisciplinary approach encourages students to pursue their passions across disparate fields of knowledge, broaden their experience beyond the classroom and engage in the community, the region and the world. Advisors are personally invested in helping students discover their passions.

Programs offered by Humphreys College are available in the fields of accounting, business administration, community studies,

The campus in 2014.

court reporting, criminal justice, early childhood education, legal studies, liberal studies, paralegal studies and law studies through the Lawrence Drivon School of Law. Master of Arts in Education degrees are offered in early childhood education, educational administration and teaching with a multiple subject credential.

Although Humphreys is a small college, it seeks to serve both general and career objectives. With this in mind, the college has sought ways to keep classes small, to offer some instruction on individualized bases, and to maintain a close relationship between faculty and students. The school seeks to provide a significant introduction to general education for students who pursue specialized occupational objectives, and to provide an appreciation of career or professional goals for students who pursue general education objectives.

While it is kept current, the curriculum today is still clearly related to the curriculum as it was when Humphreys College was founded, focusing on both liberal arts and career preparation. The continued expansion of the college—both in Stockton and Modesto—shows the school's commitment to the community and the growth of educational opportunities for all.

The trustees of the college recently elected Dr. Robert Humphreys, Jr., great grandson of the founder, to become the fourth president. He represents the fourth generation of Humphreys to lead the college and will assume the office of president July 1, 2015.

University of the Pacific

The oldest chartered university in California, University of the Pacific was founded in Santa Clara in 1851. With its move to Stockton in 1925, Pacific became the first private, four-year university in the Central Valley. Pacific is consistently ranked among the top national universities by *U.S. News and World Report* and *Princeton Review*.

Pacific is recognized for high-quality programs, dedicated faculty mentors, excellent professional preparation built on a strong liberal arts foundation, rigorous coursework and an emphasis on experiential and co-curricular learning.

In 1962, Pacific acquired a school of dentistry founded in San Francisco in 1896, adding a second campus in the Bay Area city. McGeorge School of Law, an independent law school founded in Sacramento in 1924, merged with the University in 1966, adding a third campus in California's capital city. Total enrollment at all three campuses is more than 6,000 students. With its presence in three different but uniquely California cities,

Pacific enjoys a truly distinctive footprint in California and the West.

Pacific's Stockton campus is renowned for its idyllic beauty, breadth of outstanding academic programs, vibrant and supportive campus life, and close, dedicated teaching relationships with students. Serving more than 5,000 students, the campus is home to the liberal arts College of the Pacific, a conservatory of music, and schools of business, education, engineering, international studies, and pharmacy and health sciences.

The University's new, state-of-the-art campus in San Francisco opened in 2014. It is home to the renowned Arthur A. Dugoni School of Dentistry, as well as a new audiology clinic and new academic programs in audiology, music therapy, food studies and analytics enrolling for fall 2015.

Pacific's beautiful, tree-lined campus in Sacramento, home to Pacific McGeorge School of Law, provides a focused learning environment with ties to the power and influence of the state capitol. Soon, Pacific will offer new academic programs leveraging the city's opportunities in law and policy, healthcare and business.

Noted alumni include jazz icon Dave Brubeck and his wife, librettist Iola Brubeck; former astronaut José Hernández; and former U.S. Solicitor General Theodore B. Olson.

Considered one of the most beautiful college campuses in the country, the 175 acre Stockton campus is modeled after East Coast Collegiate Gothic universities. Students learn in an inspirational setting of red brick buildings adorned with ivy, lush greenery and beautiful gardens. The meticulously maintained grounds were originally landscaped by John McLaren, designer of Stan Francisco's Golden Gate Park.

Robert E. Burns Tower, one of the tallest buildings in Stockton, fills the courtyards

✧

Above: Burns Tower at the campus entrance is a Stockton landmark.

Below: Morris Chapel, with its magnificent stained glass windows, is a popular wedding venue.

with music from the bell carillon twice daily. Morris Chapel, with its magnificent stained glass windows, is a popular wedding venue. The campus has served as the setting for many Hollywood films, including Steven Spielberg's *Raiders of the Lost Ark*.

The University brings prominent world leaders and scholars to speak on campus and presents concerts, operas, plays, films, art exhibits and multicultural programs throughout the year. The annual Brubeck Festival includes a variety of events and concerts featuring renowned jazz musicians, vocalists, and historians.

The University library's Holt-Atherton Special Collections includes the manuscripts and published essays of naturalist John Muir and the complete archives of internationally renowned composer and jazz pianist Dave Brubeck and his wife, Iola, among its extensive historical collections. These provide a tremendous resource for researchers locally and around the world.

Pacific students, faculty, and staff are passionate about enriching their communities and serving those in need. Under faculty guidance, students provide dental care and health services and information to the underserved, legal clinics for those in need, and literacy and educational enrichment programs for local schoolchildren. Students, faculty and staff contribute tens of thousands of hours of volunteer service each year.

The Center for Professional and Continuing Education offers degree completion, continuing education, workforce training and lifelong learning programs. Like the Business Forecasting Center—a go-to resource for local and regional economic forecasts and issues analyses—Pacific centers and institutes work toward solutions to local and regional issues through community partnerships, education and research.

The Pacific Tigers compete in NCAA Division I athletics primarily as a member of the West Coast Conference, fielding seven men's teams and eleven women's teams. The Tigers continue to add individual and team successes to an already outstanding performance record, including thirty-one conference championships and sixty NCAA tournament appearances.

Pacific offers more than eighty programs of study leading to undergraduate, graduate and professional degrees, as well as accelerated programs in business, education, law, engineering and the health sciences. More than eighty-seven percent of the students receive financial assistance through the University's robust financial aid program, helping to make Pacific's quality education affordable. Nearly sixty percent of students live on campus and participate in a vibrant residential life, boasting more than 100 student clubs and organizations and a comprehensive recreational program.

With a focus on teaching, close faculty-student interaction, academic excellence and real-world learning, Pacific prepares individuals for lifelong personal and professional success.

Learn about Pacific programs and activities at Pacific.edu.

✧

Top left: Community members enjoy the excitement of NCAA Division I athletics.

Above: Pacific clinics provide healthcare, legal, educational and other services to thousands of community members each year.

Below: The award-winning Brubeck Institute Jazz quintet and renowned jazz musicians perform at the annual Brubeck Festival.

CATHOLIC CHARITIES OF THE DIOCESE OF STOCKTON

Catholic Social Teaching calls the Church to protect human life and dignity in all its vulnerabilities and to participate in the social, economic, political and spiritual well-being of all people regardless of race, age, gender, religion or culture. Catholic Charities of Stockton has been an extension of the social justice activity throughout the Diocese of Stockton for more than seventy years. In the words of Bishop Stephen Blaire, the agency serves people "because we are Catholic, not because they are Catholic." Incorporated as a 501(c)3 nonprofit organization in 1980, Catholic Charities of the Diocese of Stockton is guided currently by a ten member board of directors and serves the needs of the poor and vulnerable in the six Northern California counties of San Joaquin, Stanislaus, Tuolumne, Calaveras, Mono and Alpine.

The history of the organization is deeply rooted in Stockton. The archives of the Maryknoll Sisters indicate that the Sisters were instrumental in establishing the agency around 1946. From the beginning, the Stockton office was part of the San Francisco Archdiocesan Catholic Social Service Organization. The historical predecessor of Stockton Social Service was the United Crusade, which was providing services since about 1943.

Father William O'Connor was appointed to organize and direct the Catholic Social Service Organization in 1945. The goal in the early years was to provide services through an open-door, welcoming policy aimed directly at Stockton's Hispanic population.

The agency services included help with immigration status, referral services, job placement assistance, finding homes, jobs and shelter, food and clothing and limited carfare and cash assistance. In addition, foster care for Catholic dependent children needing placement was instituted and a strong relationship was developed with the local probation department. This resulted in referral of almost all Catholic dependent children in San Joaquin County.

Simultaneously the agency procured licensing for Catholic Foster Homes services. Referrals multiplied as these services became known and the staff grew to six case workers who handled as many as 800 cases at a time. Most of this work was carried out by the Maryknoll Sisters.

In 1952 the Archbishop appointed Father Walter Doyle full-time director of the Catholic Social Services Office. Father Doyle, a professionally trained social worker, brought about some pivotal changes in the organization. In 1957 child placement services were eliminated

❖

Right: Allen Nesset has worked for Catholic Charities for over twenty years, he is the Food Bank Coordinator. Over 10,600 people were served with nutritious food in 2014, nearly half were children.

Below: Catholic Charities—Mother Lode Office.

from the agency's services because social workers could not always agree with the probation officers decision to remove all responsibility from the parents. In 1958 the agency's last foster home permit expired, leaving the sole responsibility for this service to the County Welfare's Foster Home Division. The shifts in function allowed agency workers to spend more time in the field, making referrals to foster homes and institutions and following up with youth, foster parents and institutional staff.

During the 1970s and 1980s, Catholic Charities provided services to help integrate refugees from Vietnam, Laos and Cambodia following the Vietnam War. In 1997, Family Based Immigration Services was established to assist permanent legal residents in applying for citizenship and family reunification. Citizenship education programs and English as a Second Language were established in 2010 to help legal permanent residents pass citizenship exams.

The agency continues to provide similar programs for immigrant integration and services that address the basic needs of individuals and families. The agency supports and advocates for senior independence and safety through a variety of services. Through difficult economic times that have impacted the Central Valley over the years, Catholic Charities has remained committed to providing services to the most vulnerable members of our community.

Executive Director Elvira Ramirez attributes the successful implementation and expansion of services to the dedicated efforts of compassionate staff and volunteers. Since 2009 services have grown to include a variety of senior programs such as care management and chronic disease management, which helps them remain safely in their homes as long as possible. Other new programs include supportive services to very low-income veterans and their families who are at risk of homelessness. A drop-in center for homeless and at-risk women and their children has been established in Lodi. St. Anne's Place provides day shelter, access to housing and employment resources and referral information. Additional programs include an environmental justice program and the Family Wellness

Prevention and Early Intervention Services, which provides counseling services, parent education and a youth engagement program.

With an annual budget of nearly $4 million, Catholic Charities manages more than seventy-five volunteers and employs a well-trained staff of over 100 who work out of three offices. The main office is located at 1106 North El Dorado Street in Stockton, and full-service offices are located at 400 Twelfth Street in Modesto and 88 Bradford Street in Sonora. The agency partners with other community organizations to expand and deliver quality social services to people in need.

Catholic Charities is proud to be a part of the Stockton community and remains deeply committed to its mission statement: "Catholic Charities partners with others in advocating for justice and assisting those in need by providing help for today and hope for tomorrow."

✧

Above: St. Anne's Place established in 2013 in partnership with St. Anne's Church is a day drop-in center for homeless and at-risk women and their children in Lodi, California.

Below: Maria Perez, Parent Educator Coordinator with Father David Dutra, St. George Parish and first parent support graduation class of 2013. Classes are ten to twelve weeks.

ST. JOSEPH'S MEDICAL CENTER

From its humble beginnings as a twenty-five bed hospital, St. Joseph's Medical Center of Stockton has grown to a 366 bed regional medical center, specializing in cardiovascular care, comprehensive cancer services, and women and infant's services, including neonatal intensive care.

✧

Above: Father William B. O'Connor.

Below: Dominican Sisters on the grounds of St. Joseph's, 1920s.

St. Joseph's Medical Center was originally conceived as a 'home for old men' by Father William B. O'Connor. In 1884, with the support of three generous benefactors, he purchased nearly ten acres just north of the Stockton city limits. When area physicians learned of Father O'Connor's plans, they convinced him of the need for a hospital addition to the home.

Father O'Connor selected the name of the institution and the cornerstone was dedicated on the Feast of St. Joseph Day, March 19, 1899. Under the care and supervision of the Dominican Sisters of San Rafael, St. Joseph's Home and Hospital opened on December 21, 1899.

The hospital's patron, St. Joseph, was a carpenter, a husband, a father, a dreamer, and a saint. He was known as a righteous, compassionate, and caring man. A six foot statue of St. Joseph stands above the original cornerstone of St. Joseph's Home and Hospital and greets all those who pass the main entrance of the medical center.

St. Joseph's Medical Center became part of the Dignity Health system in 1996. Headquartered in San Francisco, Dignity Health is a not-for-profit healthcare system of forty hospitals and medical centers in Arizona, California, and Nevada, providing high quality, compassionate healthcare.

St. Joseph's Medical Center is the largest hospital, as well as the largest private employer, in Stockton with around 2,200 employees and more than 400 physicians. Nationally recognized as a quality leader, St. Joseph's is fully accredited by The Joint Commission and is consistently chosen as the "most preferred hospital" by local consumers. The hospital contributes millions of dollars in community benefit and uncompensated care each year, with $76 million being contributed in 2014.

Medical services provided by St. Joseph's Medical Center include cardiovascular services, diagnostic imaging, emergency and trauma, gastroenterology, home health, intensive care, neonatal intensive care, neurosciences, obstetrics/labor and delivery, oncology, orthopedics, outpatient nutrition services, palliative care, pediatrics, physical therapy, pulmonary and cardiac rehabilitation, and surgery.

The Heart Center at St. Joseph's has a legacy of innovation and dedication to providing excellent cardiovascular care to the community. Since performing the first open heart surgery in San Joaquin County in 1974, St. Joseph's Heart

Center has had a long history of medical "firsts" in the community, including the first STEMI heart attack receiving center and designated Stroke Center. St. Joseph's quality outcomes for cardiovascular care have earned regional and national recognition. The Heart Center participates in clinical research studies both nationally and internationally to advance the treatment of cardiovascular disease. Highly trained physicians, nurses, and multidisciplinary support staff make it possible for patients to find the wide variety of services they may need all under one roof. St. Joseph's Heart Center features cardiac surgery, including new, less invasive surgical approaches, cardiac catheterization, balloon angioplasty, stenting, and additional intervention treatments.

St. Joseph's Regional Cancer Center is the only cancer center in San Joaquin County to be accredited by the Commission on Cancer of the American College of Surgeons. The Cancer Center is staffed by Board Certified Radiation Oncologists and houses two linear accelerators offering the highest quality radiation therapy available in the area. Each year, the Cancer Center delivers more than 10,000 treatments to cancer patients. Cancer services include steriotactic ablative body radiotherapy (SABR), intensity modulated radiation therapy (IMRT), Mammosite, high dose rate brachytherapy, dedicated inpatient oncology, clinical trials, I.V. chemotherapy, a cancer resource center,

cancer navigators, and a full spectrum of patient and family support services.

St. Joseph's Medical Center is the county's first hospital to be designated a Baby-Friendly® birthing facility. Family-centered care which promotes and strengthens family relations with premature infants is part of the expanded twenty-two bed Neonatal Intensive Care Unit.

The excellence of St. Joseph's Medical Center has earned numerous awards and certifications. The center was awarded the prestigious Distinguished Hospital Award in Clinical Excellence in 2013, as well as the Cardiac Care Excellence Award. The center received the Vascular Surgery Excellence Award for two years in a row in 2012 and 2013, and was rated number one in California for vascular surgery. In 2013, St. Joseph's was "Best Rated" (five out of five stars) in heart failure treatment, hip fracture treatment, neurosurgery, sepsis, respiratory failure treatment, and gynecologic surgery.

St. Joseph's Medical Center, Dignity Health and its Sponsoring Congregations are committed to furthering the healing ministry of Jesus. St. Joseph's is dedicated to delivering compassionate, high-quality, affordable health services; serving and advocating for those who are poor and disenfranchised; and partnering with others in the community to improve their quality of life.

✧

St. Joseph's Medical Center—today.

LINCOLN UNIFIED SCHOOL DISTRICT

Lincoln Unified School District has a long and proud tradition of excellence in education. The board of trustees and district staff are committed to providing the highest learning standards in a safe and welcoming educational environment. Our goal and responsibility is to help each student develop an enthusiasm for learning, a respect for self and others, and the skills to become a creative independent thinker and problem solver.

Lincoln USD is located in northwest Stockton and has an enrollment of more than 9,200 transitional kindergarten through twelfth grade students following a traditional school year calendar.

✧

Above: Don Riggio School is the district's magnet arts school, emphasizing instruction in the fine arts while maintaining a strong academic program.

The district provides a wide variety of educational programs, services and settings, including preschool programs, traditional transitional kindergarten through grade six and transitional kindergarten through grade eight programs, as well as rigorous middle school and secondary programs. Don Riggio School is the district's magnet arts school, emphasizing instruction in the fine arts while maintaining a strong academic program. Lincoln High School is one of the finest high schools in the state, providing opportunities in advanced academics, fine arts, and sports. The district also offers an alternative high school and independent learning programs, all of which have been recognized statewide for excellence.

The district's focus on the needs of the individual student is evidenced not just by the broad range of programs offered to students, but also by the ongoing training offered to staff. The commitment is real, and has the support of staff and the community.

Lincoln High School, the district's comprehensive ninth through twelfth school, offers a broad spectrum of courses to meet the needs of students. Included in these programs are fifteen advanced placement (AP) courses and ten honors courses, all recognized by the University of California for their rigor. The Career and Technical Education Department has course pathways aligned to fifteen industry sectors. Many support systems exist to help students be successful, including tutoring services, the Multilingual Center and the Academic Success Center.

In addition to the district's strong focus on academics, its commitment to the visual and performing arts is central to its identity. All students receive musical instruction in kindergarten through sixth grade. Students can elect to take band, string or choir electives beginning in grade four. Middle and high school students regularly receive county, regional and all-state recognition for excellence in performance. The Lincoln High Visual and Performing Arts Department offers thirty-six separate courses.

The district's alternative education programs, Sture Larsson High School, John

McCandless High School and the Civic Pride Independent Academy, are all housed at one site, allowing the district to offer a wider range of college-prep and elective courses. All three of these programs are of high caliber and recognized statewide for their excellence.

Lincoln Unified has an extensive and competitive sports program. There are twenty-three varsity teams, as well as freshman and junior varsity teams. Lincoln Unified belongs to the CIF Sac-Joaquin Section, and regularly competes in section and regional finals. There is great community support for each of the teams.

A new charter school in Lincoln Unified is scheduled to open in August 2015, a kindergarten through grade six site with a special focus on science, technology, engineering and math (STEM). First through sixth grade students attending the STEM school will receive 27.5 hours a week of instructional time, and four additional hours a week of STEM-focused classes after the school day.

Another hallmark of Lincoln Unified is its strong student leadership program districtwide. This program produces capable, confident students who are able to serve both their schools and their community. In the 2014-2015 school year, the student regents for both the California State School Board and the University of California Board of Regents were participants of Lincoln's student leadership program. This was the first time in record that both positions were filled by students from the same school district, and is a reflection of the quality of the student leadership program.

The commitment to student leadership extends to the board of trustees. The board annually selects a high school student to serve as student trustee. This student can make and second governing board motions and place a preferential vote.

Lincoln Unified serves as a model for integrating the community into school programs and planning. Lincoln Council PTA, Lincoln Latin Leadership, Lincoln Unified Music Boosters, Lincoln High School Athletic Boosters and the ROP community partners all play critical roles in the support and development of student programs. Several of these parent support groups have won statewide awards for their innovation and advocacy. In addition, parents and community members serve on a great number of school and district level committees. This high level of parent involvement is an integral and valuable part of the district's culture.

The Lincoln Unified community and staff are committed to the welfare and success of its students and jointly strive to leave a legacy for generations to come.

For additional information, please go to www.lusd.net or call 209-953-8712.

STOCKTON GOLF AND COUNTRY CLUB

100 YEARS... AND COUNTING!

A lush landscape of old-growth trees flourishing near the fairways joins the noble San Joaquin River to welcome both discerning golfers and social enthusiasts to the second-oldest club in the valley, the magnificent Stockton Golf and Country Club.

Foxes hunt along the water hazards and a host of egrets, herons, and waterfowl swoops above as one passes the tree-lined entrance and glides slowly through a green expanse to the lavish split-level clubhouse with spectacular views of the course and the river. This dramatic waterway and its parade of towering ships combines with a landscape created one hundred years ago to prove an attraction irresistible to those seeking the rich traditions of a first-rate experience and grand recreation.

In 1914 local citizens carved a 9-hole golf course from sixty-eight acres of tidal swampland and drove over lumpy county lanes through peat storms to reach the course—one of only twelve in the state. Hospitality awaited, however, at the elegant original clubhouse overlooking the channel.

So noted was the clubhouse for its comfortable elegance and bonhomie that the first golf pro, Peter Hay, labored to emphasize the attraction of the course he designed. His mission successful, he went on to become the first golf pro at the legendary Pebble Beach. The Peter Hay Golf Course there is a 9-hole par-27 course, a fifty-seven year attraction for the Monterey Peninsula.

The expanding golf enthusiasts' desire for an 18-hole club resulted in an expansion to 117 acres in the early 1920s. An associate of famed golf course designer, Alister MacKenzie, drew up the plans. Walter G. Hunter's work was later given to Sam Whiting for the formal design. Whiting later left his mark on the Olympic Club and Harding Park courses in San Francisco.

His result here featured 18-holes covering 5,165 yards with a par-71. Area organizations donated the nearly 1,000 trees and shrubs. Willie Locke of San Francisco, an expert on western grass greens, was brought in to design and supervise the greens.

"The course has stood out over the years because of its 'stout holes,'" says club historian Peter Ottesen. This combination of tightness of the fairways has attracted golfing legends Walter Hagen and Ben Hogan, along with Hollywood celebrities such as Bob Hope, baseball great Dizzy Dean, and hotel legend Conrad Hilton.

Ricky Barnes, a PGA tour player, holds the course record of sixty-one along with Stan Mathews and University of the Pacific's Byron Meth.

The original clubhouse, an elegant three-story manor, bowed over the years to a second, and now the current, retreat, an $8 million ranch-style rendezvous created in 2006 by Michael Donaldson and built by Gary Bloom. With its breathtaking views of the San Joaquin River and sprawling golf course, the club's ambiance is enhanced by expansive windows, outdoor terraces, and a variety of dining facilities.

The facility offers its members a championship par-71 golf course stretching to 6,480 yards, state-of-the-art fitness center, exquisite lounges and dining rooms, ballrooms, and a sparkling pool.

Above: Original clubhouse with snow on the roof, c. 1914.

Below: West Side Clubhouse, 2014.
PHOTO BY KEVIN RICHTIK.

O'CONNOR WOODS CONTINUING CARE RETIREMENT COMMUNITY

O'Connor Woods, located on a beautiful thirty-four-acre campus in North Stockton, is a Continuing Care Retirement Community (CCRC) conceived, planned and developed by St. Joseph's Medical Center in collaboration with the seniors of San Joaquin County.

O'Connor Woods, which celebrates its twenty-fifth anniversary in 2015, provides the complete range of residential and assisted care needs for seniors, from active independent living, through assisted living and skilled nursing care. An independent, not-for-profit corporation founded and created by St. Joseph's and the Dominican Sisters of San Rafael, O'Connor Woods follows a long tradition of quality and commitment to the community, going back to the founding of St. Joseph's Hospital and Home for Old Men by Father William O'Connor in 1899.

Key individuals in the vision of O'Connor Woods were Sister Mary Gabriel, president emeritus of St. Joseph's Hospital; Ed Schroeder, CEO of St. Joseph's Hospital; and Carol Cox, vice president of special projects for St. Joseph's.

Planning for the community began in 1984 and construction began in 1988. The site chosen was the former Holt Ranch, where century-old oak trees provided an appealing landscape. Two original homes and a pool house were incorporated into the design. The property was home to dozens of critters, including skunks, raccoons, beavers, squirrels and Swainson hawks. Construction was delayed when nesting hawks were discovered.

O'Connor Woods opened in June 1990 offering 219 one- and two-bedroom apartments and sixteen cottages. Garden Oaks, the first assisted-living building, along with St. Catherine's Chapel, were added in 1991. Meadowood, a 100-bed skilled nursing facility, was built in 1997 with the support of Crestwood Hospitals.

Oak Creek assisted living was built in 2000, along with fourteen additional independent living cottages. To complete the continuum of care, Laurel Pointe Memory Care and A Day Away, a senior adult day program, were added in 2014.

The O'Connor Woods campus is today home to almost 500 residents, most of whom live independently in cottages or apartments, with the balance of residents in the supportive environment of assisted living or skilled nursing. In addition, the community provides a complete fitness center and enclosed swimming pool at the Wellness Connection, a chapel for religious services and a quarter-mile walking path among the lush gardens and trees.

There are over 300 employees and the annual revenue of the organization is $30 million.

Before her death in 1997, Carol Cox said in the publication *LifeStyles*, "We are doing everything possible to create a community based on what our residents want; comfort, security, good nutrition, healthful living, social and educational activities. We compare moving into O'Connor Woods to moving into a friendly neighborhood where you feel safe and wanted and where you'll be an active participant in the daily activities."

For more information about O'Connor Woods, visit www.oconnorwoods.org.

✧

Above: The thirty-four-acre O'Connor Woods campus is filled with century old oaks, lush gardens and walking paths. It is home to 251 independent living apartments and cottages; 85 studio, one and two bedroom assisted living apartments; 20 apartments for memory care and 100 skilled nursing beds.
PHOTOGRAPH COURTESY OF SHARON POHLMAN.

Below: The Wellness Connection on campus offers a host of land and water based classes for both residents and community members age sixty and older. They are committed to all seven dimensions of well-being.
PHOTOGRAPH COURTESY OF LYNN RICH PHOTOGRAPHY.

TRINITY LUTHERAN CHURCH

✧

Below: Trinity Lutheran Church is located at 444 North American Street in Stockton and on the Internet at www.trinitystockton.org.

Bottom: Trinity Lutheran Church with its beautiful stained glass windows. A brass plate is placed below each window by the family that made a donation for the window. The windows chronicle the earthly life of our Lord Jesus Christ from His birth to ascension.

Trinity Lutheran Church, an inner city church in the heart of downtown Stockton, was founded on the words of Psalm 102:18, "This shall be written for the generation to come and the people which shall be created shall praise the Lord."

The history of Trinity Lutheran Church began in the early 1880s as Stockton was becoming an important stopping point on the way to the gold mines. During this period, a small group of dedicated Lutheran Christians banded together with people of the German Reformed faith to worship in a church on the corner of Miner Avenue and Stanislaus Streets.

In 1882 the congregation adopted the name of "The First German Evangelical Lutheran Zions Congregation," or "Evangelische Lutherische Zionsgremeinde." Services were conducted in German, and a traveling missionary administered the sacraments before the first pastor was installed in 1883. The church also established a school in those early days and, in 1927, Albert E. Brungardt began his tenure as head of the school that lasted more than forty-three years.

The name became Trinity Lutheran Church when the cornerstone was laid for a new church at the corner of Lindsey and American Streets in 1923. Trinity Lutheran became the mother church for what would become many more Lutheran Churches in the San Joaquin Valley. As one enters, it goes without saying how much Trinity's beautiful stained glass windows are enjoyed by all who sit in our sanctuary as we worship our Lord and Savior. Sitting in a pew as the morning or afternoon sun streams through these windows is an experience to be enjoyed over and over again. As the sun streams through these windows, the life of Christ is shown in rich and vibrant colors. Since 1924 their beauty and the story they tell has richly enhanced our sanctuary in a very special way.

The origin of the windows is really quite brief. They were furnished by the Ford-McNutt Art Glass Company of Minneapolis, Minnesota, and were installed in our church by an expert from the glass company. The windows beautifully chronicle the earthly life of our Lord Jesus Christ, beginning with His birth through His ascension. On each window is a Bible verse pertaining to the scene portrayed in the window. Below each window, a small brass dedication plate shows the names of the family who gave the money for the window. It is believed that the original cost of the windows on the East and West sides of the sanctuary was $350. The two larger windows at the front of the sanctuary and at the back of the sanctuary cost more, however there is no record of that.

Today each of these beautiful windows has been declared "not merely stained glass windows, but irreplaceable works of art."

Trinity Lutheran's current pastor, Jeff Morey, who came in 2008, has worked hand in hand with a young man named Pastor Frank Saldana. He, along with his wife Kim, established what was known as The Dream Team, a dedicated group of young individuals with a passion for serving the Lord. That relationship has evolved into Trinity Lutheran's community outreach in Stockton, which is known as I Action.

Services at Trinity Lutheran Church are conducted at 9:00 a.m. each Sunday, followed by coffee hour, fellowship and Bible classes. In addition, the church has a Thursday morning Bible class at 10:00 a.m. Trinity also supports a Cambodian congregation led by Lay Minister Peter Sok. This group meets at 10:30 a.m. each Sunday.

Trinity Lutheran Church is a family of God's people challenged and equipped by God's Word to reach out to all the community by worshipping, teaching, and serving through Christ's love.

The quintessential American success story is still alive and well in the career of Steve Bestolarides, who represents the Third Supervisorial District on the San Joaquin County Board of Supervisors.

The son of Greek immigrants, Bestolarides was born in Stockton and raised in San Joaquin County. Like most immigrants, his parents emphasized the importance of education and the value of religion and urged their son to make the most of the opportunities offered by their adopted country.

Bestolarides earned a Bachelor's Degree in Business Administration from the University of the Pacific and advanced to a Master's Degree in Finance from National University. He had a successful career in banking and business before entering public service.

Bestolarides was appointed to the Stockton Planning Commission in 1993 and served two terms as chairman. He was first elected to the Stockton City Council in 2002 and established a reputation as an independent decision maker and became known for making fiscal responsibility one of his top priorities.

He was elected to the board of supervisors in 2008 and served as chairman of the board in 2012. He represents a diverse district that covers the northern and western portions of the City of Stockton, the City of Lathrop, and the northern area of the City of Manteca and areas of the Delta.

Bestolarides sits on numerous committees, including the San Joaquin Council of Governments, Health Commission–Health Plan of San Joaquin, Hospital Joint Conference Committee, and Medical Executive Committee. He also serves as chairman of the San Joaquin County Employee's Retirement Association Board, serves on the Caltrans Rail Task Force Steering Committee, San Joaquin Regional Rail Commission, San Joaquin Area Flood Control Agency, County Facilities Committee, Health Care Services Review Project, Deferred Compensation Committee, San Joaquin Valley Regional Policy Council and the California Partnership for San Joaquin Valley.

When Bestolarides is not pondering the future of San Joaquin County as a supervisor, he enjoys his major hobby—motorcycles. Harley-Davidsons in particular. Bestolarides has attended the 95th, 100th, and 105th anniversaries of Harley-Davidson in Milwaukee, which attracts hundreds of thousands of motorcyclists from throughout the world.

Those many journeys and experiences have contributed to the collections of Harley Memorabilia that he displays in his office. Being a strong advocate for those with Special Needs, a memorable charitable ride was driving a young man with special needs in his side car. This simple gesture elicited an indescribable joy for both rider and passenger.

Bestolarides and his wife have two sons, Danny and Paul. Bestolarides is proud of his sons. Youngest son, Paul, is currently pursuing a Master's degree in Humanities and Religion. Oldest son, Danny, attends an Adult Day Program and is the inspiration for Bestolarides' passion to advocate for those with developmental disabilities. Danny has Down syndrome and congenital heart disease. Bestolarides' wife, Doreen, is a registered nurse with a background in critical care and currently a Special Needs RN. She is also a strong community advocate for Special Needs.

Bestolarides' passion for his community is evident in his stewardship and commitments. Family, Faith in God and education are the foundation for his success.

✧

Left: Steve Bestolarides.

Right: Left to right, Danny, Steve, Doreen and Paul Bestolarides.

FAMILY RESOURCE AND REFERRAL CENTER OF SAN JOAQUIN

❖

Above: Joan Richards, founder of the Family Resource and Referral Center of San Joaquin.

Below: The Podesto Teen Impact Center operated by Family Resource and Referral Center in Partnership with the City of Stockton.

Family Resource and Referral Center of San Joaquin serves as a critical link to quality child care services for parents, child care providers and children in San Joaquin County. The nonprofit organization promotes community awareness about the needs of children and families and participates in building community coalitions to develop solutions to these needs. FRRC also serves as a clearinghouse for information on child care services, parenting, nutrition, health and child safety.

Annually, FRRC makes nearly 1,600 child care referrals and provides child care assistance to 5,000 families or 11,000 children so parents can work while their children learn. Nearly 7,000 children receive healthy meals and snacks through the Child Care Food Program. FRRC's subsidized child care programs infuse approximately $25 million into the local economy on an annual basis.

FRRC opened in January 1980 under the direction of its founder, Joan Richards. The organization grew from Stockton Metropolitan Ministry, which was responsible for organizing St. Mary's Interfaith Dining Room, the Stockton Homeless Shelter and the Emergency Food Bank. The Reverend Bob Green, Reverend El Hoffman, and Dr. Robert Morrow, a professor at the University of the Pacific, were instrumental in the early growth of the organization.

"FRRC stayed true to its mission and aware of the needs of children and families in the community," said Richards, as the organization entered its thirty-fifth year of service.

FRRC is responsible for the formation of dozens of local initiatives to promote a strong and sustainable child care infrastructure, including support for the formation of the First 5 San Joaquin Children and Families Commission. The organization's executive director now serves as First 5 Commissioner. FRRC recently received the designation by the California Public Utilities Commission to be the provider of 211 Information and Referral Services for San Joaquin County.

FRRC also operates the Teen Impact Center on North El Dorado in partnership with the City of Stockton, and a pre-school, Grigsby Learning Village, on Grigsby Place. The partnership with the Teen Impact Center provides vital services for twelve to eighteen year old youth.

The organization's Child and Adult Food Care Program now serves ten counties, including San Joaquin, Amador, Calaveras, Sacramento, Yolo, Sutter, Placer, Los Angeles, San Bernardino and Riverside.

Headquarters for FRRC are located on the waterfront at 509 West Weber Avenue in downtown Stockton. The organization has close to 100 employees. FRRC operates with an annual budget of nearly $33 million, with $25 million of that amount returned to the community in the form of child care payments from federal, state and county funds.

For additional information about Family Resource and Referral Center, or to get involved, visit the website at www.frrcsj.org.

Zeiter Eye Medical Group has served the eye care needs of Central Valley residents for more than half a century. The ophthalmology practice is built on the vision of its founder, Dr. Henry Zeiter, who opened his first office in downtown Stockton in 1962. Since then, Zeiter Eye has become one of the largest groups of eye care providers in Northern California, with fourteen doctors in seven locations, including offices in Stockton, Lodi, Manteca, Tracy and Sonora.

From its inception, the mission of Zeiter Eye Medical Group has been to exceed its patients' expectations by providing unprecedented medical and surgical eye care with the highest degree of respect and consideration for each patient.

The practice has evolved into providing full-service eye care, offering all subspecialties including cataracts, glaucoma, diabetic retinopathy, macular degeneration, eyelid problems and occulofacial plastic surgery. Zeiter Eye also provides routine eye exams, glasses, contact lenses, and LASIK surgery.

With more than fifty years' experience, the physicians of Zeiter Eye know the importance of staying on the cutting edge of technology. Zeiter Eye offers state-of-the-art testing to its patients and was the first practice in Northern California to provide laser precision cataract surgery using the LenSx Laser. The practice services an estimated 25,000 patient visits each year and annually performs more than 5,000 surgeries.

"We've always been the largest practice in the Central Valley and take pride in having the best equipment and the latest technology," says Dr. John Zeiter. "We are consistently purchasing the latest equipment to stay on the cutting edge of medicine. In addition, we built a state-of-the-art Surgical Center with two operating suites for the efficiency and convenience of our patients. All of our doctors are well trained, but we also understand the importance of compassion. Compassion is becoming a lost art in medicine today, but we have maintained a love for what we do as well as a passion for treating our patients as individuals."

The professional staff includes three generations of Zeiters. Dr. Henry Zeiter was joined in the practice by his son, Dr. John Zeiter;

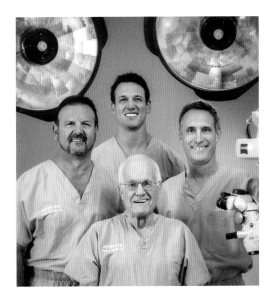

his nephew, Dr. Joe Zeiter; and Joe's son, Dr. Joseph Zeiter, Jr. In addition, the physician staff includes Dr. John Canzano, Dr. Richard Wong and Dr. Harold Hand. The staff at Zeiter Eye totals over 100 dedicated team members.

In addition to their commitment to patient eye care, Zeiter Eye Medical Group believes in giving back to the community. This includes philanthropic contributions to the local arts and music organizations, homeless shelters, hospitals, schools, and nonprofits that support women and children. Zeiter Eye also performs approximately 100 free cataract surgeries annually to the uninsured, impoverished members of our community.

For over fifty years, Zeiter Eye's focus has remained the same: Provide the very best patient care, invest in the best technology, and retain top talent to further improve its patients' vision.

✧

Above: Dr. Henry Zeiter (seated) with (standing, left to right): Dr. Joseph Zeiter, Dr. Joseph Zeiter, Jr., and Dr. John Zeiter.

Below: The Zeiter Eye Medical Group location in Weber Ranch Professional Park.

ZEITER EYE MEDICAL GROUP, INC.

SAN JOAQUIN REGIONAL TRANSIT DISTRICT

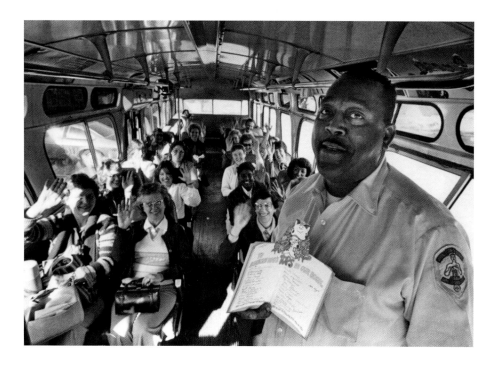

✧

*Above: Coach operator Clarence
Washington receives a thank you gift from
guests, c. 1965.*

*Below: San Joaquin RTD buses in front of
Stockton Civic Memorial Auditorium,
c. 1996 and 2014.*

The San Joaquin Regional Transit District provides safe, reliable, and efficient transportation systems for the Stockton metropolitan area, as well as intercity, interregional, and rural transit services countywide.

Currently, RTD operates a fleet of 120 buses that serve all of San Joaquin County; an area of 1,426 square miles. Annual system-wide ridership totals more than four million trips. RTD employs more than 300 people, including contractors, and operates with an annual budget of $33.2 million.

In response to the need for public transit, three private transportation companies were consolidated into what became the Stockton Metropolitan Transit Division (SMTD) and began operations on June 1, 1965.

As Stockton continued to grow, so did SMTD and its need for facilities, prompting a move in 1979 from its original location at Channel and Grant Streets in downtown Stockton to a new location at Wilson Way and Lindsay Street. A marketing contest in the eighties led to the adoption of a new logo and SMART as the Stockton Metropolitan Transit District's official brand.

In 1994 legislation expanded SMTD's service area to all of San Joaquin County and renamed it the San Joaquin Regional Transit District. SJRTD began to provide intercity, interregional commuter, and countywide general public Dial-A-Ride services.

To emphasize its regional commitment, the district developed a new logo and branding in 2004 and the system is now known as San Joaquin RTD or RTD for short. The same year it introduced its first diesel-electric hybrid buses.

In 2005, RTD acquired property and began servicing buses at its 'County Yard' at Filbert and Myrtle Streets, and opened its long-planned Downtown Transit Center in 2006. The DTC is the transfer point for nearly all of RTD's routes, and serves as the regional public transportation hub for residents of Stockton and San Joaquin County.

In 2007, RTD introduced Metro Express, the county's first Bus Rapid Transit route, on the Pacific Avenue corridor. RTD added a second Metro Express corridor along Airport Way in 2011, and a third—along Hammer Lane—in 2012. In FY 2014 the three corridors provided forty-eight percent of RTD's system-wide ridership. Metro Express and all of RTD's Stockton routes use hybrid buses; and in 2013 RTD introduced northern California's first zero-emissions electric buses.

RTD's use of hybrid buses demonstrates its leadership in the adaption of technologies that improve the environment and provide better service for its communities and community, and has been nationally recognized for its environmental efforts and innovations. Similarly, RTD leads and supports programs that benefit the community it serves, such as its Stuff the Bus annual food drive that has collected and distributed more than 200,000 pounds of food over the last fourteen years.

In 2016, RTD will complete the construction of its Regional Transportation Center, a consolidated facility that will provide the capacity required to meet the growing transportation of San Joaquin County for years to come. Accordingly, system-wide ridership is expected to increase nineteen percent from 2015 through 2018 along with the growing populations of Stockton and San Joaquin County.

The opening of the San Joaquin Pride Center in 2011 was a milestone long in coming for the socially conservative city. The Pride Center provided a public space where it was safe to gather and educate—and be educated—about acceptance and tolerance.

Prior to the LGBT civil rights movement, during the 1950s and 1960s; hiding one's sexuality or transgender identity was a fact of life. For those in Stockton who could not, they were treated as second-class citizens. Certain parts of Stockton were known to be risky ventures for LGBT people, and the smaller, more rural areas surrounding Stockton became 'do not enter' zones.

In 1972, The Imperial Pearl Court (now known as Imperial San Joaquin Delta Empire) was created just three years after the Stonewall Riots. Formed by Empress I Monique and Emperor I Terry, the Court's primary focus was a social group which held events like The Hooker's Ball, 3Ms Pageant, Closet Ball and Coronation at local bars like The Gay 90's and Paradise. Eventually the group evolved into a fundraising machine to fight the impact of the AIDS crisis.

The Delta Women group held its first meeting in February 1988. As far as can be determined, it is the oldest and longest-lasting organized group exclusively for Lesbians in the Stockton area.

In 2005 the Central Valley Stonewall Democratic Club was formed and moved Stockton into the forefront of the LGBT civil rights movement, in particular for its support of out-Lesbian candidate for city council, Susan Eggman. Susan's eventual election victory in 2006 made her the first openly LGBT elected official north of Fresno and south of Oregon, and was a clarion call which led the movement out of its closet, leading it out of the bar scene and into a full-blown social and civil rights movement.

In 2009, Elena Kelly formed the Stockton Transgender Alliance. With more than 200 active participants, this group is vital to making sure the community's most at-risk are being served.

Because of the efforts of many individuals and organizations, the San Joaquin Pride Center (SJPC) was founded in 2011 and easily opened its doors within four months. From the inaugural Pride Festival, attended by 4,000 people, to its outreach and education efforts, SJPC is making a difference by advocating for the LGBT community.

The organization has developed successful youth programs, peer-led groups, counseling services and cultural programs. It hosts the Stockton Transgender Alliance and has focused on anti-bullying and sensitivity training within local school districts. Through a partnership with the Stockton Unified School District, SJPC is helping empower youth to become leaders and form Gay and Straight Alliances (GSA) in high schools. Studies show that schools with GSA's have less violence and bullying towards all students.

The San Joaquin Pride Center has quickly become the central hub for the LGBT community with the county and serves as a vital and necessary advocate for acceptance and tolerance of LGBT people.

SAN JOAQUIN PRIDE CENTER

FILIPINO CENTER PLAZA

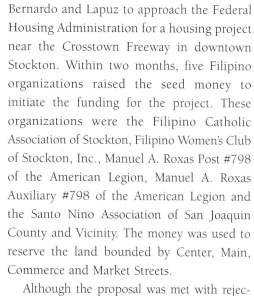

❖

Top, left: The Filipino Center Plaza Building when it was newly built.

Top, right: The Filipino Center Plaza Building—present day.

Below: Members of the board of directors standing left to right, Dr. Jose Bernardo and Moreno Balantac. Seated left to right, Doris Unsod, Attorney Tom Zuckerman and Narcy Giva. Not in the photograph—Melvin Lagasca, Phillip Nisperos, Lois M. Sahyoun and Denise Rico.

The Filipino Center Plaza is a project that has been completed through communal effort and Bayanihan spirit made possible by the Associated Filipino Organizations of San Joaquin County.

In 1967, Jose Bernardo and Ted Lapuz surveyed the downtown area of Stockton, which was the hub of 'Little Manila' and the home to thousands of single Filipino men who provided sweat and stoop labor for the San Joaquin Valley's burgeoning agricultural industry. The survey made evident the need for housing for single Filipino men.

The results of the survey prompted Bernardo and Lapuz to approach the Federal Housing Administration for a housing project near the Crosstown Freeway in downtown Stockton. Within two months, five Filipino organizations raised the seed money to initiate the funding for the project. These organizations were the Filipino Catholic Association of Stockton, Filipino Women's Club of Stockton, Inc., Manuel A. Roxas Post #798 of the American Legion, Manuel A. Roxas Auxiliary #798 of the American Legion and the Santo Nino Association of San Joaquin County and Vicinity. The money was used to reserve the land bounded by Center, Main, Commerce and Market Streets.

Although the proposal was met with rejections by the Federal Housing Administration, Bernardo and his team did not give up and more than forty Filipino organizations rallied under one banner. It was during this time that the Associated Filipino Organization of San Joaquin County (AFO) was formed and became the sponsoring nonprofit organization for the Filipino Center Plaza, with Lapuz as its first president and Bernardo as the project's advisor.

After a third rejection from Sacramento FHA, the AFO appealed to the FHA in San Francisco and was finally approved in April 1971. Funds for the project were committed and the groundbreaking ceremonies were held in July of 1971. The Honorable Vice President of the Philippines, Fernando Lopez, led the groundbreaking ceremony.

On August 12, 1972, the formal dedication took place. The completed project symbolizes a living example of Filipino power born of community cooperation and unity, a true Bayanihan spirit among the Filipinos in the San Joaquin Valley.

In the words of Dr. Jose Bernardo, "This Center is the only thing which has ever brought the capabilities of Filipinos to the attention of the outside world. Suddenly, we became visible. The people and the community have seen what we can do. All of a sudden, we became part of the community."

Today, the Filipino Center Plaza is home to more than 120 families and provides various programs that cater to the needs of its residents to become independent of government aid.

CATHLEEN GALGIANI, 5TH DISTRICT CALIFORNIA SENATOR

As a fifth generation Stocktonian, California State Senator Cathleen Galgiani represents her district with a unique understanding of the area's rich history and culture. Her long career in public service has been inspired and built on the examples set by her family and their influence in the area.

The Galgiani side of Cathleen's family emigrated from Switzerland to Stockton in 1851 and established a farm on the old Linden Road, which is now known as Fremont Street. Her great-grandmother, Adeline Galgiani, was the first female court reporter in San Joaquin County and was best friends with Edna Gleason, the first woman to serve as a member of Stockton City Council. Her great-grandfather, John Mulroy, was a hay farmer who owned a Victorian home on Madison and Acacia Streets that is now a historical landmark.

"I was blessed to be able to grow up in a family that appreciated art and music," says Senator Galgiani. "My grandpa Oscar Galgiani was an artist all of his adult life. After World War II, he was commissioned to paint the murals for the first floor of our courthouse, as well as the portrait of Captain Charles Weber, founder of the City of Stockton. Weber's portrait now hangs in the City Council chambers. Both of my grandparents were very talented piano players, and my grandma Eldena played music for the Salvation Army for many years."

While growing up in Stockton, Cathleen spent much of her time at her grandparent's home on Harding Way, a culturally rich area in Boors Park. Former Senator Krittendon lived on one side, the King of the Gypsy Family on the other, and the Bishop of the Catholic Church lived across the street.

Senator Galgiani attended San Joaquin Delta College before receiving her Bachelor's degree from California State University in Sacramento. Prior to her election to the California State Senate, she served for six years in the State Assembly. She also served as the chief of staff to her predecessor, Assemblywoman Barbara Matthews. While working for Matthews, she served as the consultant to the Assembly Committee on the "Development of the 10th Campus of the University of California, UC Merced."

✧
Left: Oscar Vincent Galgiani was commissioned to paint the portrait of Captain Charles Weber, founder of the City of Stockton.

Above: A detailed plaque next to the Captain Weber painting.

Below: California State Senator Cathleen Galgiani.

Said Galgiani, "We started with land, a vision, and the promise of start up money. Now we have a university with more than 6,000 students, and we're planning to bring a school of medicine."

Galgiani's proudest accomplishment is authoring the legislation for Proposition 1A, which enabled creation of the nation's first high speed rail system which will take valley commuters to the Silicon Valley and Bay Area.

Galgiani also worked for former California First Lady Sharon Davis, and former San Joaquin County Senators John Garamendi and Patrick Johnston. Prior to working in the legislature, Senator Galgiani spent eight years as a physical therapy aide at San Joaquin General Hospital and Dameron Hospital in San Joaquin County.

Senator Galgiani has represented San Joaquin County in the Legislature for ten years, drawing inspiration from her family's rich history in Stockton.

PHOTOGRAPH COURTESY OF VISIT STOCKTON.

STOCKTON'S GOLDEN ERA

THE MARKETPLACE

Stockton's retail and

commercial establishments offer

an impressive variety of choices

SPECIAL THANKS TO

Delicato Family Vineyards

BANK OF STOCKTON

For nearly a century and a half, the Bank of Stockton has served the financial needs of the community with integrity, solid banking principles and unsurpassed service. The values and traditions instilled by its founders and enhanced through the years still guide the bank today.

✧

Above: The block which was the first location of the Stockton Savings & Loan Society (now known as the Bank of Stockton) offices at 179 El Dorado Street.

Below: In 1885 the Wilhoit brothers— George Ewell, Eugene Lovell and Arthur— pose in front of their office at 332 Main Street in Stockton. Their father and senior partner, Roley Early, arrived in Stockton in 1852 and was immediately successful in the freighting business between Stockton and Sonora. He held the office of County Recorder from 1861 to 1868, during which time he was a founding charter member of the Stockton Savings & Loan Society, known today as the Bank of Stockton. R. E. Wilhoit served as the bank's president from 1909 to 1917, after having served multiple terms on the city council, the board of supervisors, and the board of education. R. E. was succeeded as bank president in 1917 by his son E. L., who held the post until 1949. At the time of this photograph the Bank of Stockton was eighteen years old.

The oldest bank in California still operating under its original charter, the Bank of Stockton now serves seven counties with sixteen branches.

The rich history of the Bank of Stockton began in 1867 during a period of turmoil and uncertainty. The Civil War that had divided a nation had ended only two years before but visionary leaders were beginning to seize new opportunities and helping the nation recover.

The population of Stockton was only 4,429 in 1867 but the city was growing into a shipping and transportation hub. There was a vital need for a strong financial institution to provide capital and bring stability to the chaos of the post-Civil War economy.

Twenty-nine Stockton businessmen pledged to raise $100,000 in U.S. gold coins to establish a bank and on August 12, 1867, a Certificate of Incorporation was filed with the San Joaquin County clerk. The institution's original name was the Stockton Savings & Loan Society. Although the founders had vastly different backgrounds and interests, they shared a vision of a strong financial institution that would serve the growing community.

The bank's first president was J. M. Kelsey, who was then the San Joaquin County treasurer and tax collector. He also was an officer of the Union Copper Mining Company and was involved in other successful business enterprises.

The bank officially opened for business on September 20, 1867, in leased offices shared with the Union Copper Mining Company at a location now listed as 75 North El Dorado Street. The rent was $41 per month.

The bank's founders had so much faith in the future of their institution that they actually made a $1,000 loan before the first deposit came in. That first commercial deposit was made by Jones, Hewlett & Sons. H. H. Hewlett was an owner of the business, as well as an original founder and director of the bank. He served on the bank's board of directors almost continuously until his death in 1903.

Within the first twenty-four days of operation, the new bank had generated $100,000 worth of business. The quick acceptance of the new financial institution was due in large part to the reputation of its founders and the principles by which they operated. A document entitled "An Agreement with Depositors" pledged that the bank's Board of Directors would use deposits to make loans and investments, but always within the laws of California, and always with the safety of depositors to come before the profit of the corporation. These rock-solid principles have continued to guide the bank's leaders for nearly 150 years.

The bank's rapid growth soon had the directors searching for a larger location and several possibilities were considered, including the corner of Main and El Dorado Streets, and a site known as 'Weber's Hole' where the Hotel Stockton now stands, but a majority of stockholders objected, insisting that the purchase prices were too high.

By 1875, business had increased to the point where the original location was much too small to provide efficient service. The Board then signed a ten year lease to rent the McKee Building at the southwest corner of Hunter and Main Streets, later occupied by the Sterling Department Store. The rent was $220 per month, less $50 received from the sub-rental of the building's basement.

J.M. Kelsey, a founder and the bank's first president, was found dead of an apparent heart attack in a rowboat on Stockton Slough near Banner Island in February 1877. L. U. Shippee, who had huge farming interests in the region, succeeded Kelsey as president. Shippee was well known in the community for his many achievements, including bringing the first State Fair of California to Stockton. He served sixteen years until 1893, when he was succeeded by Fred M. West, who served until 1909 during a period of major growth.

It was in 1903 that the Board decided to buy what was known as the 'Arcade Property' on the northeast corner of Main and San Joaquin Streets. Three years later—in 1906—a special meeting of stockholders authorized the expenditure of $250,000 to build a new bank on the property. Incidentally, the law firm that represented the bank during the transactions has evolved through the years to the firm of Geiger, Rudquist, Nuss & Keen, which still represents the bank today.

The entire community was soon talking about the new Bank of Stockton building, an imposing seven-story structure known as 'Stockton's first skyscraper.' In 1908 the bank moved into this new location from the McKee Building, which it had occupied for more than thirty years.

During this period, Bank of Stockton President West, who was also County Treasurer, built on the bank's tradition of service to the community. West played a major role in bringing both the Santa Fe and Western Pacific Railroads to Stockton and was also the first president of the Stockton Chamber of Commerce. Several members of the West family became influential members of the Board of Directors over successive generations.

✧

Left: A rendering of the McKee Building published in Thompson and West's History of San Joaquin County in 1879. The building was built in 1875 by William F. McKee, a local businessman, and was the second home of the Stockton Savings & Loan Society, later to become the Bank of Stockton. The bank was housed here from 1875 until 1908, when it was relocated to the corner of Main and San Joaquin Streets.

Below: George West was the oldest brother of Fred West, third president of Stockton Savings & Loan Society. George owned the El Pinal Winery on West Lane.

R. E. Wilhoit, a long-time member of the Board of Directors, succeeded West as president in 1909. Wilhoit exemplified the Bank of Stockton's philosophy of community involvement and commitment. Wilhoit was forced to resign as president in 1917 because of ill health, but agreed to remain as a member of the Board. He was succeeded by his son, Eugene L. Wilhoit, who led the bank from 1917 until 1949.

✧

Above: R. L. Eberhardt is seated on the far left of this photo identified as the Port of Stockton Commissioners from 1942. They are posed with U.S. Treasury Bonds for sale during World War II. William L. Maxwell, Sr., port commissioner, bank director, and president of the Stockton Chamber of Commerce, is third from the right.

Below: The Bank of Stockton Christmas photo from 1955.

The Bank of Stockton and Eugene were instrumental in bringing the University of the Pacific to Stockton in 1924.

The financial strength and leadership of the Bank of Stockton enabled it to weather the severe economic storms of the Great Depression and the uncertainties of two World Wars. With the end of the war in 1945, the greatest migration since the gold rush hit California and the city of Stockton experienced tremendous growth. The Bank of Stockton was a major factor in encouraging and directing this growth.

R. L. "Ebe" Eberhardt, once a State Bank Examiner, became president of Bank of

Stockton in 1949. He had joined the bank as an assistant vice president and cashier in 1927 when the bank's assets totaled $9 million. Eberhardt was very active in the community, serving as a Regent of the University of the Pacific and also serving for many years on the boards of the Port Commission and the County Fair. The Bank of Stockton enjoyed strong, solid growth during the thirty-six years Eberhardt was associated with the institution. His crowning achievement was construction of a new headquarters building at Miner and San Joaquin Streets in Stockton. It was considered the most modern banking facility in the state when it opened in 1960.

'Ebe' served as president until his death in 1963. He was succeeded by his son, Robert M. 'Bob' Eberhardt, who had joined the bank staff in 1956. As one of the youngest presidents of the California Bankers Association, Bob was instrumental in bringing community banks together in order to compete with larger national banks.

In 1970 the Bank of Stockton opened its first branch, the Carson Oaks office, at Pacific Avenue and Benjamin Holt Drive. The bank continued to grow with the purchase of Mid-Cal National Bank in 1980, an acquisition that provided branch offices in Lodi, Tracy, Manteca, and Pine Grove in Amador County. The bank's Quail Lakes Delta office opened in 1990.

The Bank of Stockton acquired the deposits of the insolvent Royal Oaks Savings and Loan in Ripon in 1990, creating a new branch in Ripon.

The bank also grew in other areas under the visionary leadership of Bob. A number of new products and services were introduced during this era, all focused on the goal of providing customers with greater convenience and better service. In 1993 the Bank of Stockton became the first bank on the west coast to introduce the 'image check system' which replaced cancelled checks with images of cleared checks.

Bob died unexpectedly in 1994 while on a family vacation overseas. Bob's brother, Douglass M. Eberhardt, became the bank's eighth president, continuing the tradition of

family leadership. Under Douglass' leadership, the bank has maintained its reputation of strength and service, while becoming a leader in new banking technologies such as electronic banking, a website, and debit cards.

In 1997 the bank acquired three Bank of America branches, resulting in representation in Angles Camp and Rio Vista and a larger, more modern facility in Ripon.

In 1999 the Bank of Stockton became the first community bank headquartered in the Central Valley to reach assets of more than $1 billion. That figure is now approaching $2 billion.

The bank's growth in Stanislaus County continued with the purchase of Modesto and Turlock Commerce Banks in 2003. These institutions have long been known for exceeding customer expectations and continue to operate under the Modesto and Turlock Commerce Bank brand as divisions of the Bank of Stockton. A third division, Elk Grove Commerce Bank, noted for the bronze elk that has become a local landmark, was opened in December 2006.

The bank has continued to build on technological advances during the twenty-first century with such innovations as mobile banking products for smartphones. Along with this technology, the bank has continued to build a solid foundation of personalized service in its branches.

Douglass' leadership philosophy reflects his belief in providing superior customer service by meeting customer's needs. Whether customers are high-tech or high touch, Bank of Stockton and its divisions are poised to meet their needs.

The bank and its divisions are strong advocates of community support and donate generously to the communities it serves. Bank employees are encouraged to be actively involved in local non-profits, sharing time and talent to help their local communities.

After nearly 150 years, Bank of Stockton and its divisions operate sixteen branches located in Stockton, Lodi, Tracy, Ripon, Manteca, Oakdale,

Pine Grove, Angels Camp, Rio Vista, Modesto, Turlock, Elk Grove, and Sonora.

The bank and its divisions continue to set a precedent for superior customer service, quality banking products, technological innovation and strength for generations of families and businesses.

To learn more about the Bank of Stockton, please visit www.bankofstockton.com.

✧

Above: The Eberhardt brothers pose in costume with a cake model of the headquarters building on the hundredth anniversary of the bank's founding, 1967.

Below: The groundbreaking of the Carson Oaks branch, 1969.

FINANCIAL CENTER CREDIT UNION

✧

Above: A photograph of the "Old Courthouse," Financial Center's original home.

Below: Guy McElhaney and L. Dennis Duffy share a laugh outside of the office. McElhaney served the credit union until 1989 and Duffy served the credit union until 1999.

Financial Center Credit Union is a different kind of financial institution because of its ownership structure. The organization's straightforward mission relates directly to its business model, which is quite simple—provide credit by taking in money through members' savings and then lending it to other members for autos and other types of loans. In turn, the interest paid back on loans allows FCCU to operate and pay dividends on savings. This cooperative effort was first created sixty years ago to provide credit to the 'little guys' for the things they need. Financial Center has been working with that same purpose since its inception and will continue to do so in the future.

Financial Center Credit Union, the largest credit union based in San Joaquin County, is a member-owned financial institution offering a variety of services to its members. The focus of FCCU is taking the hopes and wishes of its members and turning them into reality through straightforward, fairly priced products and services.

These services include all the traditional bank offerings such as savings, checking, loans and credit cards, as well as easy access to discounted insurance products and financial planning. Financial Center also provides online banking, online bill pay, automated phone banking and credit union owned ATMs.

Financial Center Credit Union was born sixty years ago during an era of unbridled optimism and a post-war spirit that believed all things were possible. Six decades later, Financial Center still maintains that can-do approach.

FCCU, known originally as San Joaquin County Employees Credit Union, was chartered on October 6, 1954. The eleven pioneering members—all employees of San Joaquin County—were: Guy McElhany, Robert Schramek, John Prowse, Paul Heurlin, Lolita Calibo, Fred Perrott, Elaine Seibel, Geraldine Schook, Broughton Long, Maurice May and George Robertson.

In the beginning, there were no paid staff and it was run by volunteers. The first 'office' operated during lunch hours at a volunteer's desk in the county treasurer's office in the Old Courthouse.

Only three weeks after receiving its charter, the credit union made its first loan for $300. It was the first of many loans that helped members afford the expansive new conveniences of the post-war era by providing low-cost loans they were unable to get from a bank.

By the end of 1954, FCCU had thirty-one members, $2,605 in shares and $1,545 in loans.

In 1955, FCCU hired its first full time treasurer, William F. Haywood, who had recently retired as an attorney in the county counsel's office. By 1958 the credit union had moved into its first permanent location, an apartment house at 538 South San Joaquin Street.

Haywood passed away unexpectedly in 1962 and Assistant County Assessor McElhaney, one of the original founding members, became the credit union's first full-time manager.

The credit union's personal alternative to traditional banking—higher rates on savings and lower rates on loans—and truly personal service combined to attract a steadily growing number of members. The credit union reached $1 million in assets in 1963. Assets doubled by 1968 and the credit union built an office at 1400 North El Dorado Street. The credit union's philosophy of "members helping members" was the epitome of the humanitarian spirit of the 1960s.

L. Dennis Duffy became the credit union's first assistant manager in 1970 and placed additional emphasis on member communication and lending. By 1972 the credit union had reached $5 million in assets. Enthused by a quarterly newsletter, *Money Talks*, membership soared to more than 5,200 in 1975 and assets reached $10 million in 1976.

The organization's name was changed from San Joaquin County Employees Credit Union to Financial Center Credit Union in 1977 and the charter was expanded so that the credit union could serve other public service employees and small employee groups. Also in 1977, a new member service—share drafts—was implemented, allowing the Financial Center to become a 'full service' financial institution.

The changes resulted in an explosion of growth for FCCU. In 1978 the organization moved to a new building at 18 South Center Street, a location that still serves as

its headquarters today. The credit union closed out the decade with the installation of an in-house computer system named BURT (Bring Up Real Time). Computerization allowed all deposits and withdrawals to be posted to accounts immediately.

The 1980s was a decade of change and rapid growth for the Financial Center. Duffy was named co-manager, along with McElhaney in 1981, and a year later, several smaller credit unions, including Catholic Credit Union, merged with Financial Center. The mergers increased the credit union's assets to $25 million.

To improve member services, the first MATT/ATM was installed in 1983, providing members with fee-free cash access twenty-four hours per day. In 1985 transactions by members became as easy as picking up the phone with BURT/Audio Response. The credit union introduced its Visa card in 1988.

Membership continued to grow because of the mergers and convenient new services, and in 1989, Financial Center opened its first branch at Sherwood Mall.

At the end of the decade, Financial Center Credit Union had $90 million in assets as well as new leadership. McElhaney retired as CEO after seventeen years with FCCU and Duffy became the new CEO.

New technology, including the first generation of Internet banking, helped fuel the credit union's growth during the 1990s. Loans also grew substantially during the decade, thanks to several new loan products, and the institution's assets grew to $164 million by the end of the 1990s.

The decade also brought a shift in management. Michael Duffy was hired as marketing manager in 1993 and by 1996, he had been promoted to vice president/CFO. This same year, FCCU's return-on-assets ratio—3.64— was ranked in the top five among credit unions nationwide. As the new millennium began, CEO Duffy retired after twenty-nine years of dedicated service and Michael was named to succeed him.

The first decade of the new century was a period of explosive growth for the credit union, beginning with the opening of the first branch outside Stockton, the Manteca Branch.

Assets topped $200 million in 2001 and 'paperless titles' were introduced to serve the members auto loan needs. By the end of the year, the Sherwood Mall Branch had moved to a new member-owned location on Benjamin Holt Drive.

✧

Above: Built in 1978, Financial Center Credit Union's main office building has undergone several remodels over the years to accommodate the growing staff.

Below: While this picture was taken in 2014, the branch building located on Benjamin Holt Drive has largely remained the same over the years. Featuring ATMs, drive up teller window and a full-service loan department, the branch is popular among members living in the north area of Stockton.

The introduction of both electronic bill payment (BURT Pay) and twenty-four hour WEBLOAN in 2002 expanded the Financial Center's online capabilities. Toward the end of the year, a prime location was acquired on Pershing Avenue and, by spring 2003, the new branch was open for business. Assets reached $253 million by end of 2003, a year that also saw the introduction of the Visa debit card program and a remodeling of the credit union's main office.

Financial Center Credit Union celebrated its fiftieth anniversary in 2004 with a year-long celebration that included a lavish party and a special loyalty dividend for members, based on years of membership.

In 2005, Financial Center completed a successful merger with Delta Valley Credit Union, a seamless joining of two organizations with a common bond and cooperative philosophy. Loans grew by sixteen percent during the year and management began new training programs to help preserve the credit union's culture while preparing employees for the next level of activity.

Growth continued during the second half of the decade with the introduction of a member call center and the opening of a new branch in downtown Lodi in 2009.

The nation was hit by the subprime mortgage crisis in 2009, an event that led to the failure of numerous financial institutions across the country. Financial Center, however, was untouched by the financial storm.

The annual member survey in 2010 revealed that the credit union's training and emphasis on customer service had been well received. Not only did 94.6 percent of the members say their experiences 'exceeded all expectations,' but—from 2008 to 2010—member perception of the credit union's friendliness increased by 34 percent, professionalism jumped by 44 percent, knowledge level climbed by 49 percent and accuracy soared to 51 percent.

New initiatives toward paperless banking and efforts to further improve member services have continued in recent years. One of the most exciting moments of the current decade came at the end of 2013 when Financial Center's Board of Directors declared an extraordinary member loyalty dividend. Thanks to the continued success of the credit

✧

Above: Financial Center's Manteca Branch, which was the credit union's first location outside of Stockton. The branch draws members throughout the south region.

Right: Michael Duffy poses for a picture in 2013, which marked his fourteenth year as president/CEO of Financial Center Credit Union.

union's operations and its consistently high capital-to-asset ratio, Financial Center was able to return every single penny of its 2013 net profit to the member/shareholders. This amounted to more than $4.8 million. The credit union has now paid more than $131 million in dividends to its member/shareholders since it was founded in 1954.

Sixty years of growth for Financial Center has seen outstanding loans grow from $1,545 to $154,087,683 at the end of 2013. The credit union has grown from thirty-one members in 1954 to more than 33,000, which includes more than 180 various sponsored groups such as local governments, medical and legal groups and the Stockton Catholic Diocese.

FCCU now has nearly 120 employees.

All of the operations are housed within San Joaquin County, including the member call center. The main office is located at 18 South Center Street in Stockton, the Benjamin Holt Branch is at 435 West Benjamin Holt Drive in Stockton, the Pershing Branch is at 4603 North Pershing Avenue in Stockton, the Manteca Branch is at 206 East Yosemite Avenue, Manteca, and the Lodi Branch is at 200 South School Street in Lodi.

Financial Center is committed to improving the quality of life for its members as well as the greater San Joaquin County community. The credit union supports a wide range of nonprofit organizations and events throughout the county each year. The focus is on organizations and events that benefit local children, families and those less fortunate, including St. Mary's Interfaith Community Services, Mary Graham Children's Shelter Foundation and SEEDS Assistance.

✧

Above: Financial Center Credit Union's northern branch, located in the heart of downtown Lodi. Opened in 2009, the branch draws members from north Stockton, Lodi, Galt and surrounding areas.

Below: Located at Pershing Avenue and March Lane, members throughout Stockton tout the friendliness and professionalism provided by this and the other FCCU branches.

VISIT STOCKTON

✧

Top: Visit Stockton staff, left to right,
Heather Duffett, Megan Dole, Wes Rhea,
Tim Pasisz, Megan Peterson and
Monica Slingerman.

Above: Annual Tourism luncheon.

Visit Stockton, formerly known as the Stockton Convention & Visitors Bureau, was organized in 1979 to promote and market the city as a meeting, event and travel destination. The 501(c)(6) nonprofit organization also promotes Stockton by increasing awareness and enhancing the image of the city's diverse cultural, historical and recreational assets.

The staff of Visit Stockton promotes the city, San Joaquin County, and Northern California through advertising, public relations, business development, online/electronic means, and attendance at consumer and trade shows.

Visit Stockton coordinates three major annual events: Stockton Restaurant Week, the Great Stockton Asparagus Dine Out, and Stockton Beer Week.

Under the leadership of then Board President Gordon Medlin and Director Joseph Travale, the organization founded the Stockton Asparagus Festival in 1986 as an effort to promote tourism and help build a positive image for Stockton and San Joaquin County. The popular festival became an independent organization in 1993 and ran each year until 2014.

Convention and tourism promotion endured some rocky times in 2003 when the City of Stockton, facing severe budget challenges, eliminated $284,000 in annual funding for the Convention & Visitors Bureau, causing the organization to shut its doors. At the same time, the Stockton Sports commission moved under the auspices of the City of Stockton Parks and Recreation Department. Soon after, the city contracted with the Greater Stockton Chamber of Commerce to provide minimal visitors services at a cost of $97,000 annually. This began the rebirth of the Stockton Convention & Visitors Bureau.

In 2007 the SCVB, in partnership with the Stockton Sports Commission and the City of Stockton, formed the Stockton Tourism Business Improvement District (STBID), beginning a self-assessment of Stockton hotels to fund the operations of the SCVB. The district was reorganized and expanded in 2010. At that time, the Stockton Sports Commission ceased operation, and the SCVB took over sports marketing. In 2014, Visit Stockton successfully renewed the STBID for a ten year term, providing stable funding through 2025.

The effort by Visit Stockton to bring in new sports events and tournaments and enhance the many events the city has hosted for years has been very successful. This effort is led by Tim Pasisz, sports development director for Visit Stockton.

Under the leadership of Pasisz, Visit Stockton has been successful in securing the NCAA Division I Women's Basketball Championship Regional games at the Stockton Arena in 2017. In addition, Visit Stockton landed the prestigious 2018 NCAA Division I Golf Regionals, which will be played at The Reserve at Spanos Park.

Pasisz searches for events that will benefit Stockton and works with officials at such

city-run facilities as the Stockton Arena and Banner Island (Stockton) Ballpark, as well as those at University of the Pacific and San Joaquin Delta College. The deal to bring the 2017 women's regionals to Stockton required many months of planning and effort.

In 2014, Stockton was host to the CIF Sac-Joaquin Wrestling Championships, the United States Twirling Association National Baton Twirling Championships, and the USA Roller Sports Roller Derby National Championships, as well as many other sports-related events. The baton twirling and roller derby championships combined had an economic impact of more than $730,000 to the city, and the women's basketball regional is expected to bring in $1 million or more.

In 2013, Visit Stockton launched the Stockton Ambassador Program, an affiliate of the national Certified Tourism Ambassador (CTA) program, which provides training and certification to front-line staff and community volunteers to ensure that every visitor encounter is a positive one.

Visit Stockton hosts an annual Tourism Luncheon to recognize the Tourism Partner of the Year, Sports Partner of the Year and CTA of the Year. The event also serves as the annual report to partners and stakeholders.

Visit Stockton employs six people and operates with a budget of approximately $1 million per year. The CEO of Visit Stockton is Wes Rhea and the board president is George Kaplanis.

The offices of Visit Stockton are located on the second floor of the historic B&M Building at 125 Bridge Place, off Hunter Street between the old Hotel Stockton and City Centre Cinema. The 1860s era building was recently renovated by The Cort Company. One of the oldest buildings in Stockton—and long vacant—B&M is coming back to life as a hub for Stockton-area visitors.

For more information about Visit Stockton, check out visitstockton.org.

✧

Above: Visit Stockton offices.

Below: EVP World Finals of beach volleyball.

SAN JOAQUIN PARTNERSHIP

Grow It! Make It! Ship It!

Since it was founded twenty-four years ago, the San Joaquin Partnership has played a key role in attracting or retaining more than 400 firms for San Joaquin County. The main focus of the award-winning public/private partnership is business attraction, retention and expansion throughout San Joaquin County and its seven incorporated cities of Stockton, Lodi, Manteca, Lathrop, Tracy, Ripon and Escalon.

The San Joaquin Partnership was established in April 1991 to help shape San Joaquin County's economic future. A public/private partnership was formed as part of a forward-looking vision for the community. The new organization was charged with actively recruiting new business and industry to the county.

The first chairman of the San Joaquin Partnership was Robert K. Wheeler of General Mills, a driving force in formation of the partnership. Rick Weddle was the organization's first president and CEO. The original Board of Directors included representatives from the county's leading businesses, education institutions and government. Weddle was succeeded by Michael E. Locke, who served until 2011. The current President and CEO is Michael S. Ammann.

The organization's original Vision 2000 plan emphasized the need for a regional transportation plan, economic development, human resources and education.

In 1997 the board of directors adopted eight major goals: to attract and site new business and industry; to assist in the retention of existing business and industry; to increase awareness of San Joaquin County, statewide, nationally and internationally; to enhance the image of San Joaquin County and its communities; to enhance the quality of life and overall community wellness through increased employment opportunities; to support education and training efforts for the preparation of the current and future workforce; to enhance the cooperative countywide economic development effort; and to assist local communities in improving competitiveness.

These goals were reaffirmed in March 2001.

The Partnership's cumulative impact as the lead organization during the past twenty-three years is profound: more than 28,356 direct jobs which stimulated indirect jobs and inducted employment of more than 66,000. This translates into more than $12.3 billion in industry output, $44.5 billion in investment and more than $3.5 billion in annual labor income.

In 2013, under the leadership of Ammann, the 'Greater Silicon Valley' project was launched, in cooperation with San Joaquin County. This signaled the start of the Partnership's campaign to locate expanding Silicon Valley companies, reduce the number of commuters and generate excitement about the opportunities in San Joaquin County as a location for start-ups and as a wine county.

THE BUSINESS COUNCIL OF SAN JOAQUIN COUNTY

The Business Council of San Joaquin County is the voice of the county's top business leaders, working together to help identify, examine and resolve countywide issues. The organization's ultimate goal is to create a better business climate for new and existing industry.

The council was formed in 1987 to provide the private sector leadership needed to tackle the many regional issues facing the county.

The founders and key leaders in the early days included Fritz Grupe, The Grupe Company; Bob Wheeler, General Mills; Rudy Croce, Croce & Company; Bob Eberhardt, Bank of Stockton; George Lagorio, Lagorio Farms; Ole Mettler, Farmers & Merchants Bank; Joe Crane, Union Safe Deposit Bank; Tom Shephard, Neumiller & Beardslee; Dick Haines, Lincoln Center; Tom Matthews, Tracy Press; David Rea, Stockton Savings Bank; Fred Weybret, *Lodi News Sentinel*; and Ed Schroeder, St. Joseph's Regional Health Systems.

The council is composed of 150 private sector members and serves the needs of San Joaquin County and its seven cities.

In 1992 the Council of Governments asked The Business Council to lead a campaign for passage of Measure K, a one-half percent sales tax for transportation projects. The measure passed with more than fifty percent approval and has provided matching funds for San Joaquin County projects. The council also provided the campaign leadership in 2006 to renew Measure K for an additional thirty years. A two-thirds vote was needed to pass Measure K and it received an eighty percent yes vote. Matching funds for San Joaquin County's transportation projects are now secure through 2041. As a result of this successful campaign, Highways 99, 120, 205, and Interstate 5 have all been—or will be—improved to new freeway standards, thus enhancing intermodal opportunities throughout the region.

One of the council's top priorities is the protection and restoration of the Delta along with the creation of new water resources for the state. The council actively participates in these two important water issues.

As a leader in building relationships between business and education, the council founded San Joaquin A+ and co-founded the Community Partnership for Families. The council continues to serve as an active participant as we touch young lives with numerous educational literacy initiatives.

The Business Council actively participates with associations that provide an opportunity to reach into areas of concern affecting the San Joaquin Valley, the Delta, and throughout California. These organizations include the California Partnership for the San Joaquin Valley (CPSJV), Regional Economic Association Leadership (REAL), Restore the Delta and the Delta Coalition.

After twenty-seven years of effective leadership, The Business Council's priorities remain unchanged—land use issues, infrastructure and education.

BANK OF AGRICULTURE & COMMERCE

✧

Above: Arthur Berberian, one of the founders of BAC.

Below: The first BAC location opened in Brentwood in 1965.

For fifty years, Bank of Agriculture & Commerce (BAC) has provided comprehensive financial and banking services to three counties contiguous to the Delta. These include Contra Costa, San Joaquin and Stanislaus Counties.

"We're a classic community bank, a privately-owned institution serving small to mid-sized area businesses, professionals and individuals with a variety of deposit accounts and loan products," explains Bill Trezza, the bank's chief executive officer.

The Berberian Family has lived and operated businesses in the Central Valley for more than half-a-century. The late Arthur Berberian was one of the original founders when the bank opened in 1965. Arthur's son Ronald A. Berberian is the bank's president and chairman of the board, and he remains committed to providing BAC customers a unique community banking experience. His devotion toward customers is reflected throughout the bank's daily operations.

BAC is a strong and viable bank that has withstood the test of time. In the mid 1980s, there were over 14,000 banks in the U.S.; there are now 6,500. Since the early 1980s, Stockton has been the home base for four savings banks and six commercial banks. BAC has weathered severe recessions in each decade since, as well as a wave of continuing consolidations. It is the twenty-second oldest charter in California, and one of only two institutions home based in Stockton.

Trezza credits BAC's ability to compete and grow to a strategic decision to concentrate on community banking with an emphasis on local business, professional and individual depositors. "After the recession in the 1990s, BAC focused on basic banking. We switched our funding reliance from CDs—and other interest-bearing deposit sources—and focused on business and household checking accounts."

Another key decision came in 1994 when the bank decided to invest heavily in software programs and become a community banking pioneer in computer technology. Even before the Internet, BAC's business customers were able to track and control their accounts electronically. "This put us on an even keel with the big national and international banks," Trezza explains.

The bank's expertise lies in its ability to offer a full range of banking services to physicians, dentists, attorneys, accountants and other business entities engaged in agricultural, commercial and industrial activities. BAC customizes its banking services and products to satisfy the goals of these business establishments as well as servicing the personal banking needs of the owners or principals and their employees.

The bank is proud of the extremely high retention rate of its customers. Most key executives have been with the bank for more than twenty-five years, reflecting the strength and stability of the organization.

Despite the financial uncertainties of the past fifty years, the bank continues to prosper. Assets have grown from $40 million in 1982 to more than $500 million dollars today. With the exception of one small acquisition, the majority growth has been organic.

BAC operates ten branches with 115 employees. In addition to Stockton, it operates branches in Lodi, Modesto, Antioch, Brentwood, Concord, Discovery Bay and Oakley with a network of branches stretching from San Joaquin and Stanislaus Counties through eastern Contra Costa County.

BAC and its employees are deeply involved in their communities. They regularly provide financial contributions, serve on boards and committees and volunteer for a vast array of nonprofit, community-based organizations and causes. The long list of organizations supported by BAC includes various Chambers of Commerce, the Children's Crisis Center, Dameron and Lodi Memorial Hospital Associations, Stockton Shelter for the Homeless, Stockton Police Department, March of Dimes, Center for Human Services, United Way, Brentwood Arts Society, Stockton Symphony Alliance and dozens of others.

In 2015 management and the board initiated a branding strategy. The bank was renamed BAC Community Bank. This serves a variety of purposes. It simultaneously caps the fifty year celebration and kicks off a new era for the next fifty years. The name reinforces BAC's strong and popular brand while denoting that it's still a Community Bank, an important difference in the market place. It also reminds the public the bank serves all constituencies in our markets.

"We are a unique financial institution and try to make it easy for customers to do business with us," comments Bill Trezza. "The fact that we have survived and grown for fifty years is a testament to our commitment to meet each customer's individual needs."

✧

BAC Plaza on March Lane in Stockton.

DIAMOND FOODS, INC.

Diamond Foods, Inc. is an innovative packaged food company focused on building and energizing brands including Diamond of California® nuts, Emerald® snack nuts, Kettle® Chips, and Pop Secret® popcorn.

Diamond Foods had its beginning more than a century ago when a group of California walnut growers formed a cooperative to promote better cultivation and marketing of their product. The California Walnut Growers Association (CWGA) was organized in 1912 and soon developed its own marketing arm.

In its early days, the association encouraged efforts to pool the state's walnut crop, eliminated local brands and established the Diamond brand, standardized grading standards and constructed a central cracking plant for processing.

The walnut growers also adopted an aggressive marketing program, developing the Diamond brand packaging and becoming the first nut producer to launch a nationwide advertising campaign. In 1926 every premium nut was stamped with the familiar red diamond.

The decade of the 1920s was a period of steady growth for the California walnut growers and on its twentieth anniversary the association had more than 6,600 members in twenty-seven local associations and ten individual packing houses. Association members accounted for eighty-five percent of the state's walnut crop. The strength of the association helped members survive the depression years of the 1930s and the challenges of production and distribution during World War II.

The growing urbanization of Southern California following the war and the resulting loss of agricultural land prompted the association to consider moving its operations. After much study, the growers decided to move their headquarters to Stockton. In addition to being adjacent to a prosperous walnut producing region, Stockton had access to a deep-water port and excellent rail and highway connections.

The association purchased a forty-seven acre site on the southern edge of Stockton and constructed a $4.25 million facility that included the most modern processing equipment. The Stockton plant was officially opened in August 1956 and the city was dubbed the "Walnut Capital of the World." A 1960 expansion enlarged the facility to 550,000 square feet and allowed the processing of 130 million pounds of bulk nuts and cold storage.

The move coincided with major changes in the structure and organization of the CWGA and in 1956 the association's name was changed to Diamond Walnut Growers, Inc.

The food industry changed dramatically during the 1960s and 1970s and the association considered a number of cooperative agreements with growers of other products. In 1974, Sunsweet Growers, known for prunes, needed to modernize its production as well as its marketing and administration. In December 1974 the Diamond and Sunsweet boards agreed to collaborate. Diamond's Stockton plant became the corporate headquarters for Diamond/Sunsweet and a new two-story office addition was constructed to handle the additional responsibilities.

Consolidation efforts continued in 1980 when Diamond/Sunsweet formed a federation with Sun-Maid and the organization's name was changed to Sun-Diamond Growers of California.

The association's focus shifted more to snack foods in the 1990s, an era that saw tremendous growth in international business. In 1990 the organization's name was changed once again, this time to Diamond of California®. It would change again in 2005 to Diamond Foods, Inc.

By 2004, Diamond had nearly doubled in size, with record gross sales nearly twice those of 1999. A major milestone came in 2005 when Diamond Foods, Inc. completed its initial public offering, with stock traded on the NASDAQ Global Select Market under the symbol DMND.

A series of acquisitions in the 2000s resulted in today's worldwide premium snack food producer and distributor. Diamond acquired Pop Secret® popcorn in 2008 and Kettle Foods natural potato chips in 2010.

Today Diamond Foods has five premium product lines; inshell nuts, culinary nuts, snack nuts, potato chips, and popcorn.

Diamond sells nuts under the Diamond of California® and Emerald® brands. Diamond's quality begins in the fertile soils of California's Central Valley and other nut-producing regions. As it always has, Diamond still sources 100 percent of its walnuts directly from growers throughout the state, most of which are family farmers with orchards in the heartland of California's Central Valley. Partnerships with some of these families date back to the early days of the association, crossing multiple generations.

Diamond's premium quality nuts are a testament to the hard work and dedication of its growers. In the fall, nuts are harvested, after which they take a short journey to the Stockton facility. Upon arrival, each nut is carefully selected, sorted and cleaned before shelling and packaging.

Diamond of California® offers inshell nuts for customers who value tradition and fresh, healthy, aesthetically appealing snack foods. Diamond of California® culinary nuts offer consumers a convenient recipe-ready source of nuts to enhance salads, vegetables, pastas, baked goods and other food. In addition, culinary nuts are sold to high quality food processors, restaurants, bakeries and food service companies and their suppliers. Institutional customers use standard or customer-specified nut products to add flavor, texture and nutritional value to their product offerings.

Snack nuts are sold under the Emerald® brand and deliver choice, convenience and excitement for consumers increasingly looking for healthier snack options. The Emerald® lineup includes trail mix and other snack items as well as roasted, glazed and flavored snack nut products. In addition to quality nuts and unique flavors, Emerald offers a variety of package sizes to meet consumers' needs.

Potato chips are sold under the Kettle Brand® label in the U.S. and Kettle Chips® brand in the United Kingdom. The potato chips are made with delicious blends of all-natural seasonings and cooked in small batches in pure, healthy oils. Kettle Brand® was the first potato chip brand to be verified as using Non-GMO ingredients by the Non-GMO Project.

Popcorn in both natural kernels and various flavors of microwave popcorn is sold under the Pop Secret® brand. The product line provides a tastier and better snacking experience by incorporating high quality details such as larger salt granules and Jumbo Pop kernels, which pop larger than conventional kernel popcorn.

Diamond's diverse portfolio of products is focused on energizing and adding value by making a relevant connection to the contemporary consumer. However, its deep roots in the walnut industry remain a foundation of the company's success.

Founded more than a century ago, Diamond's strong heritage is epitomized by its mission statement: "By honoring nature's ingredients we make food people love."

WELLS FARGO
IN STOCKTON

On March 18, 1852, Henry Wells and William G. Fargo founded Wells, Fargo & Co. after being inspired by the stunning news that gold had been discovered in faraway California. They imagined an express and banking business that could connect East Coast families and businesses with pioneers in remote gold fields out west. After establishing an office in San Francisco, branch offices opened in mining camps and towns throughout California.

❖

Right: Receipt for money delivered by Wells Fargo from Sacramento to Stockton in 1854.

Below: The Wells Fargo express office located on Center Street in 1860.

IMAGE COURTESY OF THE LIBRARY OF CONGRESS.

Wells Fargo first came to Stockton in 1853, offering essential banking services, reliable transportation of gold and goods, and dependable mail delivery. The company appointed J. M. Vansyckle as agent in charge of business in Stockton.

Among the many duties Vansyckle performed, the people of Stockton respected him most for his careful overseeing of banking services. He helped customers send funds to distant places by using paper bills of

exchange or checks. The Wells Fargo name on a check or exchange inspired confidence that the transaction could easily be converted back to coin or currency in eastern states or even overseas.

In 1855 a financial panic created by lost customer confidence in California banks led to runs and the closing of many financial institutions and express companies. The local newspaper praised Vansyckle for ensuring that the Wells Fargo office in Stockton "stood firm with doors open ready for depositors and met every demand." In the aftermath, Wells Fargo emerged as the most trusted name in the business.

Wells Fargo not only provided financial security to the people of Stockton, it also played a crucial role in connecting gold mining towns to San Francisco and beyond. Millions in gold discovered in towns like Sonora and Columbia rode to Stockton on stagecoaches in secure treasure boxes under the feet of the driver. A stagecoach driver was responsible for more than just moving gold. By directing coaches loaded with mail, express shipments, and newspapers, drivers brought news and connected communities.

Once express business from the gold fields reached Stockton, local agents transferred it to river steamships where Wells Fargo messengers oversaw its delivery to San Francisco. Pilsbury "Chips" Hodgkins worked as a Wells Fargo express messenger for over twenty years. Chips carefully recorded everything he carried in his journal, which shows that during his first year working for Wells Fargo he carried over $4 million in gold to San Francisco. Returning to Stockton, he always carried a variety of letters, newspapers, and important packages for people and businesses. Chips' journal entries demonstrate the variety of items Chips delivered to Stockton: gold coins to local banks, a roll of leather for a customer in Mariposa, a package of screen for Jamestown, oysters and cigars for Sonora, and a can of varnish for Mokelumne Hill.

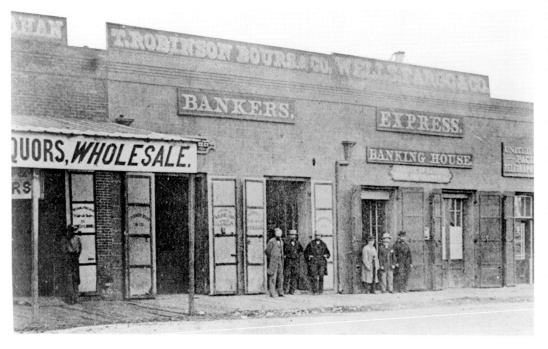

Chips had a history of going to extreme lengths to ensure timely delivery of customers' express shipments. After a steamer carrying Chips ran aground for the third time in the winter of 1863, Chips rented a small boat and rowed the rest of the way to Stockton. He arrived at the Stockton wharf just before daylight on December 1, still five hours ahead of the unlucky steamer *Helen Hensley*, to the delight of waiting Wells Fargo customers.

Wells Fargo continued to handle customers' business with the latest technology and by the fastest means available: stagecoach, steamship, telegraph, railroad, or pony express. The railroad came to Stockton in the 1860s, and over the following decades it increasingly became the chosen method for conducting business. Wells Fargo began sending express by rail in the 1860s, and by 1907 the company opened an office at the Southern Pacific Railroad depot, connecting Stockton by rail with Wells Fargo's 4,702 express offices worldwide.

Wells Fargo used its network of express offices to support the growth of Stockton's agricultural and manufacturing industries by connecting local products with national markets. In 1916, Agent J. E. Rice convinced Stockton cherry growers they could depend on Wells Fargo to arrange for buyers in other cities while also carefully delivering the delicate fruit. In addition to shipping goods, Wells Fargo agents offered customers money orders, traveler's checks, and other convenient financial services.

In July 1918 the federal government took over the nation's major express companies as a wartime measure. Wells Fargo signs disappeared from 10,000 storefronts and depots throughout California and across the nation. The Wells Fargo name continued in the banking business through the Wells Fargo Nevada National Bank in San Francisco. "Our ambition is not to be the largest bank in San Francisco, but the soundest and the best," vowed President I. W. Hellman in 1920. Conservative management allowed the bank to weather the Great Depression and wartime instability. Wells Fargo emerged in the post-war era poised to help finance the nation's economy using innovation and technology to bring convenient banking services to customers.

Wells Fargo returned to Stockton in March 1960 following a merger with American Trust Company. The merger brought many historic banking institutions into the Wells Fargo family including the First National Gold Bank of Stockton, one of the nine national gold banks established in California under Federal law in 1870 that allowed payment of paper bank notes in gold coin.

Today, the heritage of this and many other California financial institutions lives on under the familiar Wells Fargo name.

✧

Left: Stock Certificate of the First National Gold Bank of Stockton, issued the month the bank became operational in 1872.

Below: The Wells Fargo express office located at Stockton's Southern Pacific railroad depot in 1909.

Produced by Wells Fargo Historical Services. Photographs courtesy of the Wells Fargo Corporate Archives.

©2014 Wells Fargo Bank, N.A. All rights reserved.

IACOPI, LENZ & COMPANY

Iacopi, Lenz & Company, a resourceful and innovative accounting firm, provides comprehensive services to clients in a wide range of industries. A relatively small firm, Iacopi, Lenz & Company is dedicated to providing the highest quality professional services to its clients as well as giving back to the community.

The accounting firm was founded in 1978 by John T. Iacopi, who became the sole owner in 1980. Susan H. Lenz, who was with the firm from its beginning, became a partner in 1982 and the firm name was changed to Iacopi & Lenz. In 2001, Michael S. Butler, who joined the firm in 1980, and Michael D. Luis, who came in 1991, became principals in the firm. Known today as Iacopi, Lenz & Company, the firm has grown from its original 4 employees to a staff of 26 dedicated associates, including 17 certified public accountants.

Iacopi, Lenz & Company realizes that no one wants average performance from their professionals. Thus, its goal is to provide the highest quality professional services to its clients in a prompt and timely manner, and to flood its clients with service via prompt turnaround processing time offered at competitive, fair rates. The firm believes it exists to add value to its clients and strives to offer consistently creative and innovative services of high value. It presents its clients with options and works with them to sort it all out so they may achieve the very best business result. The firm delivers prompt and courteous services to its clients and prides itself on the fact that they are available to their clients seven days a week to assist with ongoing needs. The firm places its clients' best interests ahead of its own...and strives to get better and better as time goes on.

Iacopi, Lenz & Company meets the needs of its clients through general practice accounting, income tax preparation, and business consulting. The firm serves both individual and business clients and prides itself in providing personalized service, regardless of size, with each client receiving individual attention. Clients include farmers, food processors, grocery stores, restaurants, manufacturers, trucking companies, developers, nonprofit organizations, educational institutions, professional athletes, physicians, engineers and attorneys.

The firm takes a proactive approach to taxes and tax services by gaining an understanding of each client's unique needs. The staff at Iacopi, Lenz & Company uses its knowledge of current tax legislation to provide tax planning that identifies ways its clients may reduce their current and future tax liabilities. The firm prepares tax returns for individuals, partnerships, corporations, nonprofits, trusts and estates. The firm also provides experienced representation for its clients before federal and state tax agencies.

❖

Below: John T. Iacopi and Susan H. Lenz.

Through its extensive accounting services, Iacopi, Lenz & Company delivers meaningful, well-organized financial information accurately and promptly, including audits, reviews and compilations, as well as bookkeeping, QuickBooks support, and financial statement preparation.

Iacopi, Lenz & Company also offers consulting services to its business clients and provides guidance to clients who are considering acquiring, selling or merging a business or planning for business succession. The firm also provides litigation support, forensic accounting, expert witness testimony, and wealth transfer and estate planning services. The staff includes certified valuation analysts to perform business appraisal services for business planning, gifting, marital dissolutions, and litigation purposes.

The firm is dedicated to providing professional accounting services and is passionate about its commitment to the firm's clients. In 2013, and again in 2014, Iacopi, Lenz & Company received the 'Best of San Joaquin County' award for CPA firms and bookkeeping services.

Iacopi, Lenz & Company maintains an environmentally conscious office that is committed to its profession and the community. The firm's clients appreciate the continuity and longevity of its staff. More than half the staff has been with the firm for over 20 years, with 7 of them over 30 years. The firm culture is working together as a family, supporting one another, sharing knowledge and collaborating with those "family" members who have specialized expertise. They are all members of the Iacopi, Lenz & Company family with the goal of providing consistently excellent client service in a timely manner.

Members of the firm have contributed to the accounting industry by writing articles for accounting publications, speaking at professional seminars and forums, and chairing committees of professional organizations. Members of the firm also serve as board members and officers for local schools and charitable organizations, and they are proud of their involvement in civic, educational and community organizations.

In 2013 the firm received the Public Service Award for Firms from the California Society of CPAs, an award given to only one CPA firm annually. The firm also received the 2014 Action on Behalf of Children (ABC) award in the business category for its tireless efforts on behalf of the children of San Joaquin County.

Through its thirty-seven years in business, Iacopi, Lenz and Company has continued to expand and deliver a wide range of accounting services while helping to meet the needs of its clients and the community. As the firm's motto says, "Come Brainstorm and Create with Us!"

✧

Below: Left to right, Michael S. Butler, John T. Iacopi, Susan H. Lenz and Michael D. Luis.

PHOTOGRAPHS COURTESY OF CAROLINE PHOTOGRAPHY.

DAVE WONG'S RESTAURANT

Never in their wildest imaginations did David and Raymond Wong think that two boys from mainland China could come to the United States, open their own restaurant, and exemplify the American dream. But, that is precisely what happened.

✦

Above: Raymond (left) and David (right) Wong working at On Lock Sam's Restaurant.

Below: Dave Wong's Restaurant & Deli on March Lane. The first Dave Wong's location is on North Pershing Avenue.

David and Raymond, immigrants from Canton, China, began their pursuit of the American dream at On Lock Sam's Restaurant in downtown Stockton in the late 1960s. Dave was a busboy and then a waiter; Raymond a prep cook and, ultimately, head cook.

By the early 1970s, the Wongs had become very popular with customers; Dave was always joking and providing excellent service and Raymond became very adept with the wok. In 1975, David and Raymond decided to risk their life savings and pursue their dream of owning their own restaurant.

The grand opening at 5620 North Pershing Avenue was a huge success, and although the hours were long and things were not always easy, the effort proved worthy of the sacrifice. By the early 1980s it was not uncommon for customers to wait two hours on the weekends for a table at Dave Wong's.

As time went on, a second generation of Wong's was ready to work in the restaurant and in 2002, a second location was built at 2828 West March Lane with a more modern restaurant, bar and deli. The original Pershing Avenue location is now a deli only, with both locations open seven days a week.

The menu at Dave Wong's Restaurant has evolved over the years from mainly Cantonese to a more spicy and varied selection from other regions of Asia. The original cuisine is still available for those who grew up with the Wong family and you might even catch Dave greeting customers with his signature laugh, and Raymond stirring up a wok or two.

The décor is a mix of contemporary and classic design. A large mural in the main dining room is the work of one of the restaurant cooks. A talented artist from China, he painted the beautiful mural from atop a scaffold.

Dave Wong's Restaurant is honored to be serving its second and third generation of Central Valley families as well as UOP students, grads, and travelers alike. A popular dining destination and a favorite among the locals, Dave Wong's Restaurant has served Stockton and the surrounding communities for forty years. They invite you to visit soon and "Taste the Flavors of the Orient."

For more information about Dave Wong's, please visit www.davewongsrestaurant.com.

✧

Above: Dave Wong's dining room decorated for the holidays. The mural features artwork by one of the restaurant's cooks.

Left: David (left) and Raymond (right) Wong today.

MCDONALD'S OF SAN JOAQUIN COUNTY

The Schrader' Family's first McDonald's Restaurant on Pacific Avenue.

Jean and Don Schrader opened their first McDonald's franchise on February 10, 1966, at 4515 Pacific Avenue in Stockton. This location would be the first for a family business that would include multiple McDonald's franchises in Stockton, Manteca, Lodi, Tracy, Lathrop, Galt, and Martell.

Jean and Don were high school sweethearts at Emporia (Kansas) High School and, after graduating from college, they moved to Great Bend, Kansas, where Don taught and coached and Jean was a medical technologist. Their three children—Susan, Craig, and Nancy—were born in Kansas. Susan was born with Downs Syndrome.

In 1962, Don went to work for the McDonald's Corporation in Chicago as a restaurant manager trainee. They were transferred to San Jose, California, where Don opened the first McDonald's in San Jose and Susan began attending special education classes.

Don was promoted to assistant professor at Hamburger University in Elk Grove, Illinois, where McDonald's provided training for new franchise operators and company employees in the basement of an operating restaurant. Unfortunately, this small town did not provide any special education classes for Susan, and she began to regress.

In 1964, Don requested a transfer back to California so Susan could continue her development. The timing could not have been

better as McDonald's was starting to build new restaurants in the San Francisco and Sacramento areas. Susan was able to resume her education and Don assisted the new franchisees in the opening of their new restaurants throughout Northern California.

As Don visited these new locations in Northern California he made it a point to see what kind of special education classes were offered. While visiting Stockton in early 1965, he found the offering of special education classes to be outstanding, which still holds true fifty years later.

In the three and a half years Don had worked for McDonald's Corporation, he had noticed his colleagues being transferred throughout the United States as McDonald's was building new restaurants very rapidly. He knew that if he was to continue to grow with the company, the family might have to move again—and once again disrupt Susan's development.

In 1965, McDonald's had a policy that company employees could not open their own franchise until they had worked ten full years for the company. Don was aware of the new franchise being built in Stockton and he and Jean had visited the special education schools in Stockton together. They decided they would try to leave the company early and open their own franchise in Stockton.

At a meeting at the Hyatt Hotel in San Jose, Don met with McDonald's founder Ray Kroc and asked if he could leave the company early and open the new McDonald's franchise in Stockton. Kroc, who was aware of Susan's special needs, said yes.

Today, son Craig and his wife, Cathleen, have franchises of their own, as does daughter Nancy.

Jean and Don have six grandchildren. Son Craig and daughter-in-law Cathleen have three children: Carli, Meghan, and Dylan. Daughter Nancy has three boys: Corey, Brad, and Taylor Johnson.

Carli was awarded her first franchise in Manteca in 2014. This makes four generations of the Schrader family who have been involved with McDonald's as Don's parents were involved in the first restaurant. Don and Jean's other five grandchildren are in the McDonald's Next Generation Program. Carli's sister, Meghan, is a dental hygienist, and her brother, Dylan, is working in the family restaurants. Nancy's sons, Corey and Brad, are also in the McDonald's restaurants and Taylor is attending the University of Pacific.

McDonald's of San Joaquin County is very active in the community and is very proud of contributions such as the Ronald McDonald House in Sacramento and Camp

Ronald McDonald in Susanville. The Ronald McDonald facilities provide a home away from home for sick children and their families receiving treatment in area hospitals.

McDonald's of San Joaquin County is also involved in a long list of other activities, including World Children's Day and the Hanot Foundation. McDonald's of San Joaquin County contributes to numerous local schools, hospitals, and churches, participates in a number of fundraisers for charitable organizations and helps sponsor various runs/walks/and other activities for dozens of organizations.

❖

Above: Don and Jean Schrader at a McDonald's Convention.

Below: The Schrader Family.

HOWARD JOHNSON INN

The Howard Johnson Inn at 33 North Center Street is the perfect hotel choice whether Stockton is your destination or if you are just stopping for the evening. Overlooking the waters of the Stockton Marina in the downtown financial district, the Howard Johnson Inn is conveniently located between Interstate 5 and Highway 99.

If you are planning a business trip, Howard Johnson Inn offers a conference room that can accommodate up to fifty participants.

You will sleep soundly in your comfortable, well-appointed room at the Howard Johnson Inn. Rooms are equipped with high-speed Internet, cable television and all the comforts of home to include refrigerators and microwaves. Pick up your complimentary newspaper in the lobby and enjoy a free Rise & Dine continental breakfast. Non-smoking rooms are available and Howard Johnson Inn is a pet-friendly hotel. A relaxing, refreshing outdoor pool is available for your pleasure. Free outdoor parking for cars, trucks or RVs makes it easy to explore all Stockton has to offer.

You will find numerous dining options within one-half mile, including Misaki Sushi & Bar and Q Korean BBQ. Xochimilco Café and Casa Flores serve tasty Mexican dishes, while French 25 offers authentic

New Orleans-style fare. Moo Moo's Burger Barn offers gourmet burgers with a 1950s diner theme. Starbucks Coffee and Coldstone Creamery are also located nearby.

Ballpark, and the Stockton Memorial Civic Auditorium. The Regal City Center Stadium 16 and IMAX shows all the latest movies. Directly across the street from the hotel is the Weber Point Event Center, home to numerous outdoor events and concerts throughout the year. You can take a one-mile trip to the Port of Stockton or visit the University of the Pacific or San Joaquin Delta College, located only three miles from the hotel.

Guests always find plenty to do and see while visiting Stockton. The Howard Johnson Inn is within walking distance of the Bob Hope Theatre (a renovation of the historic Fox Theatre), Stockton Arena, Banner Island

Howard Johnson Inn has a multilingual staff to assist you. For more information about the Howard Johnson Inn, or to check rates or make a reservation, check the website at www.hojo.com/hotels/california/stockton.

The Howard Johnson Inn would like to say 'thank you' to the many business and civic leaders in the City of Stockton who have supported the Howard Johnson Inn. We would like to give particular thanks to the visitor's bureau (Visit Stockton), the Chamber of Commerce, Judith Buethe Communications and the Atlas Hospitality Group.

Howard Johnson Inn has been owned by Pink Ocean Hospitality, LLC since May 27, 2011. We are proud to do business in the City of Stockton.

LINDSAY FURNISHED APARTMENTS

George Washington Trahern arrived in Stockton as a young man on August 1, 1861.

He was born in 1844 in the Republic of Texas and was part of the Mier Expedition in the Mexican/American War. He became a cattle baron and owned the Trahern Ranch five miles west of Ripon, California. Sometime in the 1870s he built a mansion at 624 El Dorado Street on the southeast corner of El Dorado and Park Streets across from today's Cesar Chavez Library. Next door on the northeast corner of El Dorado and Oak was a similar mansion owned by J. M. Kelsey.

G. W. Trahern died in October of 1909. By the 'teens' both mansions were considered "White Elephants." The Kelsey mansion was barged over to Monte Diablo and relocated next to the school and became a retirement home. It no longer stands today.

The Trahern mansion was purchased in 1919 by William E. Tretheway, president of Stockton Iron Works. He had the Trahern mansion moved eight blocks to a site at Lindsay and Stanislaus and had it raised. A basement with concrete walls was constructed and an entire first floor—built of brick—was added underneath the old mansion. A full-height addition was made to the Stanislaus Street side and to the rear. The original hipped roof of the mansion is still intact and a flat roof covers the addition.

Old cobblestones were salvaged from a repaving project downtown and used for paving the driveway next to the building. As late as the 1970s, a brick garage existed behind the building where the six foot retaining wall exists today. This wall was the side and back of the old garage. Carports were added in the back and are now garages.

The architect for the conversion to apartments was Walter King of San Francisco.

In the conversion process, King stripped the old house of its Victorian elements except for the cornice, which remains today and was replicated on the new portions of the building. Windows were rearranged to suit the new floor plan. The entire building, including the added basement and first floor, was stuccoed over and the Victorian double porch was removed. Over the front entry, tiers of balconies were built where the porch once stood. The second and third floors still boast their front grand hallways replete with Victorian trim and twelve foot ceilings. The original front entrance to the mansion remains today on the second floor, which used to be the first floor of the mansion. The original Victorian staircase remains as well, leading from the second floor to the third floor. The end result was the twenty-four unit apartment building that exists today.

The Tretheway Apartments opened for business in 1921. The building was purchased by Lea Smith Tino and The Smith 1989 Trust in 2004, but restoring the building to its former glory was a major project because it had suffered from abuse and neglect. Today, the Lindsay has the charm of Victorian with all of the modern conveniences that would be found only in a luxury hotel or a bed and breakfast in Europe.

RIGHT: PHOTOGRAPH COURTESY OF BILLY LOVCI.

Lea and Tony Richards, a professional architectural designer from San Francisco, believed that a historical building such as this deserved to keep its integrity by retaining its aesthetic charm. Tony wanted to keep it as original as possible down to the trim. For example, the spindles in the staircase were butchered by a previous misguided worker. Tony had an artisan from San Francisco make the replacements.

"We reglazed the claw foot tubs and tried to save much of the built-in cabinetwork," Lea explains. "We added air conditioning and laundry facilities for added comfort, as well as full refrigerators, microwaves, toasters, coffeemakers, dishware, all cookware utensils, linens, plus great artwork. We provide off-street parking and each of our twenty-four units is equipped with Wi-Fi and television with movie channels."

Lea added the furnished designer décor to finish the Lindsay Apartments. Carefully chosen antiques and modern furniture keep the building current, yet warm and cozy.

"To date, we usually have a full house of short and long term tenants that come from all across the U.S. to stay with us," adds Lea Tino.

"All you need to bring here is your suitcase, computer and cat," says Lea. "The Lindsay is known today as the "best kept secret" in downtown Stockton. We have worked with the Stockton Police and started several neighborhood watch teams. Our furnished stays are not only sought after but we enjoy all of our repeat customers."

Lea also met with the mayor of Stockton to request that all property owners take full responsibility for their buildings. "Now is the time to be assertive to keep our city beautiful and crime free. We do our part. If reoccurring crimes continue, fine the owners," She says, "We are family-owned and live here too. We are proud of what we've accomplished over the years."

Lea Tino is a Certified Tour Ambassador and a member of the Chamber of Commerce. She is also a Certified Crime Stopper for the City of Stockton.

For more information, check the website at www.lindsaystudioapartments.com.

Web page created by Carl J. Street (www.cjstreet.com) of Hayward, California.

Or look us up on our new Facebook page titled "Lindsay Furnished Apartments."

❖

PHOTOGRAPHS COURTESY OF BILLY LOVCI

ARROYO'S CAFÉ

Arroyo's Café was established in 1946 as a small Mexican restaurant nicknamed the 'Bean Palace' by the customers who loved the authentic Mexican dishes prepared by Jesus Arroyo.

✧

Above: Front of El Ranchero Grande in the late 1950s. Insets are Jesus and Guadalupe Arroyo.

Below: Mario, Mariana and Mario inside Arroyo's at Quail Lakes.

Arroyo, a native of Mexico with only an elementary school education, came to Stockton as a young man after working as a laborer in the fields of Montana and for the Purina Grain Company at the Port of Stockton. He began his own business by renting a small kitchen. He did so well he was able to purchase the El Rancho Grande Restaurant on West Washington Street in 1948. That same year he brought his wife, Guadalupe, and their family to Stockton.

The restaurant has had a number of locations over the years. Three of the moves were forced by downtown Stockton redevelopment

projects. The name Arroyo's Café was first used in 1955.

"My father was the hardest working person I have ever known," comments his son, Mario Arroyo. "He would come to work early in the day and still be there at four or five in the morning. In the early days, the café was located in what was known as 'Skid Row' and he would prepare bag lunches for field workers on their way to work before getting his restaurant ready for the day's business.

"There are many stories of my dad helping people throughout his life," Mario continues. "He helped some buy a home or start a business and he helped Mike Torres buy a tour bus for his band."

Louie Asborno, who started eating at the restaurant as a young man and now brings his great-grandchildren, remembers "guys being broke and looking for something to eat. Jesus would get them some food and then give them a stack of dishes to wash." Mario says this demonstrates that his father had a soft heart combined with the mind of a businessman.

In 1980, Jesus turned the restaurant over to his sons Mario and Richard, but was always close by to give advice and be a helping hand. Sadly, Jesus died in 1995 and Guadalupe in 1997.

Of Mario's five children, Mario Fernando, Mariana and Madeline, and Rick's oldest daughter, Stephanie, are involved in the business today, with Mario taking the lead. Michael and Madison are Mario's other sons. Angela is Rick's youngest daughter.

Arroyo's Café has a number of long-time employees including Guero Carlos, who has been cooking so long that Mario says he cannot remember the business without him.

Now located at 2381 West March Lane, overlooking Quail Lake, Arroyo's Café has become famous for its authentic Mexican menu and warm, personal service. Arroyo's sponsors an annual car show to raise money for victims of violent crimes and supports a number of other community projects including a yearly Christmas toy drive with the Stockton Police Department, a fundraiser for the City of Hope Breast Cancer Research Hospital, and St. Jude's Children's Hospital.

AMERICAN HOMETEX, INC.

American Hometex, Inc., an importer and wholesaler of quilts and bedding products, was founded in 2000 by Eugene Meng.

The Hometex Collections offers the U.S. market a complete line of quilts and other patchwork items, table and bed linens, and needlepoint tapestry products. From the simplest placemat to the most complex quilt, the Hometex Collections reflects the artistic pride and superb needlework passed down from generation to generation in the villages of China.

Most exciting of all, the Hometex Collections are available in extraordinary American designs sure to please the most demanding U.S. customers.

Before founding American Hometex, Meng was an employee of Shandong Artex Corporation in Qingdao, China. In 1992, Meng helped Shandong Artex Corp. set up their overseas company called Shantex, Inc. in Hayward, California. Based on the experience he gained at Shantex, Meng formed American Hometex, Inc., utilizing his strong contract suppliers in China and expanded sales to $5 million in 2007.

The company moved to the Dallas, Texas, area in 2003 but returned to Stockton in 2010 to take advantage of less expensive warehouse facilities. All of American Hometex products are made in China, so the location change from Texas to California helped the company save about fifty percent of its ocean freight cost and shorten the shipping time from four weeks to about two weeks. In addition, the relocation cut the company's monthly heating cost from $4,000 to $500.

During its eight years in Texas, American Hometex formed a stable sales team and began selling to such well known retailers as JCPenney Outlet Stores, Garden Ridge Stores, and Lid'l Dolly Dresses. A sales team is still working in Texas and Arkansas, using remote access to process sales orders each day.

Although still a relatively small company, American Hometex has managed to become a very stable company despite six years of economic recession. The company is now developing a number of new products which will be introduced gradually to the U.S. market. This is expected to raise this Asian-run company to a new level.

To learn more about American Hometex, visit www.americanhometex.com.

ANGELINA'S SPAGHETTI HOUSE

✧

Below: Angelina's original menu, 1976.

Bottom: Sam Taylor and Angelina DeMartini opening night, December 27, 1976.

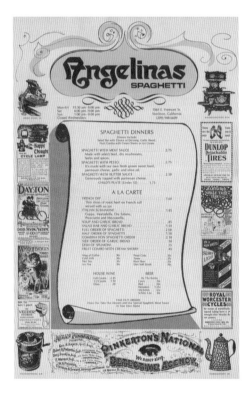

Angelina's Spaghetti House has become one of the region's most popular restaurants with those of all ages because of its warm and inviting atmosphere and varied menu.

The concept for the restaurant came from John Boggiano, son-in-law of Angelina DeMartini. Angelina, the restaurant's namesake, came to America in 1913 with the knowledge and skill to prepare the delicious meals from the province of Genova. John noticed that friends truly appreciated the fine food and believed it should be offered through a restaurant.

In 1976, John's son-in-law, Lawrence Sambado, learned that the building that housed the former Johnny Hom's restaurant on Fremont Street was for sale. The building was purchased and plans for the new restaurant began. Steve Copello, Angelina's nephew, was brought in to open and manage the restaurant, and Steve brought in his good friend, Sam Taylor, to help him. The original owners were John Boggiano, Mario Boggiano, Lawrence Sambado, Robert Costigliolo and Steve Copello. Sam Taylor joined the ownership later.

Steve and Sam, the two active partners, were recent college graduates with no restaurant experience, but they worked tirelessly throughout the

summer and fall of 1976 to remodel the restaurant. On December 17, 1976, they served their first plate of pasta to a paying customer. "When we opened, a full spaghetti dinner, including salad bar, garlic bread and dessert, was a mere $2.75," Steve recalls.

Steve remembers that non-Genovese patrons were often puzzled in the beginning. "Our gravy was brown, and pasta with pesto was green. Nowadays, everyone knows what pesto is, but back in the '70s, we had quite a few plates come back to the kitchen because the spaghetti was green."

Rita Boggiano, Beverly Sambado, Barbara Costigliolo and Marianne Boggiano all worked to adapt Angelina's recipes to the large scale needed. Irma Copello, Steve's mother and Angelina's niece, was responsible for the restaurant's signature dessert, Dolce. At home, Dolce was made only for the most special occasions, but it is offered daily at Angelina's.

Angelina's has about twenty-five full-time employees, some of whom have been with the restaurant more than thirty years. General Manager Michael Zidich, Craig Kaiser, and Betty Angeli, now retired, have given more than eighty-five years' service.

Over the years, Angelina's Catering has grown to become the area's premier caterer. In addition to Steve and Sam, event guests look forward to seeing Gretchen Murray and Bobby Bisla as they organize an elegant sit-down affair for 600, or a more intimate or casual dinner.

Angelina's is an enthusiastic community supporter, providing gift cards, sponsorships, reduced prices for non-profits and gifts and dinners for auctions. Angelina's regularly supports Saint Mary's Dining Hall, United Way, Lodi Memorial Foundation, Hospice of San Joaquin, the American Cancer Society and others.

Angelina's Spaghetti House is located at 1563 East Fremont Street in Stockton. Angelina Foods, Inc., is comprised of the restaurant, delicatessen, cocktail lounge, catering business and off-site sales of Angelina Ravioli and Sauces, which is made in-house.

For more information about Angelina's Spaghetti House, visit www.angelinas.com.

be part of the second oldest shopping center west of the Mississippi. Lincoln Center and its merchants play an active role in giving back to the community, supporting a long list of charitable causes and organizations.

The shopping center is an integral part of Stockton's history and, with Lincoln Center's excellent management and commitment to the community, the 'Big L' is certain to shine above Stockton for many more years to come.

LINCOLN CENTER

Lincoln Center, Stockton's premiere shopping and dining destination, began more than sixty years ago as the dream of Greenlaw Grupe, Roy Sims and four other men of extraordinary foresight. Their vision for north Stockton included a complete planned community with homes, schools, churches, recreation and commercial areas.

The founders of Lincoln Center acquired 1,800 acres from Stockton business leader Benjamin Holt and formed a corporation called Lincoln Properties, Inc. Stock in the new corporation sold out in only two weeks. More than 700 homes had been constructed by the end of 1951, followed by the opening of Lincoln Center.

The Center opened with 25,000 square feet of space that housed sixteen neighborhood stores. Demand was so great that ten additional stores were soon added to the complex at the corner of Pacific Avenue and Benjamin Holt Drive.

Today, Lincoln Center—marked by the 'Big L'—is located on both sides of Benjamin Holt Drive and is approximately thirty-five acres. More than ninety merchants operate retail stores, restaurants and service businesses, many of which are locally owned and family-operated.

These merchants are dedicated to quality and service and are proud to

GREATER STOCKTON CHAMBER OF COMMERCE

Above: Greater Stockton Chamber of Commerce Committee's advocate for and assist members and the business community by providing ways to reduce their costs of doing business!

Below: The Annual Greater Stockton Chamber of Commerce State of the City address draws close to 1,000 people each year to hear the Stockton Mayor's plans for the upcoming year.

PHOTOGRAPH COURTESY OF ARTURO VERA.

For more than a century—114 years and counting—the Greater Stockton Chamber of Commerce has promoted the economic vitality of the greater Stockton community. The Chamber provides strong business development and advocacy programs, including regulatory, permitting and workforce issues.

The Chamber was founded in 1901 when the City of Stockton was largely an agricultural hub of about 18,000 people. It has been an integral and important part of the city's growth into a dynamic, thriving community of 300,899 people in a county of 710,731 residents. While agriculture remains a vital part of the local economy, the Chamber has played an essential role in helping diversify the economy of Stockton and San Joaquin County and has been at the forefront of many issues as the strongest voice in the region.

The mission of the Greater Stockton Chamber is to aggressively develop and promote an economically vibrant business community. A number of local, state and national award winning programs have been developed by the Chamber to help its members succeed. Some are designed to help members directly

with their day-to-day operations and marketing efforts and others act as business advocates and watchdogs. All programs are designed to improve the local business environment now and for the future of the entire community.

The multiple programs of the Chamber work for its members in a variety of ways. The Government Relations Council acts as a political watchdog and advisor to local and state legislators. The Chamber also works very closely with our important nonprofit community partners. The Chamber works to improve the education and quality of the local workforce through programs like the Business Education Alliance and the Stockton Chamber Apprenticeship Program. Environmentally friendly business practices are studied and implemented through the Chamber's Green Team San Joaquin. The future leaders of the Central Valley are identified and educated through the Chamber's Leadership Stockton program.

The Greater Stockton Chamber hosts a variety of events each year to help members become more involved with the community and to spread the word about their businesses and services. The Annual ATHENA Award event recognizes an outstanding businesswoman who serves as a role model for all women and men alike. The Industrial and Technology Barbeque is an annual event in which the Chamber honors new or expanded manufacturers, technological companies and industries located in San Joaquin County. The Annual State of the City, cosponsored with the Port of Stockton and the City of Stockton, showcases the city's economic, educational and industrial development. Monthly Networking mixers also connect businesses with the community.

For more information about the Greater Stockton Chamber of Commerce, check the website at www.stocktonchamber.org.

Angel Sepulveda State Farm Insurance is a new business with a very bright future. Founded on September 1, 2014, the agency is growing rapidly with clients in Stockton and throughout California. The State Farm Insurance agency, located at 6838 Pacific Avenue, offers auto, home, life, health, banking and business insurance.

Angel Sepulveda worked several years for an agent in Sonora, California, before deciding to become her own boss and run an agency of her own. "I saw how I could create an atmosphere and opportunity for others to help give back to the community," she says. "I could have gone to any city in the state, but chose Stockton because I see the opportunity here and believe I can make a difference."

Buzz Garvin, an agent in Sonora, mentored Angel and encouraged her to open her own business. He continues to provide advice and support.

Angel grew up in Stockton and went to junior high and high school here. Although she has not lived in the city since graduating from high school, she says she is excited and happy to be back. "Stockton has a great history and is filled with some amazing people I'm looking forward to helping," she says. "My team and I are more than just insurance; we want to instill confidence in what we do, and also find and create ways to give back to the community. Stockton continues to grow each year and I believe local business owners should make an effort to help make the city great."

Angel says she continues to be surprised by how well things have come together since she opened her business. Her mom and an uncle helped to paint, clean and organize the office and her husband and daughter come to the office to help out on weekends. "I work very long hours, so my Mom has taken time out of her life to take my daughter to school a few days each week. I am awed and humbled by my family and their willingness to help and see me succeed," she says.

Angel Sepulveda State Farm Insurance is active in the Greater Stockton Chamber of Commerce, Hispanic Chamber of Commerce, Rotary Club of Stockton, and supports

✧

Angel Sepulveda.

such organizations as Toys for Tots and sports programs at local high schools.

"This is an exciting time for me, the team and the agency," says Angel. "We are in the beginning stages of what will be a successful and growing business. It's exciting to watch the team grow and learn and to help them create paths to success."

HILTON STOCKTON

The Hilton Stockton Hotel offers an upscale experience to visitors to the San Joaquin Valley with a stunning five story atrium lobby, beautifully appointed guest rooms, and the city's largest hotel banquet and meeting facility. The Hilton Stockton is the top choice for both business and leisure travelers who will enjoy excellent customer service and a facility and rooms unmatched in the San Joaquin Valley.

The Hilton is conveniently located just off Interstate 5 in an upscale suburban location, with many of Stockton's most popular dining, shopping and recreations venues nearby. The hotel is located only minutes away from the University of the Pacific, San Joaquin Delta College, Stockton Arena, Banner Island Baseball Stadium, the Bob Hope Theater, Spanos Park Shopping Center, Weberstown Mall and Sherwood Malls.

The Hilton offers 198 guest rooms and suites featuring contemporary décor with comfortable furnishings, handsomely appointed bathrooms and select amenities. All beautifully appointed rooms feature items from the Hilton Serenity Collection. The Serenity Bed includes an exclusive Suite Dreams mattress and box springs, Super Topper mattress pad, down-filled comforter, and Touch of Down pillows, 250-thread-count sheets. Guest will stay connected with complimentary wireless Internet available in all rooms and public areas of the hotel. Guests may also stay connected with the Hilton Connectivity Station located in the lobby that is designed to meet the changing needs of hotel guests and the ways they work, seek information and communicate while traveling. The Hilton Fitness Center offers guests a fully equipped fitness center with both cardiovascular and strength training machines.

The Orchard Restaurant, the hotel's onsite restaurant is open daily for breakfast with both served breakfast and breakfast buffet options. You can enjoy freshly brewed coffee at the Starbucks coffee bar located in the main lobby, or visit the Canal Street Grille and Bar open for lunch and dinner featuring cuisine of the San Joaquin Valley.

With more than 13,000 square feet of flexible and versatile meeting space, the Hilton Stockton is the perfect location for small business meetings, weddings, conferences, trade shows and reunions. Over the years the hotel has hosted many local, regional and state meetings conventions and has been the headquarters hotel for many local citywide events, and sports tournaments.

A number of famous celebrities and political figures have stayed at the Hilton Stockton, including President George W. Bush in 2006. Senator Bob Doyle, Senator John McCain and Michael Dukakis all stayed at the hotel during their presidential campaigns. Famous entertainers who have stayed at the Hilton Stockton include Bob Hope, Bob Dylan, Dave Brubeck and Neil Diamond.

The Hilton Stockton is proud to be with the most recognized name in the industry, Hilton, which remains synonymous with the word "hotel." Hilton is where the world makes history, closes the deal, toasts special occasions and gets away from it all. The flagship brand of Hilton Worldwide continues to build upon its legacy of innovation by developing products and services to meet the needs of tomorrow's savvy global travelers while our team members shape experiences in which every guest feels cared for, valued and respected.

"It has been, and continues to be, our responsibility to fill the earth with the light and warmth of hospitality."

For more information about the Hilton Stockton, visit www.stockton.hilton.com.

The mission of Green's Nutrition is to educate and support its customers by helping them achieve optimum health through the use of natural products. A full-service health food store, Green's Nutrition carries a wide range of top quality nutritional supplements, toxin-free skin care, and healthy groceries.

"We pride ourselves on providing quality products and personalized customer service," says owner Eunice Green, who has a doctorate in natural health. "We strive to answer our customer's questions and help them make smarter and healthier decisions when buying natural products."

What sets Green's Nutrition apart from other health food stores is its 'Herb Vault' that contains more than 400 bulk herbs—both medicinal and cooking herbs and spices. The herbs and spices are kept in an actual bank vault, left from the days when the building was a Wells Fargo bank.

Green's also has a massage therapist, and herbalist Chris Devincenzi, who is in charge of the vault. He and Eunice offer advice to customers about herbal formulas for various health conditions.

Green's began in June of 1995 when Eunice purchased Lundy's Nutrition Center, then located on Waterloo Road. A few years later the name was changed to Green's Nutrition. Eunice explains that she purchased the business because of her passion for natural health. She had been studying and learning about herbs, aromatherapy and nutrition for many years as a hobby and the purchase provided the perfect opportunity to turn her hobby into a career.

Rebekah Robinson, affectionately known as Dr. Doolittle, had been with Lundy's for five years and stayed on when Eunice purchased the store. Rebekah is very good with people and pets and creates formulas using both Bach Flower and homeopathic remedies.

Green's offers many educational opportunities, including herb, nutrition and essential oils classes taught by the owner and other employees. Eunice feels strongly that education is a key factor in improving health and often brings in experts to conduct consumer lectures.

In 2010, Green's Nutrition moved from its relatively small space on Waterloo Road to a much larger and more convenient location at 1906 Pacific Avenue on the Miracle Mile. The store now has six well trained and educated employees who stay in touch with new research and products.

Eunice is grateful to the City of Stockton, which provided expansion funds through a special program. This was invaluable in expanding inventory for the larger location. The Bank of Stockton has also been very supportive of the business. The owners of the Green's nutrition building, Mike and Lisa Whirlow, have also been very encouraging and supportive.

✧

Left: Owner, Dr. Eunice Green and her staff are happy to help their customers with any health questions or concerns.

Below: Green's Nutrition carries supplements, gifts, grocery, homeopathics, and the largest selection of essential oils and bulk herbs and spices in Stockton.

Many of Green's Nutrition customers have been shopping with the store from its beginning and have become almost like family. Eunice has nurtured and cared for many children who are now adults and is now taking care of the nutritional needs of those children's children.

GREEN'S NUTRITION

MISAKI
SUSHI & BAR

Located in the heart of downtown Stockton, Misaki Sushi & Bar was the first sushi restaurant to open successfully in the downtown area, and is the anchor restaurant for the Regal Stockton City Centre Stadium 16 IMAX Theater. Misaki serves a wide variety of Japanese entrees that include sushi, sashimi, and traditional Japanese dishes. In addition, Misaki has a full bar with a large selection of Japanese sake.

Misaki was founded in 2005 by Jacky Trinh, Andrew San, Toan Le, and Vi Banh. Jacky and Andrew had the idea of opening their own business but were not sure of a location. After an extensive market analysis they drove to Stockton and discovered a beautiful cinema complex adjacent to the downtown waterfront. Jacky and Andrew knew they had found their ideal location and immediately starting writing a business plan and securing investors.

As new business owners trying to establish a customer base, the founders of Misaki often found themselves developing friendships and new customers through sake bombs.

"It was very difficult to introduce the idea of sushi and raw sashimi to locals who had never tried Japanese cuisines," Andrew recalls. However, after a few sake bombs, the idea to be more adventurous and order something other than chicken teriyaki was more palatable. Once our customers tried the sushi and sashimi they were hooked and have become repeat customers.

"Our mission is to introduce and deliver fine sushi and Japanese cuisine paired with friendly customer service in a fun, easygoing and relaxed environment," Andrew explains. "We accomplish this mission by being very selective with our suppliers and training our staff to be interactive and responsive to our customers." The combination of good service and great food has helped Misaki maintain an average yearly growth rate of five percent.

Misaki has more than thirty-five employees and often provides the first work experience for young Stocktonians. Misaki also prides itself on being a good community member by promoting the revitalization of downtown Stockton and participating in local charitable events. Misaki hosted a golf tournament to help raise money for a customer who suffered an aneurysm and is a sponsor of the annual Stockton Police Youth Activities boxing event hosted by Steve Salas. Misaki is also a proud sponsor of Arturo and Ana Vera's fundraisers to benefit Art Expression of San Joaquin.

The founders of Misaki are constantly looking for ways to improve the delivery of its food and service. They believe that the continued success of Misaki depends on the long-term relationship it has with its customers and the community. Going forward, Misaki Sushi & Bar will continue to focus on these key items.

Remo and Marion Canepa started their car wash business in 1955. What most people do not know is that their initial venture almost turned into disaster.

They invested in a neighbor's invention designed to wash cars by spraying them with water, soap, and wax as they moved through a wash bay on a conveyor. The equipment was controlled by "electric eyes" that, unfortunately, shorted out when they got wet. When the problem became evident, the inventor disappeared, leaving the Canepas with useless equipment.

Undeterred, Remo and Marion responded to this setback by washing the cars by hand, using steam guns, mitters, and lots of manpower. But Remo knew there had to be a more efficient way of doing this work. So in 1961, they built a second car wash at the downtown location with better, more reliable equipment—push bars, side and top brushes, and quiet blowers for drying. They also opened a detail shop designed to service cars for local auto dealers.

The new car wash soon was running at peak capacity. Building on that success, the Canepas decided to expand and build another car wash on the north side of Stockton. They purchased property at 6230 Pacific Avenue for their new state-of-the-art car wash, and built an auto lube shop next door.

The expansion continued in 1983 with Marion's idea of adding an upscale gift shop that customers could wander through while waiting for their cars. That year, *Gourmet* magazine wrote, "All trends start in California...and at Canepa's Car Wash, customers walk through 1,500 feet of gift shop before reaching the cashier," highlighting this innovative retail strategy.

In 1986, Remo researched the new concept of "touchless car washing" and decided to go "touchless" at the Pacific Avenue location. But despite this new technology, he insisted that every car continue to be sprayed ahead of time, since he believed this extra step would always produce cleaner cars.

Downtown Stockton had lost most of its service stations by 1990. Remo saw this as yet another opportunity. He bought property next to the downtown car wash and built a new 24/7 gas station with thirty-six nozzles, along with a new convenience store. And in 1997 the old equipment at the car wash was replaced with the most modern technology.

Today, the company has three locations and sixty-five employees, many of whom have been with the business for years. Canepa's Car Wash has been voted *The Record*'s "Best of San Joaquin" each year since the list began in 1998.

With the business in its second generation of family ownership, five of the six Canepa children work for the company in various capacities. Although Marion has retired, daughter Rene continues to run the gift shop. And Remo, "The Boss," is now gone—the man who single-handedly managed the business and greeted his customers every day. It now takes four of his sons—Steve, David, Jeff, and Paul—to fill his shoes and continue the legacy started by their parents sixty years ago.

✧

Bottom, left: Remo, Marion and Umberto Canepa, c. 1961. Canepa's motto was, "We can wash any car!"

Bottom, right: Four Generations of hard work and dedication to service, has been a hallmark of Canepa's.

AREA WIDE EXTERMINATORS

✧

Below: Award presentation from the
San Joaquin County Board of Supervisors,
for area wide community involvement.
Left to right, Ed Simas, Doug Wilhoit,
Evelyn Costa, Jim McGaughey, Carole
Smith, George Barber and Bill Souza, 1991.

Bottom: Greater Stockton Chamber
of Commerce, president of the board
installation for Carole Smith and family.

Area Wide Exterminators, a family-owned company, has been in operation for more than thirty-five years. The company provides a wide range of pest control services, including general pest control, termite, and bedbug, bird and bat services, to San Joaquin, Sacramento and Stanislaus Counties and Sacramento.

Area Wide Exterminators was founded in Stockton by the Smith family in 1979. The Smiths' goal was to be self-employed in a service industry that could benefit from their attention to detail and customer service. Al Smith was well respected in the realtor industry and building trades and knew he could make a difference in termite control. He had worked in the trade since 1968. Carole Smith ranked number three in the U.S. for recruitment and sales in the skin and healthcare industry. Since two different licenses are required in California, one for pest and one for termite, Carole obtained the pest control license. Both Al and Carole are now fully licensed and driven to provide each customer a safe and healthy environment.

In the fall of 1979, Al and Carole refinanced their home for $20,000, which they thought would be enough to start a business and provide working capital for the first year. They rented a 1,000 square foot building, bought a truck, and leased a rig from a local home supply and tool rental company for their first three termite jobs. Their original $20,000 investment was gone within the first six weeks of operation, but the Smiths were determined to make their business a success.

Al took care of the termite department. Carole took care of the pest department. Al remembers a skeptical realtor, Bernice Huston, who insisted on going under a house and into the sub-area with Al because she wanted to see the termites and damage noted on his report. She was convinced and became a faithful customer who generated a lot of business for AWE.

Al has come across a variety of snakes, skunks, raccoons and possums under many houses and recalls one incident very clearly and painfully. While backing out of a crawl space, he managed to embed a two-inch sliver of wood in his backside and it took the removal of his pants and a co-worker with a pair of pliers to remove it; and to prove to him it was not a snake bite.

As AWE's reputation for quality service grew, the company expanded into surrounding cities and the company has now grown into a multimillion dollar business annually, employing ten to fifteen employees. The Smiths have learned that the best way to keep their family-owned business strong is to team up with people who share their philosophy.

Area Wide Exterminators' Mission Statement is to make pest control services everywhere else unacceptable for consumers who value quality service, punctuality and personal attention. These are three key areas AWE has focused on as a company and earned them an unmatched reputation in these areas. Their motto is: "AWE—Ensuring health & happiness."

Disappointment Slough

Telephone Cut

PARADISE POINT
ENGINE AND
BOAT REPAIR

✧

*Above: Richard Schwager and
daughter, Lindsay.*

Paradise Point Engine and Boat Repair have provided California Delta boaters with prompt, reliable service for nearly thirty-five years. The company is a factory-authorized Mercury, Mercruiser, Volvo, Nissan, Evinrude, Johnson and OMC repair facility.

A neighbor to Paradise Point Marina in Stockton, the facility provides access to berths for in-water repairs, moorage and boat rentals. With an adjacent haul-out facility, Paradise Point Engine and Boat Repair are equipped for any size repair—from the smallest fishing boat to a fifty foot cruiser. Paradise Point has 10,000 square foot of indoor working space in addition to water access and work berths. Haul-out capability up to fifty feet and/or thirty tons is provided on premises.

Paradise Point was established in 1980 as a partnership between Richard Schwager and Bob Breese, DBA Playmate Resorts. Schwager started in the marine industry at the age of sixteen and now has nearly fifty years of experience in the trade.

The business was run by Schwager, with Breese as a non-working partner, until 1989 when Playmate Resorts was dissolved and the marina was taken over by Seven Crown Resorts. At this point, the business and its assets were purchased by Schwager and he became sole owner. In 1994, Schwager purchased Delta Propeller Repair and brought it under the umbrella of Paradise Point Engine and Boat Repair.

The facility repairs and services all makes of inboard and outboard motors, as well as marine generators. It also provides complete marine transmission rebuild and repair capabilities as well as marine sanitation, electronic and trailer repair. Schwager was one of the first master marine mechanics in the area. He is authorized and trained in all aspects of marine engines and marine electronics and has received many awards, including a Golden Wrench Award for redesigning the gear system in one of Outboard Marine Corporation's outdrives.

A chandlery was opened at the facility in 1984, selling all kinds of boating supplies, paints, varnishes and accessories. In 1985, Schwager incorporated a complete marine electronic repair and installation facility, employing several electronic technicians. Paradise Point became the factory authorized warranty and sales outlet for nearly ninety percent of the marine electronics manufacturers.

Clients of Paradise Point include California Boating and Waterways, San Joaquin County Sheriff's Department, Mariposa County Sheriff, California Department of Fish and Game, California Department of Food and Agriculture, The Port of Stockton and many other government agencies.

Paradise Point employs five technicians in addition to Schwager's daughter, Lindsay, who manages the front end and parts department. Garland Powell, one of the best trained and talented technicians in the industry, is in charge of service.

Whether a client is looking for a brand new motor, major engine repairs, a transmission overhaul, annual maintenance, electronic upgrade or any other marine service, the staff of Paradise Point Engine and Boat Repair is ready to assist with more than eighty years combined experience.

FRED M. LEE FINANCIAL CORPORATION, DBA FINANCIAL DECISIONS

Financial Decisions specializes in the design, installation, modification, administration and recordkeeping of qualified retirement plans. The firm's mission is to assist clients in maximizing the benefits for their employee benefit plans.

Financial Decisions was organized in 1987 by Fred M. Lee, Nancy E. Lee, Kevin E. Mahoney and Michael E. Lee. Fred and Nancy were the original founders and, in the beginning, the four were the only employees.

"It all started with a dial-up modem and a Toshiba laptop," explains Fred. "After working with pension plans for eight years through investment and insurance sales, it only made good sense to offer pension plan administration for our clients. We were associated with The Guardian Life Insurance Company, the number one pension plan provider at the time, and they agreed to provide the beginning software support for accounting and administration."

The firm still owns the Toshiba laptop computer Fred used at home on the kitchen table.

Fred feels the single key event that allowed a startup company like Financial Decisions to begin pension administration services was creation of the DOS operating system and the IBM desktop computer. This new technology provided a company like Financial Decisions with the ability to offer the small business community the ability to provide a 401(k) plan to their employees.

Fred says the most important key individual in the firm's success is his wife, and company CFO, Nancy Lee. "We purchased another small company in 1997 and that put our organization on a higher level," he explains. "Today, with the help of two sons and a cousin, their efforts have again moved us to a higher level of service for our clients."

Financial Decisions has grown from the four original employees to seventeen employees and $2.5 million in annual revenue. The firm services more than 350 company retirement plans and over 400 individual clients. The company is continuing to grow on an average of five to ten percent each year.

Company employees are involved in a number of charitable community activities, including American Cancer Society, Children's Home of Stockton, Stockton Symphony, Red Rhino Orphanage Project, Hospice of San Joaquin, Greater Stockton Emergency Food Bank, and Stockton Shelter for the Homeless. The firm is a member of the Stockton Chamber of Commerce.

Financial Decisions is now transitioning its management from the original founders to the next generation of leaders, including a new CEO Michael E. Lee. The company is partnering with regional firms in the western U.S. to provide services to retirement plans and is moving from local-only services to a more regional presence.

STOCKTON AUTO GLASS

Stockton Auto Glass, a full service glass replacement company, has served the San Joaquin Valley with quality products and services for more than half a century.

The company was opened by Ted Bregman and George Highiet in the summer of 1961. Bregman had begun working for Stockton Auto Wrecking in 1946, following his discharge from the U.S. Navy, where he had served during World War II. When the auto wrecking company closed, Ted was approached by his close friend, George Highiet, and they founded Stockton Auto Glass. The new business, which focused strictly on auto glass, was located at 324 North Wilson Way, across the street from its current location at 345 Wilson Way.

Ted and George worked long hours, six days a week, and developed a reputation for quality work and service. Ted's sister and brother-in-law operated an auto glass company in Sacramento and helped mentor Ted in his new business.

In 1974, Stockton Auto Glass opened a second location at 1110 South Cherokee Lane in Lodi, which soon became a successful venture.

In 1980, Ted's son-in-law, Clint Harless, joined the business after a career in the savings and loan business. Under his direction the company continued to grow by adding new locations and embracing the emerging technology that was revolutionizing the industry. Between 1987 and 1993, additional locations were opened in Stockton and Tracy, and a new corporation was formed in Sacramento called Sacramento Auto Glass & Mirror.

In 1998 the company continued to expand by purchasing Quick's Glass Service, a long-established company in Marysville. This purchase was instrumental in the future growth of the company because it introduced the residential and commercial glass business to what had been only auto glass.

Today, the company operates under the parent name of Quick's Glass Service, with a dba of Stockton Auto Glass and the dba of Sacramento Auto Glass & Mirror. A second corporation has been created for the residential business and it operates under the name of Quick's Residential Glass Installation, Inc.

Stockton Auto Glass has been recognized as the "Best in Auto Glass Replacement' in San Joaquin County for six years in a row by the *Stockton Record.*

The two companies have a total of thirty-five full-time and two part-time employees, including a number of long-time employees. Kent Solomon has been with the company since 1978, Rose Benjamin since 1979, Clint Harless since 1980, Terry Jovan since 1990, and Henry Peralta since 1995. Mario Saenz, who came in 1987, is the first and only manager of the Sacramento store. The average tenure of all employees is eighteen years.

Stockton Auto Glass and its employees are very active in the community, contributing to such organizations as the Greater Stockton Chamber of Commerce, San Joaquin County Hispanic Chamber of Commerce, Better Business Bureau, Child Abuse Prevention Council, March of Dimes, and Stockton Youth Soccer Association.

WALLACE & CO., INC. DBA PREMIER STAFFING

✧

Left: The dedicated professionals of Premier Staffing, 2015.

Right: Jennifer Wallace, president of Premier Staffing.

Premier Staffing brings people and companies together by providing excellence in temporary labor, temp-to-hire and direct placements. The firm also provides recruiting and payroll services.

The company was founded in 1977 and has been under the current ownership since 2011. Premier Staffing is proud to be the largest female-owned business in the San Joaquin Valley. The company president, Jennifer Wallace, has been with Premier Staffing for more than fifteen years.

Premier Staffing draws on a combined experience of sixty-five years in human resources issues, and takes the time needed to study each client's operations and learn their business needs. Candidates are thoroughly checked and evaluated to determine skill levels and attitudes. Because of its extensive experience in recruiting, Premier Staffing maintains an inventory of highly qualified applicants and is able to fill a wide range of client needs quickly and accurately. All employees are insured and bonded and candidates undergo a thorough interview process and evaluation that includes drug testing, employment verification, testing of computer skills, and a criminal background

check. Businesses have learned they can depend on Premier Staffing to recommend the best individual for the job.

Job seekers appreciate the fact that Premier Staffing has thirty years' experience in placing people in every field imaginable. The firm has established close relationships with many of the finest companies in the area who look to Premier Staffing for qualified and eager employees.

Premier Staffing has available positions in a wide range of businesses, including accounting, administrative, assembly, banking, bookkeeping, clerical, customer service, human resources, management, medical, technical, and warehousing.

Premier Staffing welcomes those who are looking for a permanent, temporary, or temp-to-hire position. Contributions are made on the employee's behalf to unemployment insurance, Medicare, Social Security and worker's compensation insurance. Temporary employees have an opportunity to participate in health benefits.

Premier Staffing, which has more than 700 employees, has shown strong growth and averaged a forty percent increase each year under the leadership of Jennifer Wallace. The firm is located at 8807 Thornton Road, Suite L in Stockton, California, 95209, and at www.premierstaffingstockton.com.

The company and its employees contribute time and money to a variety of organizations, including the American Cancer Society, March of Dimes, San Joaquin Housing Authority, and all area Chambers of Commerce.

Whether you are a company seeking an employee, or an individual searching for a job, you can depend on Premier Staffing for the most complete professional services available.

"We Create Safe Communities" is the guiding philosophy behind success at Delta Protective Services, a local private security company providing uniformed officers, private investigations and security training. The firm is guided by its core values of personal responsibility, honesty, excellence and commitment.

Delta Protective Services (DPS) began as a family business in 1993 when Lawrence and Kimberley Borgens started a private security company. Pairing Kimberley's police academy training and Lawrence's United State Marine Corps experience made a perfect match! Prior training in executive protection also gave Lawrence the experience necessary to work with the prestigious celebrity protection firm Gavin de Becker, Inc., as a bodyguard for celebrities, public figures, entertainers and executives in Los Angeles. Kimberley and Lawrence's teamwork and diversity provide the foundation for a thriving business.

The Borgens family started DPS from their home office, gaining their first client, Pacific Avenue Bowl. Later when they found that businesses desired vehicle patrol, the family car was mounted with magnetic signs and a marked vehicle patrol service was born.

As the firm grew, the Borgens' added employees and moved DPS from their home into the Chamber of Commerce Business Incubator, which provided needed space and helped the fledgling business grow. In 2002, Lawrence took an opportunity to work for a month providing armed security during the winter Olympics in Salt Lake City while Kimberley stayed to manage the business and their growing family. Kimberley provides what Lawrence calls an uncanny ability to read people's character.

DPS provides clients with armed and unarmed uniformed security officers, marked vehicle patrol, alarm response and private investigation. Officers are available on a permanent or temporary basis to meet the client's needs and are supervised by highly trained managers while the firms fully-staffed twenty-four hour dispatch center provides client support services. Communication is a key to DPS's success so they utilize cutting-edge technology for the benefit of both clients and staff. DPS is an established leader in special event security with years of experience managing venues like the Lodi Grape Festival, Asparagus Festival and the San Joaquin County Fair.

DPS continues to grow as a professional local firm that is well respected and recognized by the business community. In 1996 the Borgens' were awarded Small Business Persons of the Year by the Greater Stockton Chamber of Commerce. In 2006, they received a similar award from the U.S. Small Business Administration Sacramento District Office.

Their commitment to community involvement is evident with current and past involvement in many local and national civic organizations including resident of Stockton Host LIONS Club, the Greater Stockton Chamber of Commerce board, Executive Security International Alumni Association board, and volunteering at the Business Leadership Summit.

Future plans include expanding DPS from a regional company to a statewide provider of contract private security services from their home base in Stockton, California.

To learn more about Delta Protective Services, visit www.deltaprotectiveservices.com.

DELTA PROTECTIVE SERVICES

✧

Left: Lawrence and Kimberley Borgens.

YASOO YANI RESTAURANT

✧

Above: The dining room still retains the same charm it had when the restaurant opened in 1975.

Below: In the kitchen at Yasoo Yani. Shown are (from left to right) Jim Aftias, Nickolas Aftias, Rosana and Travis.

Residents of the San Joaquin Valley know where to go for an authentic taste of Greece— Yasoo Yani Restaurant at 325 East Main Street in Stockton.

At Yasoo Yani, hungry diners select from a delicious array of menu items, including the best gyros in the Valley, chicken souvlaki salads, Greek salads, falafel, grilled chicken breast and cold ham and cheese. The family-owned Greek/American restaurant is open for breakfast, lunch and dinner and also offers catering and delivery services.

The restaurant was started in 1975 by Mike Frangidikis and Nick Aftias. "When we started, the place was only half the size it is now, but we soon had lines out the door because we were offering the only Greek food in town at that time," Aftias remembers. "The kitchen was visible from the sidewalk and on Fridays we would barbeque a whole lamb on the sidewalk. The smell of our food cooking drove people crazy and they would come in just to see what smelled so delicious.

"The whole family helped build the shop, even doing the stripping and painting, sanding and installation of equipment," Aftias explains. "Everyone was involved—mom; dad; aunts and uncles; my brother, Leo; my sister Maria; and several cousins. It was a true family operation."

Yasoo Yani was so well received that it was expanded from fifty seats to about 125 in 1982, but the 3,200 square foot restaurant still retains the same charm it had in the early 1970s.

The restaurant is still a family affair with Aftias' children working at various jobs, along with aunts and uncles and a number of long-time employees who have become like family. Family members are active in their church and volunteer their services for the annual Greek Food Festival.

"We've been through a lot since the beginning and I hope to someday see the business continue to do well with my kids," says Aftias.

THE MARKETPLACE

PHOTOGRAPH COURTESY OF VISIT STOCKTON.

FACING EAST TOWARDS DOWNTOWN STOCKTON. AERIAL PHOTOGRAPH COURTESY OF VISIT STOCKTON.

STOCKTON'S GOLDEN ERA

BUILDING A GREATER STOCKTON

Stockton's real estate developers,

construction companies, heavy industries,

and manufacturers provide

the economic foundation of the city

SPECIAL THANKS TO

Cal Sheets

Port of Stockton

It is virtually impossible to overemphasize the importance of the Port of Stockton to the economy of the San Joaquin Valley. In 2014 alone, 230 commercial vessels tied up at the Port of Stockton, providing an enormous boost to the Delta business climate and promising a bright future for the eighty-two year old Port.

Just consider these hard numbers: the Port supports more than 4,500 jobs in the San Joaquin area, generating about $180 million annually in salaries and benefits. More than $1.5 billion in cargo crosses the Port's docks each year, and 2,300,000 tons of American products are exported each year. The Port contributes more than $5 million in taxes each year, helping support important services provided by San Joaquin County and the City of Stockton. Private sector investments in the Port of Stockton exceeded $2 billion over the last five years.

Without doubt the Port of Stockton is the engine that drives much of the Delta economy.

The Port of Stockton opened in 1933 as the first major inland seaport in California. However, traffic on the San Joaquin River had been a part of Stockton's history since 1846, when the first cargo boat sailed down the river. John Doak established the first ferry service on the river in 1848, and the sloop *Maria* visited Stockton that same year. In 1949, Doak brought lumber from San Francisco to Stockton and began a building supply business. By the 1850s the port had become a center of shipping and the supply center for the goldfields.

According to *Harbor of the Heartlands*, a history of the Port of Stockton by Nicholas Hardeman, the trickle of boat traffic to the embarcadero on the San Joaquin surged to flood stage during the economic boom created by the gold rush.

"Sailboats and steam boats fought for passage and dock space," Hardeman wrote. "Only one rule of the road was recognized: 'The Devil take the hindmost.' Skippers such as Doak with his cargo of Oregon lumber in 1949, when caught between too much current and too little wind, warped their way laboriously up the San Joaquin by tying ropes to trees and hauling to the cadence of a 'heave-ho' chant. Passengers queued up in long lines at San Francisco, bound for the inland head of navigation at Stockton and thence to the gold mines. Steamboats maneuvered and raced for position in the crooked channel. Boilers exploded, causing ships to sink and carrying passengers to a watery grave."

The gold rush boom became a bust by the mid-1850s, leaving Stockton businessmen in a state of shock. The more enterprising business leaders hoped to replace gold shipments with cargos of wheat grown in the rich delta soil. However, the hydraulic mining debris left from the mines, along with erosion from the era's primitive farming techniques created silting on the river at an alarming rate.

Who first conceived the notion of dredging a ship canal to Stockton is not definitely known, but the possibility was being widely discussed by 1869. Many thought it was a foolish idea and newspapers published satirical articles critical of a ship canal. Proponents, however, claimed that the ship canal would force railroads to converge on Stockton, making the city the leading commercial center of the entire valley.

William Henry Knight, a San Francisco businessman, was among the first to appreciate the benefits of a ship canal. Gradually, a number of prominent men from Stockton and San Francisco also became interested in the idea. A group of twenty-one investors joined Knight to form the Stockton Ship Canal Company in May 1870. The new company proposed to acquire rights of way, excavate a deep-water ship canal, build terminal facilities, provide towage service and a shipyard, and derive revenue from these services through towage, tonnage, tolls, and passenger fares. The company also planned to erect dikes and levees to reclaim agricultural land and to construct toll roads through the restored areas.

The estimated cost of such a massive undertaking was staggering. It soon became evident that the cost of dredging the channel and building the necessary dams would exceed $1 million, a tremendous amount

for that era. Construction of terminal facilities would add another $500,000 to the cost.

Hometown taxpayers were reluctant to invest in the risky scheme—and when potential stockholders failed to come forward, the Stockton Ship Canal Company looked for alternate financing sources. A 'stupendous lottery' scheme surfaced briefly, but the idea was dropped when it was pointed out that the state would probably withdraw the company's franchise.

The final blow came in the summer of 1871 when a severe drought sharply cut production of wheat, the San Joaquin Valley's chief exportable crop. The canal project lapsed and the company was eventually dissolved.

Several other plans for developing a port on the San Joaquin surfaced in the late 1800s, but despite heavy demands for river usage and poor navigating conditions on the river, the U.S. Congress showed little interest in helping improve conditions, and local and state support was inadequate.

This attitude began to change in 1906 when U.S. Representative Joseph Ransdell, a powerful member of the House Committee on Rivers and Harbors, toured the area and encouraged local officials to push Congress for the funds needed to construct a deepwater port. Stockton's Chamber of Commerce was tireless in its efforts to bring the city's case for improved river navigation to the attention of the federal government. However, it would be nearly twenty years before incremental improvements led to a full-scale effort to

construct a deepwater port at Stockton. As author Hardeman points out in his history of the port, "The physical and political log jam of six decades was at last to be broken. But, between the time of clearance for the big river boats in 1913 and final approval of plans for a harbor of ocean depth in 1927, there would be, politically speaking, much water over the dam and the Delta."

An economic report commissioned by the Stockton Chamber of Commerce in 1924 convinced engineers for the federal government that a deepwater channel to the inland city was justified. Meanwhile, by a vote of more than twelve-to-one, Stockton voters approved a $3 million bond issue to help make the port a reality. This was followed by a visit to the city by Secretary of Commerce Herbert Hoover, who would later serve as the nation's thirty-first president. After touring the site of the proposed project and talking with local officials, Hoover declared that 'the time has arrived' for construction of a deepwater port.

The first contract for dredging the Stockton deep port channel was awarded in 1930, sparking a flurry of construction activity. The clamshell, chain bucket ladder, dragline or drag buckets, hydraulic dredges and other specialized machines were used to remove dirt from the channel floor and create the Stockton Deep Water Channel.

In 1930, California Governor Frank Merriman broke ground for the Port of Stockton as crowds cheered and newsreel cameras recorded the historic event. With the ground broken, construction moved quickly. A belt line railroad was constructed and work began on the first dock and transit shed. The deepwater channel dredging was completed to a depth of twenty-six feet.

In February 1933, in what has been called the worst month of the worst year of the nation's worst economic depression, the Port of Stockton was officially opened. Soup kitchens and bread lines cluttered a country that was experiencing a twenty-five percent unemployment rate, but for the inland harbor town on the San Joaquin, the picture was noticeably brighter and the new Port was soon operating in the black.

The first ocean going vessel to dock at the Port was the *Daisy Gray*, carrying 75,000 board feet of lumber from the Pacific Northwest. The Port soon outgrew its original facilities and, between 1933 and 1940, there were a number of improvements, including construction of three wharves with transit sheds, additional brick warehouses, the first grain terminal, and construction of a cotton compress. In 1935 plans were approved to increase the depth of the channel to thirty-five feet.

The outbreak of World War II brought a second stage of development to the Port of Stockton. Most of the Port, along with 257 additional acres leased by the U.S. Army, became the Stockton Sub-Depot of the Benicia Arsenal. New wharves were built to accommodate thirteen vessels.

A third stage of development began with the end of the war. An oil terminal was built in 1946, the beginning of the bulk cargo business that propels the Port today. A bulk terminal was built in 1952.

By the 1950s the Port of Stockton had outgrown its historic role of exporting agricultural products and had begun playing an active role in importing, warehousing and distributing manufactured goods.

To accommodate these changes, congressional support was sought to deepen the channel to thirty-five feet. Additional warehouses and transit sheds were constructed, along with an additional transit shed and a terminal for handling iron ore. By the end of the decade, the Port would have a new $1 million dry bulk handling and ship loading facility. Five mooring platforms were constructed, the original ore loading conveyor was replaced, and a bulk wine facility and terminal for molasses were completed. In 1956 a new records system was instituted for the receipt, storage and distribution of all Port cargo.

By the end of the decade of the 1950s, the Port of Stockton had become a major economic force in the San Joaquin Valley.

The 'container revolution' of the 1960s led to the Port's fourth stage of development. While other ports rushed into the container business, the Port of Stockton made a calculated decision to create modern maritime facilities for all other types of cargo. The Port would later add the latest container facilities but the decision to handle all types of cargo greatly expanded the Port's appeal. By the early 1960s, the Port was handling 3 million tons of cargo annually.

Construction of a 750,000 square foot warehouse for distribution of soft and hard goods in 1972 soon became the major full-service distribution point for retail giant JCPenney. An estimated seventy percent of the Port's employees were involved in serving the Penney facility.

The Arab Oil Embargo of the 1978-1979 led to a large increase in coal exports from the Port, generating profits that were reinvested to upgrade and replace outdated facilities.

The Port took another big step forward in 1980 when the California Water Resources Board approved a project to deepen the channel to thirty-seven feet. The dredging began in 1982 and, in May of 1987, the Port and the City of Stockton celebrated the deepening of the Port with a mammoth two-day celebration. With a depth of thirty-seven feet even at low tide, large ocean-going vessels were able to use the Port's modern facilities. The Port's motto became, '37 Feet to the Sea'.

The Port's economic importance was enhanced in the 1990s when the City of Stockton created an Enterprise Zone that included the Port and the airport. The Port was later designated Foreign Trade Zone 231, a designation that removed many tax and duty costs.

In 2000 the Port acquired Rough and Ready Island, a former Navy base. This 1,400 acre tract became the West Complex and has played an important role in increasing the export of California agricultural products.

After more than eight decades of continuous improvement, the Port of Stockton now provides first-class warehouse storage and handling facilities and equipment to handle bulk, break-bulk, and containerized cargoes by land or sea. Situated in the hub of four major freeways, two transcontinental railroads, an international waterway and a regional airport, the Port is centrally located to provide optimum service for ships and storage of product and cargo.

In many ways, 2014 was the Port's best year ever, setting records for ship calls, and rail activity. The Port also handled more than 4.1 million metric tons of cargo in 2014, the highest level in ten years and a thirty-six percent increase over the previous year. This activity has led to revenue increasing to $54 million in 2014—another all-time record—and more than 300 jobs added in just a single year. Between the improving economy and new projects, the future looks even better.

Activity at the Port has long been a reliable economic barometer for the San Joaquin Valley. Commenting on the 230 commercial vessels that tied up at the Port in 2014, Director Richard Aschieris said, "Ports usually are the forefront of an economic recovery or decline. Things happen here first, whether it's good or bad."

"The good news is that things are better here. We're starting to see construction-oriented materials for the first time in quite a while. Our steel is increasing significantly and, in December 2014, we had the first cement imports that the Port has seen in five years."

Port officials can tick off a growing list of assets: its strategic location, the Port's ability to build facilities on its 4,000 acres, the availability of seven million square feet of covered storage, as well as the deepwater channel which provides easy access for the big ships and the goods they carry to port.

In the summer of 2014, the Port took the first steps toward adding 4.5 miles of new track. "We'd like to improve our rail facilities here," Aschieris said. "In my opinion, rail is just as important to a Port as a dock, and the additional track will enable us to handle more business."

Despite the Port's long and successful history, the presence of a deepwater port in Stockton still comes as a surprise to some. "It's the best-kept secret not only locally, but also statewide and nationally," remarks Douglass Wilhoit, Jr., CEO of the Greater Stockton Chamber of Commerce. Wilhoit estimates that fifteen to twenty percent of the Chamber's member businesses have ties to the Port.

In an effort to make people more aware of the Port and its tremendous impact on the region's economy, port officials are using new ways to connect with people in and around Stockton. The Port is active on Facebook, Twitter and Pinterest. The Port's website includes webcams that allow visitors to watch shipping activity.

One of the most important roles the Port has played over the years has been in the building of family-wage jobs for a community needing job growth. The Port's goal of creating business opportunities within its boundaries is achieved daily. These businesses have the capability of creating the types of jobs a family can thrive on and enjoy the great lifestyle possible in Stockton and San Joaquin County. The Port has long been a significant player in the community and, in the future, it will carry on as it always has...with the purpose for which it was originally conceived: To create jobs and facilitate commerce in California's heartland.

PDM STEEL SERVICE CENTERS, INC.

PDM Steel Service Centers, Inc., has been known for prompt, reliable service since 1954. The company processes and distributes its extensive steel inventory throughout the western United States and is headquartered and has two locations in Stockton, California. Other PDM service centers and sales offices are located in Santa Clara, Fresno, and Roseville, California; Denver and Grand Junction, Colorado; Boise, Idaho; Las Vegas and Sparks, Nevada; Spanish Fork, Utah; and Woodland, Washington.

PDM Steel's beginnings go back more than a century to an engineering and construction company that began in Pittsburg, Pennsylvania, and Des Moines, Iowa. That firm, Pittsburgh-Des Moines Steel Company, was founded in 1892.

PDM entered the steel processing and distribution industry in 1954 with the acquisition of the Proctor-James Steel Company in San Jose, California. A year later, Kyle & Company, with facilities in Stockton, Fresno, and Sacramento, was purchased. With four strategically located service centers, PDM was able to service customers throughout Central and Northern California.

In 1968 the existing operations were greatly augmented by the completion of their large, newly designed and built state-of-the-art service center in Stockton. This facility included the most modern materials handling and processing equipment available.

To provide the greatest possible service and selection to its customers, PDM adopted the "Common Inventory Concept," which provided customers access to a vast array of products and services like no other in the region without the burden of carrying duplicate specialized inventories in each location. Using this concept, the new Stockton facility became the geographical hub of a service wheel with spokes to all locations. An "Interplant Transfer System" was developed to quickly move inventory between service centers, providing short lead-time delivery of most items regardless of the inventory location. This concept proved to be so successful that future PDM operations were either built or expanded to provide other "hub-type" distribution facilities.

As a result of PDM's success, a new service center was established in Sparks, Nevada, in 1974. In 1977 another new service center was established in Spanish Fork, Utah. This location has since been expanded several times and now serves as the hub for the Intermountain Region.

In 1997, PDM purchased General Steel, a carbon steel service center in Vancouver, Washington. This operation was relocated to a newly-designed and built facility in Woodland, Washington, in 1999 and became the hub for the Pacific Northwest.

PDM began servicing the Las Vegas and Southern Nevada market in 2003. In 2008 the Las Vegas operation moved into a newly built facility. This operation houses a complete product offering with a multitude of processing capabilities and now services Southern Nevada, Southern Utah, and Northern Arizona.

A sales office and transfer yard was also established in Grand Junction, Colorado, in 2008 to aid company expansion into Colorado and New Mexico. That same year, PDM acquired the Engbar Pipe and Steel Company in Denver, Colorado, expanding service and product offerings throughout the entire state of Colorado and parts of Wyoming.

As customers' needs and demand for pre-production, tight tolerance processing grew, PDM responded by investing in new and automated highly specialized processing equipment. The company brought in the latest automatic saws with computer controlled feed-in and feed-out conveyors, enhanced plate burning, including high definition plasma and laser cutting. Other enhancements have included plate machining centers, press baking, rotary beam splitting and cambering.

The Service Center division of PDM was acquired in 2001 by Reliance Steel & Aluminum Co. of Los Angeles, the largest metals service center company in North America. PDM Steel Service Centers, Inc., now operates as a wholly owned subsidiary of Reliance.

A major change also occurred in 2013 when PDM acquired the Stockton, California, location of another Reliance subsidiary, known as the Ferralloy Western Division and wholly owned Specialty Steel Service, located in Roseville, California. These companies specialize in flat rolled steel product distribution, and expanded PDM into coil slitting, greater cut-to-length capabilities, and a variety of additional product offerings. Now known as Ferralloy PDM Steel Service, this facility is one of the largest flat rolled facilities in the western U.S.

PDM Steel attributes the firm's growth and success to its strong emphasis on customer service. PDM does everything it can to provide customers with innovative product solutions, not just steel. They operate their own fleet of trucks, deliver material up to eighty feet long, up to 80,000 pounds, and offer vast processing capabilities, expansive inventories, one-stop shopping, and unparalleled customer service.

Whether it is a delivery at a remote mine forty miles down a dirt road in the middle of Nevada, a power plant off the beaten path in Eastern Washington, or a high-tech manufacturer in San Francisco, California, most customer orders are delivered no later than the next day.

PDM Steel has come a long way since its founding in 1954. Currently, PDM employs more than 400 people with twelve locations including 148 in Stockton and is the premier structural steel supplier in the west.

The company attributes its success and continued growth to its focus and commitment to its customers providing steel service "When and Where You Need It!"

M. CALOSSO & SON, INC.

A family-owned business now in its third generation, M. Calosso & Son was established in 1924 by Michael Calosso. "He migrated from Italy through Ellis Island. His job for the first few years was as a teller and driver for A. P. Giannini, the legendary Bank of America founder," explains Mike Calosso, a grandson who now runs the business. "My grandfather was an engineer from the old country so he built his own practice in San Francisco. However, the weather didn't agree with him and with the help of Giannini, he obtained fifty acres and moved to Stockton."

Calosso began farming the acreage but had to take a ferry to San Francisco to get the materials for his produce boxes. He began providing boxes for his neighbors as well, and in 1924 he decided to give up farming and become a box manufacturer.

✧

Above: John Calosso, 1928.

Right: Left to right, Nona (grandmother in Italian), Uncle John and Aunt Nina at the M. Calosso Box Plant, 1924.

Below: The original M. Calosso Box Plant in 1924.

The ability to change with the times has enabled M. Calosso & Son, Inc., to survive and prosper for ninety years. The Stockton-based firm manufactures and distributes packaging for asparagus, cherries, bell peppers, peaches, apples, potatoes, squash, eggplants, walnuts and other products. Calosso also produces custom-made boxes and displays for wineries.

In the early days, Calosso traveled among the numerous camps that were set up where the produce was being harvested and packed. In addition to providing boxes for the produce, he supplied the camp workers with forks, knives, spoons and other essentials.

Michael ran the company until 1958, when his son, John, took over the operation. John operated the company until 1978, when he was succeeded by his son, Mike.

Mike literally grew up in the business and has been with the company all his life. "I was brought up the old way. I played sports,

I came to work Friday after school and worked Saturday and Sunday, if need be," he explains.

Mike recalls that his father refused to allow him to answer the phone when he started with the company. "My first job was running a box machine," he explains. "The second year I worked on a truck but my dad still refused to let me answer the phone. When I asked him why, he replied, 'When you're operating the box machine you know how many boxes you can manufacture in an hour and you've got to figure why someone is not producing the same amount. When you're on the trucks, you get to know your customer's needs and the time frame you have to meet those needs. When you answer the phone you learn nothing.' It was an old-fashioned lesson."

Mike joined the family business full-time after graduating from Sacramento State. When the company was incorporated in 1967, his dad became president, his mother was vice president and Mike was secretary-treasurer. He still serves in that capacity, with his wife, Susan Gay Calosso, serving as president, son-in-law Jeff King and David Heinze serving as vice presidents. Jeff has been with the company for fifteen years and David for thirty-four years.

Growth was slow but steady in the early days but business began to pick up when the operation was moved to a new location in Stockton in 1952. The firm's original building on East Miner Avenue was 10,500 square feet. The company now operates from a 57,000 square foot facility situated on three acres. The company also leases a 140,000 square foot space across the street.

Calosso feels the key to the company's survival for nine decades is a willingness to change with a constantly evolving produce supply industry. Originally, the company manufactured and supplied wooden boxes for many farmers and retailers. Over time, there was a massive shift from wooden crates to cardboard containers. This meant the company had to overhaul its entire mode of business, shifting from wooden boxes that were nailed or stapled together to corrugated boxes that are glued together.

This revolutionary change meant the installation of new types of equipment.

The company has also adapted to the demands of the marketplace. Calosso now provides plastic clamshell containers and bags for vegetables and fruit for large retailers such as Costco and Walmart. The cherry and walnut markets have expanded in recent years, while markets for apples and asparagus have fallen off. The ability to adapt to these changes has allowed the company to increase its market share. The only wood crates manufactured by the company today are specialty boxes.

M. Calosso & Son, Inc. has 31 permanent employees, although the figure increases to 55 to 60 during cherry season. The company's containers are distributed to a customer base of about 300 throughout Northern California.

"We're doing very well," says Mike. "We've moved with the times and changed with the times. My son-in-law, Jeff King, and David Heinze, are bringing in new business every year and they are the driving force now. We just want to maintain our growth every single year, not growth by leaps-and-bounds, just steady growth. I think we've been successful because we're determined to provide a service that other companies can't give."

✧

M. Calosso & Sons Plant, 2005

COLLINS ELECTRICAL COMPANY, INC.

Above: Left to right, "The Original Three," John Nomellini, Henning Thompson and Gus Sanguinetti calling out bids for the day.

Top, right: Vern Gomes laying out the electrical installations at the San Luis Reservoir Dam, 1953.

It was Christmas 1927 and the founder of Collins Electrical Company, Willard J. Collins, owed one of his employees, Gus Sanguinetti, $2,400 in back wages. Collins, short of cash, offered Gus half of the business to square the account. Gus quickly accepted the deal.

A year went by and Collins once again owed Gus several thousand dollars in back wages. Gus took the other half of the business in lieu of the back pay and became sole owner on January 1, 1929. The acquisition included the business as well as an Overland touring car, a Model T Ford and a Dodge truck.

A colorful character who also played in popular bands of the day, Gus' motto was 'Work Hard—Play Hard.' This attitude has survived the decades and remains part of the company culture today.

The great economic depression of the 1930s began shortly after Gus took over the business but he somehow managed to survive the hard times and keep the business going.

John Nomellini, Gus' brother-in-law, and Henning Thompson joined the firm around 1937 and became part owners of the business. Gus told them both shortly before they shipped out for military duty in that he would make them his partners when they returned from the service. True to his word, John and Henning became Gus' partners in the business. John's role became the field production superintendent and Henning ran the office as the company's accountant. In those days, people came to work in the dark and left long after dark on weekdays and then returned on Saturday morning for an additional half day of work. Nomellini's motto was "sempre avanti" or "always forward" and the work ethic was strong at Collins Electric. Back in the 1940s and 1950s, Collins Electric's workforce included over 1,000 active electricians, operated out of seven branch locations and had the reputation of being the best electrical subcontractor in the state of California. In addition to the original three, other past Collins owners include Carrol Keys, Frank Truco, Glen Lively, Bill Evans, Joe Bacigaloupi and Gene Gini. At present the company is owned by Gene, Dianne, Kevin and Brian Gini. Craig Gini is vice president.

By yesterday's standards the company would appear to have scaled back, however, if you look at how technology continues to change electrical installations, what you will find is you do not need as many electricians today as were needed back then to complete the same work. Methods of installation, tooling, and planning have reduced the man-hours it takes to build a construction project today.

Eighty-eight years after Sanguinetti took his first share of the business and started to grow that business by partnering with Nomellini and Thompson, Collins Electrical Company, Inc. (CECI) remains today one of the leading electrical construction and engineering firms in Northern California with annual revenues exceeding $100 million.

CECI is involved in all facets of electrical contracting on hospital, educational, commercial, entertainment, energy and infrastructure projects throughout the Central Valley and Bay Area. Over the past decade, CECI has

excelled in the area of Pre-con design-build and design-assist services and has established a reputation as a premiere specialty contractor known for quality proposals, conceptual pricing, expertise, and excellence in fast-track, Pre-con design-build delivery methods.

CECI also maintains a service and maintenance department, organized specifically for small, competitive tenant improvements and responsive emergency service needs on all types of commercial and industrial applications.

The company believes that communication is crucial to the success of any project, from conception through completion. Collins works with owners, general contractors, architects, public entities, consultants and subcontractors to produce a superior finished product at a fair market value.

Some of the company's more recent projects are the Stockton Waterfront Arena-Hotel-Baseball Field, St. Joseph's Hospital, Pacific Ethanol, Amazon Distribution Center (Patterson), Kaiser Hospital (Modesto), and various State of California courthouses throughout the Central Valley.

With offices in Stockton, West Sacramento, Dublin, Modesto, Fresno and Marina, Collins employs an office and field staff of more than 300 consisting of a solid workforce in the field and a superior internal staff dedicated to the company.

The company supports multiple civic and community activities either through corporate donations or through encouragement and support of its employee's participation. Organizations consistently supported include the American Cancer Society, Children's Home of Stockton, Bishop's Awards and SEEDS program, Lincoln High School's Window on Your Future and Sober Grad Nights, the Chinatown Music & Arts Festival in Fresno, the Dominican Hospital Foundation in Santa Cruz and the Greater Stockton Chamber of Commerce.

For more than eight decades, the growth and success of Collins Electrical Company, Inc., can be attributed to the company's simple mission statement: To be the best electrical contractor and engineering firm in our field; experienced, responsive, competitive and on-schedule. These qualities translate into excellence and trust...the same trademarks that have carried our reputation since 1928.

To learn more about CECI, check their website at www.collinselectric.com.

✧

Above: TID Almond II Power Plant—280 megawatt power plant in Modesto, California.

Below: Stockton Sports Arena—downtown Stockton Waterfront.

A. G. SPANOS COMPANIES

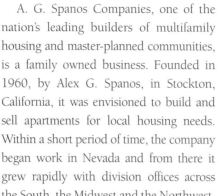

A. G. Spanos Companies, one of the nation's leading builders of multifamily housing and master-planned communities, is a family owned business. Founded in 1960, by Alex G. Spanos, in Stockton, California, it was envisioned to build and sell apartments for local housing needs. Within a short period of time, the company began work in Nevada and from there it grew rapidly with division offices across the South, the Midwest and the Northwest.

Today, A. G. Spanos Companies, still headquartered in Stockton, have built more than 130,000 apartment units and over two million square feet of office space. Operating on the principles of its founder, the company has earned a reputation for integrity, high quality, and excellence.

In 2005, Alex turned over operation of the business to his two sons, Dean and Michael, who are dedicated to continuing their father's legacy. His two daughters, Dea Spanos Berberian and Alexis Spanos Ruhl are also members of the company board.

The change in leadership marked the beginning of a new era in the firm's growth and direction. In 2008 the company began exploring urban infill opportunities and recently completed a nationally recognized apartment project in Denver. The company also continued to enhance and expand on its environmental preservation and sustainability initiatives including the AGS Conservation and Resource Management Plan, which promotes educational programs for Kindergarten through

twelfth grade; the Shin Kee Wetlands & Habitat Restoration Project on the eastern edge of the Sacramento/San Joaquin Delta, which provides habitat suitable for the federally-protected Giant Garter Snake and the Delta smelt; and the Preserve in Stockton, which represents a first-of-its kind opportunity in central California to master plan a community based on the principles of One Planet Living. The project is envisioned as a model for an environmentally sensitive, economically sustainable, whole community development, continuing the Spanos legacy of market leading development.

More recently, a joint initiative by the Spanos organization and the County of San Joaquin to promote renewed economic activity resulted in the designation of the County by the State of California as an innovation hub. iHub San Joaquin is one of sixteen such innovation hubs in the state directed to help drive regional economic growth and job creation.

The Spanos family is also involved in the National Football League. In 1984, Alex achieved yet another lifelong dream by purchasing the San Diego Chargers. The team is managed by his son Dean, who serves as chairman and president.

In 2002, the autobiography of Alex, *Sharing the Wealth—My Story* was published. The book is a moving recollection of his humble beginnings, his road to success and advice on how to achieve one's dreams. In his autobiography, Alex wrote, "I grew up with a feeling of responsibility, not only to my immediate family, but also for my country, my city, my world." This philosophy has found confirmation in the many charitable and civic contributions made by the Spanos family to the Stockton community, the state and the nation.

✦

Above: A. G. Spanos Companies'
headquarters in Stockton.

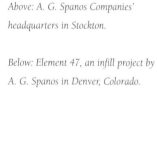

Below: Element 47, an infill project by
A. G. Spanos in Denver, Colorado.

GOLDEN STATE LUMBER

Golden State Lumber has provided quality building products across Northern California since 1954. Golden State is prepared to provide all the building products needed from foundation to rooftop. Whether you are building a room addition, custom home, multifamily development or commercial or industrial project, Golden State has the lumber, hardware, milling services and expertise to get the job done on-time and under-budget.

"What sets us apart is the individual service we provide," says Ralph Panttaja, the company's vice president. "Our goal is to provide our customers with the materials and technology needed to work faster, more efficiently and within budget. When our customers succeed, we succeed."

The family-owned company was founded sixty years ago when Glen Nobmann purchased a lumber yard in Richmond. His son, Lee, led an expansion of the company that made it one of the largest building products suppliers in the region. Lee's daughter, Jessica Scerri, now serves as the firm's CEO.

Golden State moved to Stockton in 2003 and also has locations in San Rafael, Brisbane, and Newark. The company employs about 350 people, including eighty-five in Stockton.

The sixty acre state-of-the-art facility at 3033 South Airport Way in Stockton provides customers with an expert sales staff, optimizer saw, milling services, dry timbers in stock, multiple lines of engineered lumber and a design team to help engineer any project.

In addition to lumber and plywood, Golden State offers a wide selection of tools, engineered wood, hardware and fasteners, doors and windows, decking and fencing, insulation, waterproofing, exterior siding, interior moulding and trim.

Golden State has the ability to keep projects 'green' and LEED certified by matching the customers design to the latest environment-friendly products.

"We take pride in our value-added programs, which set us apart from our competition," says Panttaja. "We prefabricate walls and concrete form panels. We precision end-trim floor systems and framing components. We are continually looking for ways to help our customers be more successful."

As the premier Northern California supplier of building materials, Golden State Lumber is dedicated to keeping customers informed and ahead of the industry.

To learn more about Golden State Lumber, visit www.goldenstatelumber.com.

DELTA GLASS CO.

✧

Above: Delta Glass Co. is located at 3005 East Main, Stockton, California. Visit www.deltaglassco.com or call 209-466-5581.

Below: Nelson Palmer.

From replacing broken windows in residential homes to large commercial glass installations, generations of Stocktonians have learned to rely on Delta Glass Co.

Delta Glass provides the best in glass repair and installation services for both residential and commercial properties. The company uses only the best parts and materials and the quality of workmanship and attention to detail are second to none.

The company was founded in 1955 by Nelson Palmer. Kenneth Frost, Sr., later joined Palmer as a partner in the business. The business was located on East Main Street, only one block east of the current location at 3005 East Main.

Palmer's son, Mark, joined the firm in 1970 after serving an apprenticeship in the trade, and took over his father's portion of the business when he retired in 1985. Frost's son, Ken, Jr., later assumed his father's role in the firm. The company suffered a big loss when Ken, Jr., died unexpectedly in 2011.

Delta Glass has earned a reputation for quality repairs and installations, coupled with competitive pricing. Among the firm's well-known glass installations are the School of Pharmacy at the University of Pacific and the Eagle Ford showroom. The skilled craftsmen at Delta Glass understand the need to have residential and business windows repaired quickly and are equipped to provide fast service for windows, safety door glass, and storefront glass. They can also provide services for fire-rated and bullet resistant glass.

Delta Glass offers homeowners a wide selection of glass repairs and installations, including custom mirrors and shower door work. Delta's technicians treat customer's homes as if it were their own. You can depend on Delta for single pane and dual pane window and door glass, patio door glass, shower door glass, mirrored closet doors, tabletops, screens, and a variety of parts. No job is too small or too big.

In recent years, Delta Glass has done work for a diverse type of customers ranging from Delta College, San Joaquin County, property managements, apartment complexes, and all residential and commercial work. The company has three superb and dedicated technicians in the field: Bee Lor, James LaBarber and Toua Lee and one office manager, Jennifer Sutherlin.

Palmer decided to retire in 2015, however, he will still be around to advise and consult. The business was purchased by Jennifer Sutherlin and her family members, Andy and Lisa Isgrigg. Jennifer has been in the industry for fifteen years and joined Delta Glass nine years ago. Andy has been in the window industry for thirty years. The company is now going through the transition to the new ownership, but Sutherlin and Isgrigg say they are committed to building on the company's hard-earned reputation.

"We have good glass mechanics and we're honest and personable," says Palmer. "We've always tried to affiliate with our customers and many have become like family. We don't look at the bottom line as much as we try to concentrate on maintaining our reputation and relationship with our community, as we have tried to operate consistently year after year."

With products at every price point and for every age and function, Dorfman Pacific, Inc., has a hat for every head. The company, now in its ninety-third year of business, is the largest wholesaler of hats in the nation.

Dorfman Pacific offers its customers an impressive selection of brands; including Stetson Cloth, Woolrich, Cappelli Straworld, Inc., Tommy Bahama, Scala, Callanan, Indiana Jones, Stacey Adams, Biltmore, Santana, Justin, Larry Mahan, DPC, Tropical Trends, Outdoor Design and Panama Jack. The product line includes both men's and women's headwear and accessories and the company also specializes in custom and stock embroidery, custom lettering styles, screen printing and rhinestone applications. Dorfman also does private label for many of the largest department stores and specialty accounts in the nation.

The company has only one goal in mind: providing each customer with superior service and the best selection of headwear in the industry. We value long term relationships and have many independent and corporate customers that have been with us for over fifty years.

Dorfman Pacific began in 1921 when Arthur Hyman and Jack Dorfman established the Dorfman Hat and Cap Company in a small storefront in Oakland. The company was founded on the concept that retailers would support a headwear business offering quality products backed by a commitment to strong service. The company remains successful today because of its adherence to that policy.

During its nine decades in business, Dorfman Pacific has changed continuously to keep pace with customers' headwear needs, while maintaining its commitment to customer service, product quality, on-time deliveries and competitive prices.

In 1988, Dorfman Pacific relocated its distribution center to a 275,000 square foot state-of-the-art facility at 2615 Boeing Way in Stockton. A huge inventory of products is kept in our state-of-the-art distribution center, ready for shipment anywhere in the world. A team of sales representatives is ready to serve any location in the world and an in-house sales staff is available to help place orders.

Dorfman Pacific and its employees have donated more than $3 million to charities

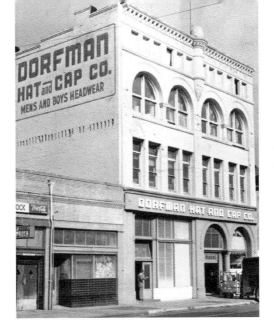

DORFMAN PACIFIC, CO., INC.

✦

Left: Dorfman Hat and Cap Company on Tenth Street in Oakland.

Below: Striving towards energy independence, the distribution center is a state-of-the-art facility at 2615 Boeing Way.

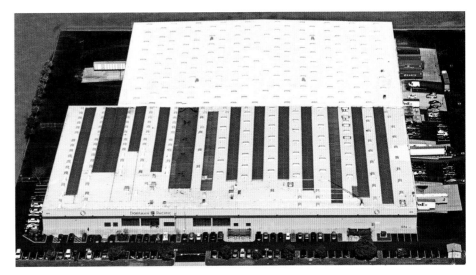

worldwide and are especially passionate about giving back to the Stockton community. The company has teamed with local food banks to donate hats, gloves and scarves to families in need during winter. In addition, the company partners with the United Way to sponsor local programs to aid needy children and the poor.

Dorfman Pacific is also very proud of its commitment to being the "greenest" company in the headwear industry and operating one of the greenest distribution centers in the United States. Dorfman generates eighty-five percent of our energy via solar panels, skylights, motion sensors, low wattage lighting, reflective white roofing, recycled boxes, electric hand dryers, electric fork lifts and carts, high efficiency air conditioning units, waterless urinals and two new electric commuter cars.

As Dorfman Pacific nears a century in business, it still maintains the same goals that have assured its growth and success in the past—quality products, superior service and the best selection in the industry.

GEIGER
MANUFACTURING
COMPANY

More than 100 years ago, Geiger Manufacturing started serving local industries. Today its work can be found throughout the United States.

✧

Top: Geiger Manufacturing in 1934.

Above: Joe Geiger, Sr., (wearing a Derby Hat) and his crew.

For the past twenty-seven years, this firm, which builds machinery to its customers' design as well as its own, has been managed by Roger Haack.

It all began in 1904 when Joseph Geiger, a machinist at the old Sampson Iron Works, started Geiger Iron Works, a jobbing machine shop, on Main Street, just off Stockton Channel. Most of the early work involved making machines for the former Holt Manufacturing Company. However, Geiger found time to design and construct an asphalt paving plant that contributed to the development of paved highways in California to replace the old dirt roads.

When the Main Street shop was destroyed by fire in 1913, Geiger moved his operations to the present site at 1110 East Scotts Avenue. A community-minded Geiger served on the commission that was successful in establishing California's first inland deepwater port on Stockton Channel, not far from Geiger's original shop.

Geiger, who had a way with words as well as tools, was accosted one day by an employee who said, "I think I'm worthy of a raise." The master machinist replied: "Some days you're worth it; some days you're not. Today you're not."

Company records reveal that in 1910 the total monthly pay of the firm's seven employees amounted to $444.60. By the time of Geiger's death in 1930 the business had been incorporated. His widow assumed the presidency, serving until 1938, when she died and was succeeded by their son, Joseph Donald Geiger.

During World War II, the firm manufactured practice bomb casings and submarine doors and young Geiger was instrumental in forming the Stockton Manufacturers' Association for producing machinery and other heavy equipment for the Mare Island Navy Yard. Many years after the war, Joe had the pleasure of meeting Admiral Chester Nimitz. In response to Nimitz' inquiry as to what Joe had done during the war, Joe explained he made submarine doors, a complex and critical part of submarine construction. Nimitz shook his hand and thanked him and his workers for keeping so many submariners safe during the great naval maneuvers of the war.

During the period of Joe's management, the company grew and greatly expanded its machining capabilities to become the largest jobbing shop in the valley. When Joe died in 1969, at only fifty-five years old, ownership and management passed to his widow, Carolyn. Carolyn ran the business for nearly twenty years, retiring in 1988. During that time, she recruited a young foreman, Roger Haack, who succeeded her as president on her retirement and continues his leadership today.

Over the years, Geiger has produced tomato and celery transplanters, silkscreen printing presses, paper box folders, machine bottle washers and fillers, and can making and mining equipment. It repairs machines for businesses all over the west, such as large centrifuges used in sewer plants.

Geiger Manufacturing continues to explore new fields, such as an experimental asparagus harvester, where the company can use the talents of its skilled machinists to develop new products. Geiger Manufacturing is a part of Stockton's past and a participant in its future.

The Holt family and the name Caterpillar® have been synonymous from the very beginnings of the iconic brand. Today, Holt of California is the exclusive Cat® dealer for sixteen California counties, offering a complete selection of new Cat equipment.

C. Parker Holt, the father of Parker and Harry Holt, was a long-time employee of Caterpillar Tractor Company, specializing in international sales. Their grandfather, Charles Henry Holt, and a grand-uncle, Benjamin Holt, established Stockton Wheel Company in 1883. They later formed Holt Manufacturing Company in Stockton.

To provide flotation on the soft peat lands of the San Joaquin Delta, Benjamin Holt invented a farm crawler tractor in 1904 and named it 'Caterpillar.' He copyrighted the name 'Caterpillar' for his track type invention with the U.S. Patent Office in 1910.

Parker and Harry became the Caterpillar/John Deere dealer for the Santa Paula and Santa Maria area in 1939. When the dealership in Stockton became available, the two brothers gave up the earlier venture and moved to Stockton in 1940 as a Caterpillar/John Deere dealer for San Joaquin and Calaveras Counties.

One of the first D10s, the largest track-type tractor built by Caterpillar, was used in building the New Melones Dam. In addition, equipment was sold and supported for building most of the major infrastructure throughout Holt Bros. territory, including Comanche, Don Pedro, San Luis, Delta Mendota and California Aqueduct.

When John Deere decided to build construction equipment in 1961, Holt Bros.

gave up that dealership and added Stanislaus, Tuolumne, Mariposa and Merced Counties to their Caterpillar territory.

Parker and Harry retired in 1986 and the dealership was sold to Parker's son-in-law, Victor Wykoff, and long-time employee, Ronald Monroe. In 1998, Holt Bros. merged with Tenco Tractor to expand the company's territory to the north, and the name was changed to Holt of California. The dealership is now run by the Wykoff, Beatie and Monroe families.

Holt of California now has fourteen locations throughout Northern Central California and the company management is spread out to different locations to be closer to their employees and customers. The company currently has about 600 employees.

The firm's customer base includes contractors, farmers, hospitals, food processing firms, data centers, trucking firms, aggregate mining operations, manufacturers and many others. In addition to the 'open-to-the-public' locations, the dealership has a service center on the Gallo campus in Modesto dedicated to supporting all the mobile support equipment for the winery and glass plant.

For more than eight decades, Holt of California has partnered with its customers to provide equipment solutions and the best product support in the industry. Holt of California has earned a reputation as a leader, with its employees as the heart and soul of the business. The dedication of its employees and their high level of commitment to exceed customer's expectations has brought Holt of California the distinction of being the top equipment supplier in its territory.

HOLT OF CALIFORNIA

SUST MANUFACTURING COMPANY, INC.

Sust Manufacturing Company, Inc. is the culmination of a dream for Peter H. Sust, whose family fled Cuba to escape communist rule and find freedom and opportunity in the United States.

For more than thirty-seven years, Sust Manufacturing Company has provided its customers with general machine shop and fabrication services. These services include designing and building custom components and complete custom production machines serving a wide variety of industries throughout the world.

Sust Manufacturing Company has designed and built machinery for the pencil making industry, aerospace, wood machining, plastic pipe manufacturing, some of the largest electrical power generating wind mills, automobile component manufacturing, the electronics industry and many others.

Sust Manufacturing Company is much more than the story of a successful company. It is the embodiment of the drive and determination of a Cuban immigrant to make the most of the golden opportunities he found in the United States.

Sust was born in Cuba, and as a boy lived in a neighborhood where famous writer Ernest Hemingway was a frequent visitor. Other neighbors included Che Guevara and Fidel Castro, whose son, "Fidelito," played baseball with Sust as a child.

When Castro seized power and installed a Communist regime, eleven year old Sust and his sister were sent by their parents to live with an aunt and uncle in Tampa, Florida. The family later relocated to Stockton where the parents were able to rejoin the family.

"When Castro began plucking grade school children from their homes against their parents' wills and shipping them to Czechoslovakia for indoctrination, my parents knew it was time to leave," Sust writes in his memoir, *A Boy from Cuba*.

"Although I could not define the values my family was instilling in me back then, I certainly absorbed those principles that would help me throughout my entire life," Sust writes. "Watching my family get on with their lives as Cuba changed so drastically was a major life lesson to me; one that I understand much more now than I did as a boy."

Sust has always been eager to learn. Beginning with various jobs suitable for a young boy, he continued his practical education when he started working at the California Cedar Products Research Laboratory. After serving on active duty in the United States Air Force he returned to work at the Research Laboratory. After a few years he started a manufacturing company with his friend Ed Morton from the Research Laboratory. "Ed was a very smart man and a great machinist," says Sust. "Unfortunately, he passed away not long after we started the business."

Sust and current general manager Richard G. Swartzer have worked together for the last thirty-seven years.

"The United States has been a wonderful home for me," Sust says. "I could never say what my life would have been like had I been born here. But I do know as someone who came from Cuba before he could be snatched up and sent for indoctrination to Czechoslovakia, the USA really is the Land of Opportunity if you are willing to work hard!"

Utility Telephone and its subsidiary web-hosting division, BroadStorm, provides telecommunications services such as DSL, hosted PBX and web-hosting telephone service to customers throughout California and Nevada.

The company was founded in 1996 by Jason Mills who began learning about the highly technical business at the age of fourteen when he began working in the switchroom at Pac-West, which had its roots as a retail phone store in 1979. As the industry grew, Pac-West became the largest TDM-interconnected entity to Pacific Bell's network in the late 1990s and Mills eventually became one of the company's key executives.

Utility Telephone was started as a reseller of AT&T's local lines in 2001 in order to sell a finished product to end-user customers, which then included long-distance and voicemail services. This was a great way for Mills to start out and build a customer base before making an investment in highly capital-intensive equipment. In 2002, Utility was able to obtain cages inside AT&T's central offices in Stockton and began offering advanced data services—the voice and data networks were still separate which was the standard in telecommunications at that time.

In 2004 the company's customer base had grown large enough to justify purchasing all the central office equipment to transfer the AT&T local lines onto their own platform, completing this process in 2007 and increasing the product line dramatically into advanced, integrated voice and data services on a single access circuit, jumping ahead in terms of network standard to be a local leader and paving the way for an all Ethernet and Voice-over-IP network.

Utility Telephone has been built on a foundation of service. The company understands that businesses rely on telephone and Internet services and makes sure that its clients can always connect with their customers and their customers can always connect with them. The company focus is on connecting businesses to their customers reliably and affordably and remaining accountable to their customers without finger-pointing between vendors.

The company has developed a business approach that takes the philosophy of 'Customer First' to a new level in the telecom industry. Utility has created a network of local support technicians who are dispatched quickly throughout the service area in response to service calls and technical support queries.

In addition to its customer-focused service, Utility Telephone has built a network around the needs of its customers. Over the past few years, the company has deployed many OC-48 fully redundant fiber rings, keeping its customers supplied with lightning-fast Internet speeds on ADSL, Ethernet over copper as well as the ultra-reliable T1 service.

Utility is equipped to provide customers with the connections they need with the most cutting-edge technology and efficient investments. For this reason, customers can rely on Utility Telephone for all their business telephone and Internet needs.

Utility Telephone's focus market is small- to medium-sized businesses, typically with ten to 200 employees located in markets with a population of 200,000 or less. Most of these customers are locally-owned businesses that value both "buying local" as well Utility's relationship-based way of doing business compared to that offered by larger impersonal suppliers.

Utility has CLEC and long-distance operating authority in multiple Western states, leaving opportunity for future growth.

Company executives see tremendous growth potential for the company, based on its commitments to customer service, state-of-the-art technology, accurate billing and entrepreneurial smarts. It continues to grow year over year by applying these principles.

✧
Above: Jason Mills.

SPONSORS

Aerial photograph taken by Visit Stockton of ship at the Port of Stockton with the Klamath Ferry in the foreground.

PHOTOGRAPHS ABOVE AND OPPOSITE
COURTESY OF VISIT STOCKTON.

PHOTOGRAPH COURTESY OF VISIT STOCKTON.

BUILDING A GREATER STOCKTON

About the Author

Alice van Ommeren

Alice van Ommeren developed into a local historian after accumulating thousands of postcards of Stockton and publishing *Stockton in Vintage Postcards* in 2004. The success of the book led her to write a historical column called "Postcards from the Past" for the *Downtowner*, once a monthly publication of the Stockton Downtown Alliance. As a local historian, she has given numerous community presentations. One notable talk was "On Location in Stockton: The Filming of *All the King's Men*," based on extensive research of the buildings shown in the movie and the use of local Stocktonians as extras. The critically acclaimed film received more than thirty awards including three Academy Awards, and forever sealed Stockton's 1940s landscape on the big screen.

The preservation of Stockton's rich culture and heritage for future generations is important to her. To that end, she served on Stockton's Cultural Heritage Board, and successfully led the effort to have the Police and Fire Alarm Station designated as a Stockton Historical Landmark and the Philomathean Club as a listing on the National Register of Historic Places. In 2010, she received the City of Stockton's "Charles Weber Award" for extraordinary achievement in preserving Stockton's cultural heritage. In 2014 she was recognized with Stockton's "Susan B. Anthony Women of Achievement Award" for her role in historic preservation and community education.